CROSSING THE INDUSTRIAL DIVIDE

THE POLITICAL ECONOMY OF INTERNATIONAL CHANGE
John Gerard Ruggie and Helen Milner, *General Editors*

THE POLITICAL ECONOMY OF INTERNATIONAL CHANGE
John Gerard Ruggie and Helen Milner, *General Editors*

CROSSING THE INDUSTRIAL DIVIDE

STATE, SOCIETY, AND THE POLITICS OF ECONOMIC TRANSFORMATION IN MALAYSIA

ALASDAIR BOWIE

Columbia University Press
New York

COLUMBIA UNIVERSITY PRESS
New York   Oxford
Copyright © 1991 Columbia University Press
All rights reserved

Library of Congress Cataloging-in-Publication Data
Bowie, Alasdair.
Crossing the industrial divide : state, society, and the politics
of economic transformation in Malaysia / Alasdair Bowie.
p.   cm. —(The Political economy of international change)
Includes bibliographical references and index.
ISBN 0-231-07212-0
1. Industry and state—Malaysia.   2. Malaysia—Economic policy.
I. Title.   II. Series.
HD3616.M32B68   1991
338.9595—dc20   *90-47683*
                                                            CIP

Casebound editions of Columbia University Press books are Smyth-sewn
and printed on permanent and durable acid-free paper

Printed in the United States of America
c 10 9 8 7 6 5 4 3 2 1
p 10 9 8 7 6 5 4 3 2 1

To my Mother,
Mavis Ellen Bowie,
and in Memory of my Father,
Robert Hunter Bowie

CONTENTS

ABBREVIATIONS

ACCCIM	Associated Chinese Chambers of Commerce and Industry of Malaysia
AICs	Advanced Industrialized Countries
APMC	Associated Pan-Malaysian Cement
ASEAN	Association of Southeast Asian Nations
AWSJ	Asian Wall Street Journal
AWSJW	Asian Wall Street Journal Weekly
AY	Asia Yearbook
BMF	Bumiputra Malaysia Finance
BT	Business Times
CBS	Currency Board System
CGC	Credit Guarantee Corporation
EON	*Edaran Otomobil Nasional* (National Automobile Distributor)
EPU	Economic Planning Unit
FAMA	Federal Agricultural Marketing Authority
FEER	Far Eastern Economic Review
FELDA	Federal Land Development Authority
FIDA	Federal Industrial Development Authority
FIMA	Food Industries of Malaysia
FMP	First Malaysia Plan
FMS	Federated Malay States
GDP	Gross Domestic Product
GNP	Gross National Product
HBI	Hot Briquetted Iron
HICOM	Heavy Industries Corporation of Malaysia
IBRD	International Bank for Reconstruction and Development

ICA	Industrial Coordination Act
INSAN	Institute for Social Analysis
ISEAS	Institute of Southeast Asian Studies
ISIS	Institute of Strategic and International Studies
ITM	*Institut Teknologi MARA* (MARA Institute of Technology)
KMM	*Kesatuan Melayu Muda* (Young Malay Union)
KMS	*Kesatuan Melayu Singapore* (Singapore Malay Association)
KRIS	*Kesatuan Ra'ayat Indonesia Semenanjong* (Association of the Indonesian Peoples of the Peninsula)
MARA	*Majlis Amanah Rakyat* (Council of Trust for the Indigenous Peoples)
MARDI	Malaysian Agricultural Research and Development Institute
MAS	Malayan Administrative Service
MB	Malaysian Business
MCA	Malaysian (formerly Malayan) Chinese Association
MCP	Malayan Communist Party
MCS	Malayan Civil Service
MIC	Malaysian (formerly Malayan) Indian Congress
MIDA	Malaysian Industrial Development Authority
MIDF	Malaysian Industrial Development Finance
MIE	Malaysian Industrial Estates
MISC	Malaysian International Shipping Corporation
MITI	Ministry of International Trade and Industry (Japan)
MMC	Mitsubishi Motors Corporation
MOIC	Malaysian Overseas Investment Corporation
MPAJA	Malayan Peoples' Anti-Japanese Army
MPAJU	Malayan Peoples' Anti-Japanese Union
NEP	New Economic Policy
NICs	Newly Industrializing Countries
NST	New Straits Times
PAS	*Partai Islam Se Malaysia*
PDA	Petroleum Development Act
PERNAS	*Perbadanan Nasional* (National Corporation)
PETA	*Ikatan Pembela Tanah Ayer* (Defenders of the Fatherland)

PIO	Pioneer Industries Ordinance
PMIP	Pan-Malayan Islamic Party
PNB	*Permodalan Nasional Berhad* (National Equity Corporation)
RIDA	Rural Industrial Development Authority
RISDA	Rubber Industry Smallholder Development Authority
SAP	Structural Adjustment Program
SEDCs	State Economic Development Corporations
SGI	Sabah Gas Industries
SMP	Second Malaysia Plan
ST	Straits Times
STM	*Syarikat Telekom Malaysia* (Malaysian Telecommunications Company)
TMP	Third Malaysia Plan
TS	The Star
UDA	Urban Development Authority
UMBC	United Malayan Banking Corporation
UMNO	United Malays National Organization
UNIDO	United Nations Industrial Development Organization
WSJ	Wall Street Journal
4MP	Fourth Malaysia Plan
5MP	Fifth Malaysia Plan

ACKNOWLEDGMENTS

This book grew out of my curiosity about how to explain successful industrial development in certain parts of the Third World (but not others) and what recent scholarship on industrial change in advanced industrial economies might have to offer in terms of new insights. I became interested in these issues as a result of my participation in theoretical exchanges on comparative political economy with colleagues at Berkeley. My introduction to Southeast Asia, on the other hand, I owe to a number of excellent teachers at the University of Auckland, New Zealand, and at Princeton University, and to the opportunity I had to work in Indonesia in the early 1980s.

In writing this book I have been assisted by a great many people, both directly in terms of insights, guidance, and criticism, and indirectly with hospitality, support, and understanding. I am acutely aware that this study could never have seen the light of day without the generosity and kindness of my teachers, colleagues, friends and family.

Financial support for my research in Asia was provided by a University of California Regents' Traveling Fellowship and a Doctoral Fellowship from the Institute for the Study of World Politics, New York. Initial formulation of the project and subsequent attendance at scholarly meetings to present the study's findings were funded by the Department of Political Science, the Center for South and Southeast Asian Studies, the Institute for East Asian Studies, the Institute of International Studies, and the Graduate Division, all of the University of California, Berkeley, and by the American Political Science Association. I am deeply grateful to all of these institutions for providing me the wherewithal to complete this book.

In Malaysia, as a visiting research associate at the Institute of

Strategic and International Studies in Kuala Lumpur, my field research was greatly facilitated by the generous support of ISIS Director-General Dr. Noordin Sopiee and his staff. In Singapore, as a visiting associate at the Institute of Southeast Asian Studies (ISEAS), full access to library and research facilities was extended to me by ISEAS Director Dr. Kernial Sandhu. Both institutions were most welcoming and the introductions provided to me by researchers at ISIS in particular were most valuable.

Besides enjoying this institutional support, I was blessed by feedback from and interaction with a wide variety of officials, scholars, journalists, business people and friends in the region. My thanks go to all those Malaysian and foreign colleagues and friends who extended their hospitality and who were patient and thoughtful in introducing and explaining the intricacies of the Malaysian scene to me. In particular, to Shingara Singh and family for accommodating me, to Jomo and James Clad for extended discussions and support, to Munira and Rudin Salinger, Nan Bonfils and Sarah Arney for sharing their appreciation of Malay culture with me, and to Tim and Jill Caughley, Fred and May McAdam, and Ed and Holly Eger, I owe a deep debt of gratitude.

In the United States, Berkeley provided the superb collegial setting in which a project such as this could be nurtured, undertaken, and eventually brought to fruition. I owe much to the Department of Political Science for important financial support, and to individuals there who have by example and by direct interest in my work given me far more support and consideration than I deserve.

Thomas Gold, Karl Jackson, Chalmers Johnson, and Robert Price have given generously not only of their time and intellect but also of their good humor and enthusiastic optimism. I am grateful to them for the insights they have contributed to this study and for their willingness to act as experienced guides through the morass of data that I have accumulated in the course of this project. In particular, my thanks go to Karl Jackson, for his infectious enthusiasm and gentle prodding, and to Chalmers Johnson, for his unshakable conviction as to the value of the study and his frequent exhortations to broaden the comparative focus of the work. Jack Citrin, Giuseppe diPalma, Andrew Janos, Ken Jowitt, and Robert Scalapino also gave carefully considered advice over the years.

The detailed critical comments and encouragement of my colleagues Glyn Morgan, Susan Sell, and Stevens Tucker have represented an invaluable contribution to this study. During two years of spirited deliberations, this very active research and writing group read and re-read every chapter of the manuscript, raised and debated theoretical and substantive issues, and suggested guideposts that were enormously useful in directing the writing of this book. I owe more to them than I can say.

Among those within the community of Southeast Asianists at Berkeley whose insights into the politics of Asia proved a bountiful source of new ideas at each step of the way, I would like to thank Rick Doner, Gerard Maré, Brad Palmquist, and Danny Unger. These friends, so much more than colleagues, have all read pieces of the manuscript and related papers and articles, and have provided knowledgeable feedback which is reflected in ways too numerous to mention in the pages that follow. Among others at Berkeley who read various sections of the draft and were generous with their time, their ideas, and their understanding were Jim Glaser, Eva Eagle, Jim McGuire, and Leslie Armijo. I would also like to express my gratitude to Merrill Shanks, Micky Skronski, Cathy Walton, Ruth Wren, Norm Gelbard, and the staff of Computer-assisted Survey Methods (CSM), the Survey Research Center, University of California, Berkeley, for computer assistance, and to Peter Ananda and the staff of the South and Southeast Asia Library at the University of California for help with documents and sources.

At Cornell, as a visiting assistant professor, I received support from the Department of Government, enjoyed access to the John M. Echols Collection on Southeast Asia, and partook of a conducive atmosphere in which to make changes to the manuscript and to present my ideas, in the form of the Southeast Asia Program, under Benedict Anderson. I wish to express particular appreciation to Milton Esman, George Kahin, and Jonas Pontussen for the interest that they have taken in my work and for their suggestions and support. I also thank Mary Callahan and Michael Malley for reading and commenting on parts of the manuscript as it neared completion.

At Catholic University, I wish to acknowledge financial assistance for wrapping up the project from the Office of the Vice-President (Academic) and to express my appreciation to James Quirk for proofing and indexing assistance.

Kate Wittenberg, Editor-in-Chief of Columbia University Press, and John Ruggie and Helen Milner, editors of the Political Economy of International Change Series, have been of considerable assistance in the realization of the finished product and the manuscript has in addition benefited from reviews from two anonymous readers, whose suggestions I value. Despite all the professional help I have received, however, those errors of fact and interpretation that remain are entirely my own.

In conclusion, I wish to acknowledge the debt of gratitude I owe to friends and family whose encouragement of my work and tolerance of its demands have made this book possible. My thanks go to Brad Palmquist and Liz Jeff, for being "family" when family was many thousands of miles away, to Lyn Spillman, for antipodean solidarity, to Sarah Hutchison, for sharing the scholar's life with me, and to my siblings, Donald, Hamish, and Fiona, and my Mother, Mavis Ellen Bowie, for believing that the project would eventually be completed, and for reminding me that there is a life out there to be lived, after all the (writing) "fun" is over.

A.B.
Washington, D.C.
January 1991

CROSSING THE INDUSTRIAL DIVIDE

WEST MALAYSIA

1

CHOOSING A DEVELOPMENT STRATEGY: BY WAY OF AN INTRODUCTION

How and why do industrial development strategies change? This study takes as its point of departure existing cross-national studies of industrial change in advanced industrialized societies (Japan, the United States, and Western Europe). Its focus is on the forces that drive state industrial strategies over time in Third World, late-industrializing contexts. Its findings suggest that the structure of society and the mechanisms by which disagreements between societal groups are reconciled have an important bearing on the choices states make between alternative development paths in countries undergoing rapid industrialization in the late twentieth century.

The case considered here is that of Malaysia, a middle-income industrializing country which, since independence in 1957, has pursued three distinct development strategies: a *market-led approach* during the country's first decade (1957–1969); a *mixed market-regulatory policy* during the 1970s; and a *state-centered strategy* for most of the 1980s. The puzzle posed by the Malaysian experience is how to explain marked disjunctures in development strategy observed over comparatively short periods of time. An appropriate place to start to "solve" the puzzle is with a consideration of "models" of development strategy choice that have already been generated in the course of studies of industrial change in the the First World.

Individual actor models of politics, for example, explain economic policy formulation by pointing to the preferences of individual economic actors. According to this approach, business, agriculture, and labor hold policy preferences shaped by their positions in the international and domestic economy (collectively, the economy's "production profile," as Gourevitch terms it).[1] They form coalitions around certain policies as a result of these preferences and it is the nature of these coalitions which determines the shape of overall economic policy. So, to understand the choice of development path in any particular country we have to understand what that country's "production profile" looks like—where do societal actors stand in the international economy? What are their policy preferences and their likely points of conflict or congruence with other actors?[2] Where we observe divergence in economic policies—between countries at the same time, or between one era and another in the same country— this approach suggests that we can explain it ultimately in terms of differences (or changes) in the patterns of preferences of societal actors.[3]

If we apply this model to the Malaysian case it suggests that a change in direction in industrial strategy must have as its precursor some identifiable change in the map of business, agriculture, and labor preferences, which in turn must have been produced by a change in the production profile of one or more of these actors.

But we will see shortly that economic actor preferences have been considerably less important in the Malaysian context than this individual actor approach would indicate, while other sorts of preferences, specifically those generated by communal groups, have been more salient in the determination of strategy. Ethnic rioting in 1969, for example, prompted significant change in the relations between the non-Malay and Malay communities and was followed by major changes in state approaches to achieving economic structural change. Economic actors (leaders in business, for example), far from initiating the changes, were forced to react to them, and when they did respond, they did so in communal rather than functional terms—the Chinese chambers of commerce, for example, voiced concern about the effect of new development choices on *Chinese* business activities, rather than on those of business as a whole.

A second type of model emphasizes the causal role of intermediate associations in determining national development choices. From this perspective, the functional positions of economic actors per se have little bearing on policy change because, to have an impact on policy, the preferences of economic actors must be marshalled and organized. Thus, to understand policy change we must focus on the role of intermediate associations (specifically political parties and interest groups) which undertake the crucial task of transmitting the preferences of individual actors to state policymakers.[4] The model emphasizes the autonomous influence these organizations can have upon policy, independent of the actors they represent.[5] The explanatory focus of this approach thus moves from the individual to the association.[6]

Intermediate association models would lead us, in the Malaysian case, to expect significant shifts in development strategy (as occurred in 1970 and in 1980–1981) to have been accompanied by major changes in coalitions of political parties or interest groups representing functional interests. As we shall see, however, functional interest groups have generally been subordinate in Malaysian politics to associations representing communal interests, and in neither instance did functional association alliances play a prominent role in precipitating events leading to policy change. Only by recasting the intermediate associations explanation to incorporate the role of associations representing communal interests can one obtain some purchase in explaining the observed outcomes in Malaysia. I will return to this point shortly.

A third political explanation of strategy change that we might consider is that which emphasizes structural characteristics of the polity or the economy as key determinants of economic policy paths. Explanations of this type usually focus on state structure, emphasizing the crucial role of formal state institutions, bureaucracies, and rules in connecting economic actors and representative associations on the one hand, with particular policy outcomes on the other. The central argument made here is that state decision-making mechanisms have an autonomous effect on policy—because they can influence both the ways in which actor preferences are aggregated through intermediate associations, and how these associations must act through the state to achieve their policy objectives.[7] So policy choices are "more than the sum of countervailing pressure from social groups." The medium through which these pressures are brought to bear on policy, namely the state, can itself stamp its own image on the outcomes.[8] Policy similarities or differences among countries, then, derive from the similarities or differences in the character of their respective states.[9]

The problem with the institutional or state-centric approach is that it requires major changes in formal state structures, in institutional rules, or in the elites that control such structures before significant changes in strategy can be expected. Industrial strategy changes of the order witnessed in Malaysia in 1970 and again in 1980 must, these theories suggest, have their roots in abrupt changes in the Malaysian polity. But in Malaysia both institutional and elite changes have been largely incremental—neither the institutions of the state nor those who have exerted control over them have experienced the sorts of upheaval witnessed, for example, in the case of the Socialist victory in France that gave Mitterrand the presidency after more than three decades of conservative rule.

A fourth set of explanations we might consider are models, often labeled functionalist, which focus on the political and economic *system*, understood as an organic whole. David Easton is among those who argue that "each part of the larger political canvas does not stand alone but is related to each other part; or, to put it more positively, . . . the operation of no one part can be fully understood without reference to the way the whole itself operates."[10] From his perspective, official economic policy can best be understood as functional—its adoption ensures the survival and stability of "the system."[11]

The usefulness of this approach in the Malaysian context (or any other, for that matter) is rather difficult to judge because "system needs" are never very clearly defined. It is conceivable that any change in policy whatever might fulfil functions (of accumulation or legitimation, in the Marxist view, or of interest articulation and aggregation, in the conservative view) necessary to sustain the system.[12] So, even if one accepts, for the sake of argument, the proposition that introduction of a state-led strategy for industrial development in 1980–1981 in Malaysia was in response to changing system needs, one is left to imagine what those needs might be and how the state-led policy might have served them.

Cultural analyses, of the kind employed by Sydney Verba, Jack Hayward, and Aaron Wildavsky, stress the central role of political culture in explaining national economic policy choices.[13] In particular, they focus on how prevailing models, ideologies, and values can affect economic actors' perceptions of reality (their "habits of mind"), leading countries to develop divergent policy responses to objectively similar challenges. For example, the cultural attitudes of civil servants and societal groups, according to Hayward, have shackled the British with incrementalist economic policies while freeing the French to undertake wholesale reform of their economy.[14] Political culture might be expected to alter across generations, ethnic groups, and especially between countries, but is likely to change only very slowly within these categories over time.

The problem that arises when we try to apply a political culture argument to the Malaysian case is that the strategy choices and changes we seek to explain have all occurred within a relatively short period of time (less than one generation).[15] Although we can see differences in political culture between the major ethnic communities within Malaysia, this cultural mix has not changed in any dramatic way in three decades, as would apparently be necessary to generate the sharply different approaches to industrial strategy witnessed during this time.

The final group of explanations we might consider are international state systems theories which explain national policies as the product either of aspects of the international political economy (i.e., they are determined by a country's position in the sequence of international economic development)[16] or of politico-military rivalries.[17] Essentially, these theories hold that the international (economic or strategic) system constrains domestic political responses to international economic crises. This approach thus suggests that major policy change observed in a context such as Malaysia's is necessarily the product of external shocks, such as the oil crises of 1973–1974 and 1979 (during which the nominal price of oil jumped to ten times its previous level, while the real price more than doubled),[18] and that the *way* in which national policy changes under such circumstances can be understood only by referring to Malaysia's position in the international division of labor.

We shall see, though, that the first major change in Malaysia's approach to industrial development in 1970 was clearly the result of *domestic* changes precipitated by intercommunal riots in 1969 and cannot easily be attributed to changes in the external environment. The second major change, although it followed the 1979 oil shock, and paralleled "radical" economic experiments elsewhere (Britain's election of Thatcher and abandonment of Keynesianism, and France's election of Mitterrand), was only indirectly oil-related. Malaysia, by 1980, was a non-OPEC oil exporter but benefited only modestly from the second series of oil price rises (oil revenues were still overshadowed by earnings from tin and rubber, the country's traditional exports).

In sum, our existing arsenal of explanatory tools, drawn mainly from cross-national studies involving the advanced industrialized democracies of Western Europe, appears to have limited application in the case of late-industrializing Malaysia. If the preferences of *economic actors*, or the actions of *intermediate associations* representing their material interests, are central in determining the shape of policy, then how might we explain policy in Malaysia, where the principal actors are communal in nature, each community encompasses a wide variety of economic interests, and where political parties and interest groups are communally based? If it is the basic *structure* of the polity and the economy to which we must attend if we are to understand how policy evolves, then how do we account for significant changes in strategy, as occurred in 1970 and again in 1980, unaccompanied by precipitating changes in structure?

If the character of *policymakers* provides the key to understanding strategy, how can we explain significant change in strategy not accompanied by major change in elite structure in the Malaysian case? If strategy is essentially *functional* in serving the needs of the system then how do we account for changes in strategy when we cannot specify what the relevant system needs are?

If long-standing national *political culture* is what really drives economic policy choice, how can we explain two broad changes in direction in one country within the span of a single generation? If the *international economic system* is the root source of national economic policy change, then why do changes in industrial strategy in Malaysia not parallel such watershed international events as the two oil shocks in 1973–1974 and 1979?

In seeking to employ these existing approaches to explain policy outcomes in the Malaysian case, we are faced with two problems. First, many of the available models (especially those identified as cultural or structuralist) rely on historical *continuities* to explain between-country variations in policy approach. Country A is said to respond to crisis in manner X, whereas country B responds in manner Y, because of long-standing differences between the two in their world views or institutional arrangements. It is difficult to account for within-country *variation* in economic strategy using models that emphasize within-country continuity (relative *invariance*) among explanatory variables.

Secondly, the models outlined here emphasize factors, such as the economic structural roots of actor preferences, which are often less important in a Third World context, while paying little attention to considerations, such as the strength of communal identity as a motivating factor in politics, which have considerable salience for economic strategy formulation among late-industrializers.

The next section introduces an explanatory model for economic strategy variation in the Malaysian case that addresses these issues and generates hypotheses applicable to other developing countries.

A THEORETICAL MODEL OF INDUSTRIAL CHANGE

The argument developed here is that changes in Malaysian economic development strategy can best be explained as products of the changing nature of a communal settlement that has prevailed in Malaysia since 1957. As the terms of this communal settlement—which concerns the distribution of political and economic power between the major communities—have evolved over time, so has the extent to which the state has been constrained in its ability independently to formulate and implement economic policy. The state in turn has responded by adopting different approaches to economic development strategy in seeking to satisfy the twin policy objectives of boosting Malaysian economic growth and advancing Malay communal interests.

In positivist terms, the model says that among national political determinants of the dependent variable (development strategy) the most important explanatory variable is the nature of the communal settlement (and the level of societal constraint on state autonomous action that it implies). In essence, the changing terms of a communal modus vivendi limit and shape the policy choices confronting state decision-makers and in particular the ways in which the state can foster economic structural change.

This approach clearly has some affinity with intermediate association models which emphasize the role of societal coalitions. But it differs from this social alliances approach in two important respects. First, we are not dealing here with coalitions of economic actors or with intermediate associations representing functional interests. The actors and associations in the Malaysian case (and in a number of other pertinent Third World contexts) are communally, not functionally, identified, their preferences being primarily the products of a

hnic solidarity.[19] We shall see shortly that these ethnic
cannot easily be dismissed as "false consciousness" or as
ks for more fundamental class or economic interests.

he Malaysian case, coalitions are not constantly forming
and reforming around policy packages, as envisioned in the Gourevitch analysis of intermediate associations. Instead, a more or less
permanent intercommunal coalition links leaders of three major ethnic groups. Political events and changing ethnic perceptions lead to
periodic shifts in the balance of power within this coalition which in
turn lead to changes in the terms of settlement between communities. But the *composition* of the coalition itself has remained essentially
unchanged.

One of the primary purposes of this model is to broaden the scope
of existing theory to encompass industrial strategy choice in Malaysia
(and, by extension, in developing communal societies elsewhere).
This is done first by extending the conventional formulation of coalitions to accommodate Third World communal coalitions and then by
demonstrating how these coalitions shape and constrain state autonomous policy-making and subsequently lead to changes in national
industrial strategy choices.

Before describing the hypothesized relationships of the model,
some discussion of the variables involved is in order. The dependent
variable, economic development strategy, is formulated here in broad
terms, to accommodate the fact that specific policies might at any one
time not conform to the overall thrust of strategy pursued by government.[20] The focus here is on the character of economic strategy as a
whole, and on commercial and industrial strategy in particular, because Malaysian decisionmakers have themselves attached great importance to industrial development; industrial expansion has consis-
tently been the center piece of national economic development strategy
since 1957.

Given this emphasis on changes in broad strategy, we need to
specify the particular dimension of change in which we are interested. We can envisage economic development strategies varying on
a number of differen. levels: they can be inward- or outward-looking,
import-substituting or export-promoting, capital- or labor-intensive,
or foreign- or local-capital-intensive, for example. For the purposes
of this study, the variation to be explained is that between two types
of strategy: those that are *market (i.e., company)-led*; and those that are

state-led. This study is thus similar to recent analyses of economic development trajectories in advanced industrial democracies which have sought to explain how strategies vary along this market-led/state-led dimension, across several countries facing the same challenges at the same time. The difference lies in the fact that in this case the variation to be explained is from time-period to time-period *within the same country* (specifically, we focus here on three decades and three different approaches).

John Zysman, writing on the role of financial systems, has identified three distinct types of strategy that have been used to address the political and economic challenges of growth and industrial adjustment. He labels them market-led, negotiated and state-led.[21] Each represents a stable political settlement, among different social groups and sectors, over the terms of industrial change—which groups are going to gain, who will be protected, and how those who gain will compensate those who lose. Zysman argues that states can, by their actions, effect different sorts of settlement. They can leave the distribution of costs almost entirely to the free market with only limited government intervention, in which case the basic choices of how to respond to changing economic conditions are left to individual firms (market-led). Alternatively, states can participate in explicit and continuing negotiation over the detailed terms of industrial change with major functional groups to arrive at a bargained adjustment strategy (negotiated). Or they can consciously mold particular sectors and shape economic outcomes by themselves becoming dominant economic players and imposing a particular distribution of costs and benefits on the market (state-led).[22]

Zysman thus suggests that we can profitably compare societies and their different approaches to economic strategy along a primary dimension that leads from market-led to state-ied. This is the dimension chosen in the present study—our task is to explain variation along this dimension within a single country over time.

The dependent variable, then, is broad state development strategy as it affects industrial and commercial activities in Malaysia, and the variation to be explained is that observed along this continuum, from a predominantly market-led approach at one time to a heavily state-led approach at another.

The independent variable here is the nature of the communal settlement reached by leaders of Malaysia's major ethnic groups in order to sustain interethnic harmony. During each of the three main periods that are the focus of this study (1957–1969, 1970–1980, and the 1980s), there has existed a settlement (sometimes tacit, sometimes explicit) with respect to the distribution of economic and political power between groups acceptible to all communities.

I use the term "settlement" advisedly. It indicates compromise and acquiescence, but not necessarily approval, on the part of all groups. In the case of Malaysian Chinese political leaders in 1980 and 1981, for example, tacit acceptance of a bold state-led challenge to Chinese business domination (e.g., in auto production) on behalf of Malay communal interests was accompanied by a sense of foreboding over the long-term effects of this incursion. Chinese leaders, who formed part of the government, did agree to go along with the initiatives of Prime Minister Mahathir and conceded publicly that the new large-scale heavy industries projects to be controlled by Malays were a legitimate initiative of government. Privately, however, they were in no way reconciled to these developments. There was a settlement, of sorts—the Chinese leadership continued to lend its political support to the Malay-dominated government while existing Chinese business was in large part permitted a free hand to dominate domestic business activity—but it fell short of consensus or approval.[23]

The question might be raised at this point: why do we find any settlement at all between ethnic communities in Malaysia? Why do groups with little natural affinity (they eat different food, speak different languages, follow different religions, and have their roots in separate subcontinents) not approach competition for economic resources and political power as a zero-sum game, in which gain for one group results in losses for others? Why do we not see the largest community, the Malays, who control the state and its instruments of coercion (the police and armed forces), simply imposing their will on the minority communities?

The explanation is in part historical, in part instrumental. The concept of a Malaysian "nation" had its origin in an explicitly negotiated "bargain" that set the stage for a peaceful transfer of power from the British in 1957. This bargain, reached between leaders of the three major political parties, representing the Malay (the United Malays National Organization—UMNO), Chinese (the Malayan

Chinese Association), and Indian (Malayan Indian Congress) communities, at the urging of the British, established the basis for a political coalition that has ruled Malaysia since independence. In an instrumental sense, leaders of each community, especially those of the majority Malay community, have been very conscious of the possibility that imposition of one community's views might precipitate ethnic violence. They have been constrained in asserting their narrow communal interests by a fear of repeating the riots that erupted in the immediate aftermath of World War II and again in May 1969 (resulting in numerous deaths and injuries from street fighting), or of rekindling the (largely Chinese) communist guerrilla insurgency that caused widespread dislocation during the 1950s. Thus intercommunal consensus in the Malaysian case can be explained as a product both of historical circumstance and of fear that absence of consensus has the potential to damage the interests of all groups.

As the nature of the settlement has changed, in response to watershed events such as the 1969 ethnic riots, for example, so have the constraints on the strategies state policymakers might employ to foster industrial growth.

Some might argue that changes in the settlement referred to in Malaysia are essentially responses to different levels of coercion, employed by a politically hegemonic group (the Malays) to force the others (the Chinese and Indian communities) to go along with its preferences. This viewpoint would suggest that what we are witnessing is coerced compliance and therefore the underlying causal variable in the present model should be coercive power.

Coercive power, however, refers to an actor's ability to induce or influence others to carry out his or her directives or any other norms he or she supports *by means of physical sanctions* (the use, or threatened use, of violent physical force).[24] In employing such sanctions the powerful attempt neither to persuade others to their point of view (to capture their commitment) nor to play upon their sense of self-interest, as is the case with the exercise of normative and utilitarian power.[25] They *force* them to comply.

In practice, however, the threat of physical force in the Malaysian case is quite remote, largely because of the perceived sensitivity of ethnic issues and the belief, alluded to above, that collective effort by any community to do physical violence to another, toward *any* end (and however successful in the short term) would eventually result in the complete destruction of the society as a whole—an outcome damaging to the long-term interests of all.

What we witness instead are ethnic groups complying with communal settlements for periods of a decade or more, either because: a) they are persuaded that such settlements serve their ideal interests and therefore feel free to make a normative commitment to them (normative compliance); or b) they see material rewards stemming from the settlements and make a utilitarian calculation that their material interests are best served by going along (utilitarian compliance).[26]

In short, it is not possible to take the causal variable here and simply reduce it to levels of coercion. The "hegemon" in this case has never been a true hegemon—Malays have never been able to turn their political dominance into complete physical or economic dominance—and the powder-keg nature of this multi-ethnic society has paradoxically rendered the threat of sustained violence, an essential component of coercive power, very remote. The major ethnic groups comply with intercommunal settlements for reasons of normative belief and concern for material self interest. As events have led ethnic leaders to change the content of the settlement (changing, for example, the balance of political and economic power between the major communities), the government's approach to industrial development strategy has changed. The connection between changes in the settlement between the major groups in society (the independent variable) and changes in industrial development strategy (the dependent variable) is the primary focus of the present study.[27]

Before elaborating this relationship I should clarify what I mean by "ethnic group" in the context of the present study and explain why ethnicity, rather than class, has been the primary cleavage base for political action in Malaysia since independence.

Ethnic identity can be thought of as embodying elements of both birth and achievement, ethnic characteristics being both "given" and "taken" to a greater or lesser degree. At the same time, ethnic group boundaries are specified with respect to both objective reality and fictive belief.[28] There is always a significant element of descent (most members, after all, are born into the same ethnic group in which they die), and descent is the starting point for group definition in most cases. But ethnic groups will differ in the extent to which they are prepared at the margin to adopt outside members *as if* they were born into the group.

At minimum, an ethnic group requires three things: the *idea* of a common provenance, whether or not there is objective evidence for such a provenance; recruitment primarily (though not exclusively) through ascriptive ties; and a conscious feeling of distinctiveness, whether or not this matches an observable, unique inventory of cultural traits (in other words, the traits by which group members choose to distinguish themselves may not be obvious to non-group members).[29]

I give prominence in my model to the settlement between ethnic groups in Malaysia as the causal variable most influential in determining industrial strategy choice. Yet many would take issue, a priori, with any analysis that seeks to give ethnic groups a causal role.

Marxists, in particular, would object. From their point of view, ethnic groups and ethnic divisions are either artifices, created and nurtured as a veil for class concerns, or historical remnants, complicating factors that obscure the class divisions within society.[30] My misplaced emphasis on ethnicity thus overlooks the essential forces rooted in the productive system which are at work; ethnic conflict is simply a camouflage for, or distraction from, the underlying class conflict. Marxist theory identifies the primary antagonism in capitalist society as that between polarized class interests in the division of labor—between the owners of the means of production, on the one hand, and wage labor, on the other hand. It is this antagonism, based on material reality, that eventually gives rise to a revolutionary struggle culminating in the destruction of the capitalist class. Class identity is always far more important in history than the petty concerns of ethnicity, because class struggle is invariably the motor-force behind historical change. It is inconceivable that material (class) concerns should be eclipsed by those of ethnicity.[31]

Conflicts between ethnic groups are, from a Marxist point of view, simply indicative of a false consciousness on the part of ethnic group members—false in the sense that it derives from belief ("ideology" —the motives, values, and expectations of autonomous actors) and is not rooted in economic material relationships which are the primary driving forces of social change.[32] Such false consciousness has sometimes been attributed to a "displacement" of social antagonisms which originate in the contradictions of the capitalist mode of production, or to simple irrationality (people lacking a clear-sighted view of where their true material interests lie), as suggested by the phrase: "Anti-Semitism is the socialism of the stupid."[33] Alternatively it is said to have its roots in the calculated, rational actions of the bourgeoisie, which manipulates ethnic identity in pursuit of its narrow class interests. Combining these interpretations is the orthodox western Marxist view that ethnic identity and culture are a "joint product of bourgeois cunning and proletarian gullibility"—the "divide and rule" thesis.[34]

Marxists, then, view ethnic groups either as epiphenomena—incidental outward manifestations of class conflict or vestiges of an earlier era—or as dependent, the product of deliberate manipulation by the bourgeoisie. In neither case does ethnicity warrant being treated as in any sense causal.

Others, however, beg to differ. Nelson Kasfir, for example, protests:

> False consciousness is still consciousness, whether or not the actor recognizes his 'true' interests. . . . To dismiss all manifestations of politicized ethnicity as irrelevant is to ignore a range of motives, many of which will, on empirical examination, turn out to be strongly felt.[35]

Kasfir joins with a wide variety of scholars in rejecting the view that ethnicity and class are antithetical principles of association and that the former is necessarily a proxy for the latter.[36] He proposes a typology of the various ways in which ethnicity and class can be related to one another as alternative and overlapping bases for social and political cleavage: class or ethnicity alone may explain political action; ethnicity and class may be equally important as organizing principles within the same political situation; the two may be in conflict; or ethnicity and class may reinforce each other. He concludes:

> In each of these four types of situations . . . the research problem is to untangle and assess the mixture of motives held by the actors. . . . the observer must seek the causes in the political situation that stimulate people to think of (and organize) themselves in class, ethnic, or other terms—or some combination of them.[37]

Thus, rather than considering class the independent variable and ethnicity as the dependent (or class perched at the top of a hierarchy of bases for social cleavage, with ethnicity somewhere below) this approach suggests that the relationship between ethnic and class identity in any society must be seen as the product of the broader social, political, and economic conditions from which both draw life and breath.[38] Simply put, there is no one pattern of political cleavage applicable to all polities at all times. As Lipset and Rokkan have observed:

> There is a hierarchy of cleavage bases in each system and these orders of political primacy not only vary among polities, but also tend to undergo changes over time. Such differences and changes in the political weight of sociocultural cleavages set fundamental problems for comparative research:
> —When is region, language, or ethnicity most likely to prove polarizing?
> —When will class take the primacy and when will denominational commitments and religious identities prove equally important cleavage bases?
> . . . what we want to know is when one type of change will prove more salient than the other.[39]

In short, the theoretical primacy of class over ethnicity may not be assumed in the Marxist fashion. The principal line of social cleavage in any system—the fault line to which all serious political upheavals are thought to be traceable—must be determined by means of empirical observation.[40]

The orthodox Marxist perspective on ethnic and communal identity has also been faulted for its limited conception of the range of observable ethnic arrangements. Specifically, the view of ethnic groups as guises for class interests is drawn for societies assumed to exhibit cultural and ethnic homogeneity or derived from the experience of stratified settings where ethnic inequality is a consequence of differential control of assets—one group usually has control over the means of production utilized by another group.[41] Such arrangements have sometimes been called "lateral" or "aristocratic," to indicate that each ethnic group in such a system is seen as being identified with a particular stratum of society.[42]

An alternative type of ethnic arrangement, however, might involve "vertical" ethnic groups that straddle a range of social strata.[43] Donald Horowitz refers, for example, to an idealized "unranked" ethnic group arrangement, in which ethnic groups are "cross-class" and ethnic divisions take the form of vertical cleavages. Ethnic groups, each representing incipient whole societies with their own internal strata, coexist side by side.[44]

The Marxist approach to ethnic conflict, as simply an outward manifestation of class conflict, cannot account for the complexities that arise when ethnic divisions cut across formal class divisions in an unranked system, such as that found in Malaysia.[45] There, each of the major communities contains its own elite strata. Among the Malays, there are high-status members of the aristocracy, the modern bureaucracy, the elected legislature, and the bourgeoisie. Among the ethnic Chinese may be found very wealthy descendants of early traders, as well as newer industrialists, professionals, and intellectuals. Among the ethnic Indians, there are prominent doctors and lawyers as well as wealthy entrepreneurs. Similarly, there are parallel representatives of the lower strata in each ethnic community. Each group has its own criteria for rank and prestige. The groups do not stand in a generalized hierarchical relationship with respect to each other, nor is one group generally seen as constituting an elite stratum above the others.[46] In essence, what we have in the Malaysian case is a society where the principal lines of stratification are vertical—separating ethnic communities which are laterally insulated from each other by cultural barriers—rather than horizontal as is the case in societies where class is the main basis for social cleavage.

From the Marxist assertion that the primary antagonism in society is necessarily between classes rather than ethnic groups, we would expect that social conflict would primarily take the form of violence between different class elements. This has not, however, been the experience in the Malaysian case. The worst outbreaks of unrest and violence (in 1945, 1969, and in numerous less serious incidents) have involved fighting between members of one ethnic group and those of another, rather than between members of different classes. In each group, representatives of different classes (e.g., the petty bourgeoisie, the rural proletariat, and agricultural peasants), have repeatedly shown themselves ready and willing to combine in confronting ethnic opponents. It is difficult to find support in the facts of the Malaysian case for the claim that ethnic groups are simply ciphers for class interests that will be revealed in their true colors in times of serious social conflict. The willingness of proletarian elements within each ethnic group to join with their own bourgeoisie and do battle with co-workers in other ethnic groups in Malaysia suggests that collectively perceived social and cultural attributes are more salient to social action there than class position.[47]

Thus far, I have focused on the independent variable in the proposed model of industrial strategy choice, specifying what an ethnic settlement is, why we see settlements occurring at all, why they cannot simply be reduced to different levels of coercion by a hegemon, what an ethnic group is, and why it makes sense in the Malaysian case to view ethnicity rather than class as the principal source of motivation for political action. But a few caveats are in order.

First, the argument here is *not* that politics in Malaysia can be understood simply by focusing on ethnic ties; other factors are at work as well. Ethnic affiliations do not govern behavior in all situations. Horowitz makes the point that "everywhere there exist buyers and sellers, officials and citizens, co-workers and members of professions; all of these roles are to some extent independent of the ethnic origins of their incumbents."[48] In Malaysia's deeply divided society, strong ethnic allegiances permeate organizations, activities and roles to which such allegiances are formally unrelated. So Malaysians do not always act as members of ethnic groups, but their primary allegiance remains, nevertheless, to their group. Classes exist and we find trade unions and business chambers of commerce, but these organizations mobilize their members on the basis of ethnic affinity (so we have Malay chambers of commerce and Chinese chambers of commerce, Malay-dominated unions and Chinese-dominated unions). The same is true of political parties; no party that has seriously attempted to develop a multiethnic constituency has ever been successful and each of the major parties today is clearly identified with a particular ethnic group. In Horowitz's words, Malaysian ethnic affiliations are "powerful, permeative, passionate and persuasive."[49]

Second, the emphasis here on ethnic identity and on the politics of *inter*group relations does not mean that *intra*group politics are unimportant. Patron-client ties and issue-specific rivalries between members of the same ethnic group often play a role in determining policy outcomes. We shall see in chapter 4, for example, that specific policies implemented by UMNO in 1970, in response to a broad Malay consensus that the government had to intervene more actively in the economy to reduce non-Malay domination, were shaped by rivalries *within* the Malay leadership of UMNO itself. Similarly, recent splits in UMNO, between the Prime Minister on the one hand, and his former Deputy Prime Minister and Trade and Industry Minister on the other, that have resulted in the formation of a new Malay party, have demonstrated that intra-Malay politics can have far-reaching implications for the country as a whole.

Nevertheless, the significant shifts in industrial strategy which this study seeks to explain (in Malaysia, we have seen two such abrupt changes, in 1970 and in 1980) are shown here to have their roots in the politics of intergroup relations, and to be related specifically to the nature of the prevailing modus vivendi between ethnic groups. To explain the original impetus for change and to understand the politics behind the choice of a particular overall strategy (market-led, mixed market-regulatory, or state-led) at a particular point in time, our principal focus needs to be on intergroup relations, rather than subgroup rivalries. Under the rubric of an existing overall strategy, particular policy choices (e.g., the adoption of the Industrial Coordination Act in 1975) may reflect the influence of intragroup coalition-building, but the overall framework itself is tied to the nature of relations *between* major ethnic communities.

Third (and this point relates to the second), while the political salience of ethnic identity in Malaysia helps explain why ethnic parties have flourished and multiethnic parties have not, the longevity of the *particular* political organizations that represent each group in the governing National Front coalition cannot be explained simply by the fact that they are ethnically identified. To explain, for example, why Malay group affiliation has focused on UMNO (why UMNO has been recognized for over forty years as the primary vehicle for Malay political aspirations) rather than on the *Partai Islam* (PAS) or some other Malay party, we have to look beyond ethnicity to factors such as the coalition-building devices that have been employed to hold the party together. For example, elaborate patronage networks, used to distribute resources which party leaders have access to as a direct result of their control over government coffers, have played an enormously important role in nurturing and sustaining the UMNO political machine. Within UMNO itself, leaders such as Mahathir owe their following and their status to carefully husbanded personal ties with supporters that reach down to the district level and, in some cases, to the village.

This story, however, is one that must be left for another time. For the purposes of this study, we need note only that the particular political organizations and particular leaders within these organizations that manifest ethnic political aspirations in Malaysia today are not the product of some ineluctable process driven by ethnic identity. A *necessary* condition for UMNO's success, for example, was that it be communally identified and that its leaders couched their appeals in communal terms, but ethnic identity is not *sufficient* to explain why the party, or particular leaders within it, have succeeded in solidifying their positions. To explain this, we need to attend to the processes of coalition-building and resource distribution that have characterized UMNO and its leaders since the party's inception. While these processes are certainly deserving of further research,[50] they are antecedent to the main focus of this study, which is concerned *not* with how existing political structures and leading individuals within those structures arrived at their present state, but *how such structures and individuals have influenced strategy choice.* We will see that, in this story of changing industrial strategy choices over time in a communally divided society, ethnic identity (and the nature of ethnic group relations) plays a pivotal role.

CONSTRAINT ON STATE AUTONOMY

Thus far, discussion of our model has focused primarily on ethnic aspects of the communal settlement. But the extent to which a communal settlement is able to shape industrial choices in any society is dependent on the level of constraint it imposes on state autonomous decision-making. It is appropriate at this point, therefore, to discuss the role of the state in all of this.

Implicit here is the assumption that the state enjoys some degree of autonomy from forces within the larger society.[51] The state can be considered neither Marx's executive committee of the bourgeoisie nor, as Dahl might have it, the product of a simple aggregation of group pressures.[52] My conception of state-society relations thus recognizes that the state may enjoy relative autonomy from society, under certain conditions. This perspective, however, begs two important questions: autonomy from whom or from what; and autonomy with respect to what issues?

In the Malaysian case, the state is autonomous, but only with respect to certain ethnic groups. What makes the issue of autonomy so important to an understanding of state industrial strategy in this case is the fact that these groups happen to control the "high ground" of the national economy. State autonomy in Malaysia is autonomy with respect to the economically dominant Chinese and Indian minority communities. The original agreement that accompanied independence guaranteed Malay dominance of the state apparatus and of the governing coalition that inherited political power from the British. State economic policies have therefore sought to address two (sometimes contradictory) goals: that of fostering overall economic growth; and that of promoting the economic well-being of the least economically-advanced (but most numerous) in society, namely the Malay community. Thus the state in Malaysia can be said on the one hand to have been "captured" by one community and therefore to be autonomous from other communities—those dominating the private sector economy. Yet, on the other hand, it has been constrained in its ability to pursue narrow (Malay) communal interests where they have directly threatened those of other communities (i.e., where there is a preception that policy is in effect a zero-sum game).[53]

We may construct a typology to explore the range of possible relationships that might exist between group settlement (or societal "common ground"), on the one hand, and constraint on state action, on the other (see table 1.1).

In table 1.1, the horizontal axis represents the scope of settlement among societal groups—the extent to which major groups in society are in broad agreement on issues affecting the distribution of wealth and power between them. When the settlement is relatively narrow in scope, as has been the case in Malaysia since 1980, agreement between groups on distributional issues is limited. Conversely, broad

TABLE 1.1
Settlement and Constraint

		Scope of Settlement	
		Broad	*Narrow*
Societal Constraint on State Autonomous Action	*Low*	Japanese Case	Malaysia 1980–
	High	Malaysia 1957–1970	Lebanese Case

settlement implies a wide-ranging consensus among groups over how the national pie (broadly defined) ought to be divided.

The vertical axis measures societal constraint on state autonomous action: where constraint is high, the state's realm of autonomous action is relatively limited as a result of pressures that societal groups are able to bring to bear on state actors; where constraint is "low," the state is able to formulate policy (in this case, industrial strategy) without being unduly constrained by pressures from societal groups.

From table 1.1 we can see that the Japanese case corresponds to a situation in which broad distributional agreement and low levels of societal constraint on state action coincide (the upper-left-hand cell). In Japan, an absence of significant religious, ethnic, linguistic, or caste divisions has contributed to the existence of relatively broad societal agreement on policy goals (distributional disputes between such groups have been rare in Japan). The Japanese developmental state, therefore, has been relatively free from policy constraints rooted in ethnic concerns and this is one of a number of factors that have facilitated high rates of economic growth in the Japanese case.

A contrasting example, involving broad agreement between groups but with high levels of constraint on state action, is exemplified by Malaysia during the first decade of its independence. The Malay-dominated state was at that time constrained from using the state apparatus to advance Malay commercial aspirations by the terms of a communal settlement which enjoyed broad support among all ethnic groups.

If we consider the right-hand column of table 1.1, characterized by limited intergroup agreement on distributional issues, we can see that the case of Malaysia since 1980 corresponds to a situation of low constraint. Where groups agree on very little, the state enjoys considerable freedom to pursue a policy agenda favoring the group that controls it. Lebanon provides the contrasting case—there, limited agreement between Islamic and Christian communities has rendered the state impotent, constrained from pursuing *any* agenda at all, for lack of sustained support from any quarter.

It is possible, therefore, to identify real-world situations that correspond to each of the four cells of table 1.1. Now let us consider the relationship between agreement and constraint in the case of a country like Malaysia, where differences between communal groups are highly politically salient. In Malaysia, the principal source of societal constraint on state autonomous action is the nature of the prevailing ethnic settlement. In other words, although it is not difficult to identify real-world cases elsewhere in which societal consensus and societal constraint on state action move in *opposite* directions (i.e., where a broader consensus is associated with less constraint [Japan] or, alternatively, a narrower consensus leads to a highly constrained state [Lebanon]), in the Malaysian case the two variables are closely interrelated and move together. Implicit in the communal settlement over distribution of wealth and power is "agreement" on who should control the state and on the extent to which the state apparatus should be constrained in making decisions which might impinge upon the *ideal* or *material* interests of groups party to the settlement. Hence the intercommunal agreement in Malaysia *embodies* agreement on whether, and to what extent, the state should enjoy autonomy to act.

The model advanced here, relating communal settlement (the independent variable) to industrial strategy choice (the dependent variable), is represented in table 1.2.

Table 1.2 has three analytic categories and generates three sets of hypotheses about how particular strategy choices are made in communal societies. These analytic categories are shown to correspond to three empirical stages in the evolution of economic strategy in

TABLE 1.2
Communal Settlement and Strategy Choice

	Communal Settlement (Independent Variable)		
	Broad**	Medium	Narrow
Societal Constraint on State Autonomy	High	Medium	Low
Industrial Development Strategy (Dependent Variable)	Market-led	Mixed Market-led and State-Regulatory	State-led
Level of State Intervention	Low	Medium	High
Empirical Referent: Malaysia	1957–1969	1970–1980	1980–

**Although the term "settlement" implies broad agreement, breadth, in the case of the independent variable used here, refers to the range of issues on which communal leaders find they are able to settle their differences.

Malaysia. In the first column, corresponding to the 1957–1969 period in Malaysia, there is broad agreement among communal leaders as to the appropriate distribution of political and economic power between communities. The state's ability to act autonomously, free of constraint from the communal agreement, is limited and the result is a low level of state intervention (corresponding with adoption of a market-led industrial development strategy).

On the other hand, when there is relatively little accord over appropriate economic and political roles for the different groups and the communal settlement is therefore limited in scope (as shown by the righthand column), the state is less constrained in the manner by which it chooses to pursue its twin goals of promoting economic growth and serving the interests of the group or groups that control it. The result is a state-led strategy wherein the state uses public resources in a manner that is designed to foster growth but which at the same time benefits one group disproportionately in comparison to all the others. This is the outcome that we observe in Malaysia beginning in 1980.[54]

Between the two extremes is an intermediate case, associated with moderate communal accord, a moderate level of constraint on state action, and a strategy that mixes market-led adjustment with an increasing degree of state intervention through expanded regulation of economic activities. This parallels the situation observed in Malaysia between 1970 and 1980.

Driving the model overall are changes in the nature of the communal settlement. Agreement in 1969, for example, that the interests of all communities in Malaysia were best served by encouraging the expansion of existing (foreign and non-Malay owned) industry, was replaced, as a consequence of the 1969 riots, by a Malay belief that continued laissez-faire growth would inevitably disadvantage Malays while favoring the non-Malay community. As the common ground between communities became more limited, industrial strategy choice was affected.

It should be emphasized at this point that the intercommunal settlement, and the societal constraint on state autonomous action that it implies, represents just one of a number of political and economic factors which conceivably might exert influence over industrial strategy choice in a communally divided society. Among economic factors that might be causal, for example, are the existing structure of the economy (i.e., how well-developed it is), the level of industrial development thus far attained (i.e., whether existing market opportunities have been exhausted), and external economic conditions, particularly the country's position in the international division of labor. Relevant political factors might include calculations as to which choices stand to yield the most benefit to supporters of the ruling elite or to dominant sub-elites.

This study does not deny the potential relevance of such factors to an analysis of industrial choices. It suggests, however, that, among political factors affecting industrial strategy choice in Third World communal societies, the nature of relations between major communities has a central role, and the relationship between communal settlement and strategy choice is therefore deserving of more attention in the literature than it has enjoyed thus far.

The model outlined in table 1.2 describes a relationship—between the scope and nature of the settlement over political and economic objectives and level of state intervention—that is at odds with that observed in the case of Japan, for example. The experiences of Japan, and of some of the newly industrializing countries (NICs), suggest that broad agreement over national economic goals, or at least lack of focused opposition from the disorganized and pliant "masses" to goals enunciated by the state, provides the state with room for autonomous action in fostering industrial development.[55] The findings of this study show the reverse to be the case in Malaysia, where broad societal agreement represents a tight constraint on state actions.

The difference may be explained by observing that intergroup settlement, in the case of a communal society, entails agreement over the *distribution* of economic (and political) resources. The state is free to pursue overall economic growth objectives *within the constraints imposed by this distributional agreement*. The societal "consensus" found in the Japanese and East Asian NIC cases, on the other hand, concerns overall *growth* goals and is based on a lack of organized opposition to state initiatives rather than broad support for those initiatives. The state in these cases has been able to pursue such growth goals, until relatively recently, without being too concerned about the distributional consequences.

The contrasting experiences of Japan and Malaysia suggest that we need to consider the degree of communal fragmentation existing in a society if we are to understand why a broad societal settlement in Malaysia (and in comparable cases elsewhere in the developing world) constrains the state while in Japan and the NICs broad acquiescence to state action prevails and appears to free the state from constraint.

At this point it is appropriate to turn to the empirical content of this study. The next section introduces state and society in Malaysia and describes the origins of the negotiated intergroup settlement that is central to my analysis.[56]

THE CASE: MALAYSIA

Malaysia provides a compelling example of the influence that communal arrangements can have on industrial choices in a developing Third World society. Chapter 2 describes in broad terms the historical and social context for this study. What follows is a brief orientation to the political constraints on economic management posed by intergroup relations in Malaysia.

At independence, Malayan society comprised three major ethnic communities—the indigenous Malays (who then accounted for 50 percent of the population), and two sizeable immigrant communities, one Chinese (37 percent) and the other Indian (11 percent).[57] The Malays, descendant from migrants who had traversed the land-bridge from Central Asia, were heavily concentrated in rural areas where they were primarily engaged in subsistence agriculture. Malay ownership in the commercial sector was limited. Malays owned only 10 percent of registered businesses, paid only 4 percent of income taxes and held only 1.5 percent of shares in publicly listed companies.[58] But they were involved in urban areas as laborers (in the construction industry, for example) and, among the elite strata of civil servants, Malays far outnumbered any other group. So Malays were well-represented among the most politically powerful and those holding positions in the well-paid and relatively extensive state bureaucracy, while at the same time dominating the ranks of the least well-off rural peasantry.

The Chinese, originally drawn to the Malay Peninsula by the lure of profits from trade and tin (a tin boom began in the 1840s), represented a substantial permanent community by the time of independence. In the latter part of the nineteenth century, thousands of laborers had been shipped by Chinese entrepreneurs from southern

China to the alluvial tin deposits of Perak, Selangor, and Sungei Ujong to provide coolie labor for the open-cast mines. These laborers joined traders who had preceded them to the trading ports of the straits settlements (Singapore, Malacca, and Penang). Thus, while the wealthier Malayan Chinese were concentrated in towns and cities of the coast, dominating locally owned commerce and small-scale industry (the largest companies were still at this time foreign-owned),[59] the Chinese workers were found predominantly in the tin-mining areas inland, in Perak and Selangor.

The Malayan Indian community originated with the Malayan rubber boom at the turn of the century. To tap the rubber trees, which had been introduced to Malaya from South America (by way of Kew Gardens, London), large numbers of Tamils (as well as speakers of Telugu and Malayalam) were imported by British plantation interests from South India. This migration of labor satisfied a conscious colonial policy which sought to preserve an ethnic balance between Malays and Chinese. Indian tappers were joined, in the years following World War I, by urban traders, businessmen and professionals from the Punjab who set themselves up in towns along the peninsula. The result was a substantial permanent population of Malayan Indians, comprising, as was the case with the other ethnic groups, a mixture of rich and poor, proletarian and bourgeoisie, rural- and urban-dweller.[60]

The sorts of occupational tasks that elite members of each ethnic group undertook were generally quite distinct—the Malays were hereditary aristocrats, bureaucrats, and politicians, and, at a lower level, school teachers and village headmen; the Chinese were traders and businessmen; the Indians were professionals and shopkeepers. The same was true for workers from each group—the Malays worked in the fields; the Chinese labored in the tin mines; and the Indians tapped the rubber trees. Because of this functional or occupational specialization, different ethnic groups tended also to live in separate areas. Ethnic occupational specialization and geographic separation were encouraged by a colonial policy of assigning to elements of each community specific roles in the economic division of labor. The employment of Malay workers as tin miners or rubber tappers, for example, was officially discouraged because it was felt that the "proper" place for Malay workers was in the rice fields.[61]

When the British began preparations for eventual Malayan independence, soon after World War II,[62] it was clear that they saw the indigenous Malay leaders as the rightful inheritors of the sovereignty which had been wrested from the Malay sultanates during the original colonial occupation. At the same time, however, colonial administrators made it clear that they were not prepared to leave government in the hands of just one community, for fear of communal violence of the sort that led to the partition of India and Pakistan in 1947.

The leaders of the three major ethnic groups responded to these conditions by turning an ad hoc local electoral alliance linking the major Malay (UMNO) and the major Chinese party (the Malayan Chinese Association) into a national coalition of the three main ethnic political parties.[63] Labeled simply the Alliance, this coalition was based on an intercommunal settlement that satisfied the British conditions for the granting of independence: the Malays would dominate government (UMNO would be the leading party in the coalition, Malays would dominate positions in the civil service, and the head of state, the king, would be constitutionally elected by his peers from among the rulers of the traditional Malay royal families) with the support of the immigrant communities, in return for a Malay commitment to accord the Chinese and Indians full citizenship rights and not to challenge (or interfere with) Chinese and Indian commercial freedom.

How this intercommunal settlement evolved, leading to different levels of constraint on the state actors in economic policy-making and subsequently to markedly different approaches to industrial development strategy in succeeding decades, is the subject of the chapters which follow.

Chapter 2 provides a brief overview of Malaysian history and a discussion of how the explicit negotiation of a communal modus vivendi set the scene for the country's independence in 1957 and for the first attempt at formulating a national industrial policy.

Chapter 3 analyses the market-led strategy that dominated the state's approach to industrialization during the first decade or so after independence (1957–1969). Extensive state intervention in the traditional rural sector was sanctioned during this period because the beneficiaries were mainly Malay and it was implicit in the intercommunal settlement that the Malay-dominated state would play an active role in improving the economic condition of rural Malays.

However, this same settlement placed severe constraints on the extent to which the state could intervene in the Chinese- and Indian-dominated modern commercial and industrial sector. Noninterference here had been part of the price the Malay leadership had paid to secure the agreement of Chinese and Indian leaders to constitutional arrangements that guaranteed Malay political hegemony. Thus the independence settlement established a political climate in which the state had little choice but to leave industrial development to non-Malay entrepreneurs and foreign companies.

Chapter 4 describes the watershed events of May 1969, when Malay resentment at the terms of the intercommunal settlement spilled over into the worst urban ethnic violence in the country's independent history. It describes how the terms of the bargain changed in response to the riots and then how these changes affected the state's approach to industrial development. After the riots, Malay leaders were able to secure grudging acceptance, by the leaders of the other communities, of state-sponsored efforts to enlarge the Malay role in commerce and industry. They subsequently began to employ increasingly intrusive state policies designed to benefit Malays while limiting the entrepreneurial freedom of non-Malay business.

Chapter 5 examines the state-centered industrial development strategy put in place by the Malay-dominated state in 1980, in response to Malay perceptions that Chinese failure to embrace earlier affirmative action goals for Malays indicated that the intercommunal bargain had finally unraveled. The large-scale state-controlled industries established under the guise of a NIC-type model posed a challenge to historical non-Malay economic dominance of the local economy. The NICs presented proximate exemplars of rapidly industrializing developing societies, but their example was used primarily for the purpose of justifying a heavily statist policy of industrial change that served a domestic communal agenda.

The book concludes with a review of the theoretical argument of chapter 1 in light of the empirical evidence presented in chapters 2–5, and an elaboration of the broader implications stemming from this study which can inform our understanding of the recent developmental experiences of late-industrializing countries in the Third World.

2

COLONIAL AND PRECOLONIAL MALAYA

Some knowledge of Malaysia's colonial and precolonial past is necessary if one is to understand the context for industrial development in independent Malaysia since 1957. The treatment here is selective—it focuses on those aspects of Malaysia's history which have had a lasting impact on economic policy-making.

The historical events of most importance for this study began in the late nineteenth century when the British established direct colonial rule over Malaya. In 1874, the governor of three British settlements on the Straits of Malacca ordered British "intervention" in three previously independent Malay sultanates in response to demands for protection from British commercial interests. By 1890, the British, who only sixteen years earlier had claimed but a few small trading ports, controlled the entire Malay Peninsula. Before discussing the consequences of this colonization, however, several aspects of precolonial Malay society deserve mention.

The Malay people are descendant from migrants who reached Malaya from the North about 2000 B.C. In precolonial times, they lived in small villages scattered along the coastline and inland rivers, surviving largely by subsistence agriculture (although they did trade for some goods, notably salt).[1] Their living conditions were relatively comfortable; land was plentiful and the soil and climate generally bountiful.[2] This, though, was later to prove a mixed blessing, for while Malaysia was able to prosper as an exporter of crops such as rubber and palm oil, the favorable rural surroundings discouraged indigenous Malays from investing in commerce. Unlike the immigrant Chinese and Indians, who were physically separated from their homelands, the Malays had an ethos of return to the village, where land and food were always plentiful. This engendered a sense of economic security that discouraged Malays from "bare-knuckle" competition in commerce with urban non-Malay entrepreneurs.[3]

The village in Malay society was usually under the control of a district raja who, in turn, acknowledged the authority of a state sultan. But rulers in Malay society had limited authority. If their demands were deemed excessive, or if they failed to protect their people against attack, subject populations were likely simply to "disappear," into the jungle. Farmers generally did not invest in long-term improvements (such as irrigation), or accumulate material possessions, because they wanted to be able to "vote with their feet," if necessary. This attitude proved an obstacle to state efforts to encourage Malay investment after independence. Accumulation was seen historically as counterproductive because it attracted the unwanted attention of authority and cut off the possibility of flight.[4]

Malay rulers supported themselves by levying taxes on trade in pepper, salt, and other imported items. This traditional approach to revenue collection, which placed a heavy burden on non-Malays who were the majority of the traders, is the basis for the present pattern of reliance on Chinese and Indian (and foreign) commercial activities to generate the resources necessary to finance social programs (most of which benefit Malays).[5]

Because Malaya stood astride a major trade route linking India and the Far East, contacts with foreign traders were frequent. Ports along the Straits of Malacca had, by the fifteenth century, become important trading centers and many foreign merchants established semipermanent residence in Malaya, thereby founding immigrant communities that today account for 40 percent of the population of Malaysia. More than half the residents of Malacca, for example, were foreign traders, including Gujerati and other Indian seamen and merchants, Burmese, Chinese, Javanese, and other Indonesians, as well as smaller groups.[6] The Chinese were particularly active; in the first half of the nineteenth century they were the first to expand their commercial activities inland, where they developed open-caste tin mines and smelters.[7]

Soon Europeans were drawn by trade to Malacca. The Portugese attacked and occupied the town in 1511, intending to gain control over commerce in Indonesian spices and Southeast Asian tin and over imports of Indian textiles to the region. But their efforts to establish a trading monopoly over the area failed (they were opposed by the Sumatran kingdom of Aceh and the former Malaccan dynasty, exiled in Johor) and their legacy was limited.[8] They did however manage, in trying to enforce the trading monopoly, to destroy a preexisting class of indigenous Malay traders. This was significant because it meant that, from the Dutch time forward, commerce in Malaya was almost exclusively the domain of non-Malays.[9] The Dutch, like the Portugese, sought commercial goals in the region and in 1641 their forces drove the Portugese from Malacca. They took Malacca not to establish a monopoly but to secure the sea route to Java and Batavia, where the Dutch East India Company was active. The Dutch impact on Malay society, however, like that of the Portugese, was slight. This was not the case with the British.

The first Englishmen to frequent the Malay Peninsula were private traders such as Francis Light, who claimed the island of Penang for the British East India Company in 1786.[10] The company was reluctant to extend its activities eastwards from existing trading ports in India and Ceylon, but agreed to pursue Light's initiative because Penang was attractive as a haven for company ships during the northeast monsoon.[11] So began the first phase (1786–1874) of British involvement, during which the crown acquired three trading ports on the Straits of Malacca (Penang, Malacca, and Singapore) and annexed parts of the island of Borneo.[12] These straits settlements (as they became known) existed as tiny enclaves surrounded by Malay sultanates which extended from Singapore in the South to Siam in the North.[13] The thrust of British colonial policy towards the sultanates was to maintain tidy, peaceful relations with the indigenous rulers, so that trade could continue unimpeded by local squabbles.[14] This policy of cooperation and noninterference remained in force until the early 1870s, when the demands of rapidly expanding European industry necessitated a change in the British approach.

Before describing this change, though, we might pause to review those aspects of pre-1874 Malay society that have had a continuing influence on economic policy-making: the environment was bountiful year-round, so there was little incentive for Malays to put aside "for a rainy day," (i.e., to save); peasants avoided investing in improvements or accumulating material wealth because they wanted to be able to escape predatory rulers; there were extensive trading contacts with foreign traders, many of whom settled and established permanent immigrant communities; and Malay rulers made their living from taxes on this trade (thus the burden of supporting the state fell disproportionately on non-Malays). Trade eventually attracted European attention and the Portugese, Dutch, and British in turn operated trading ports on the Straits of Malacca, but before 1874 their presence had limited impact on Malay society as a whole. Each of these aspects of precolonial and colonial Malaya has been of importance for economic development since independence.

BRITISH COLONIAL RULE

Rapid industrialization in mid-nineteenth-century Europe led to greater demand for tin from Malaya than could be supplied by traditional Malay methods.[15] This caused Chinese and British merchants in the British settlements on the Straits of Malacca to respond by forming joint ventures with local Malay rulers to undertake large-scale commercial production of tin in the inland river valleys of Malaya. Such ventures usually had three partners: the Chinese, using their links to clan associations and secret societies, imported and organized coolie labor from South China; the British supplied the capital and supervised the marketing of the output on international metals markets;[16] and the rulers granted access to the deposits, in exchange for a share of the profits (in the form of export duties on tin, import duties on miners' supplies, and receipts from tax-collecting monopolies granted to Chinese entrepreneurs).[17] This association of non-Malay trading and commercial interests in the straits settlements and Malay rulers in the tin-producing areas of Perak and Selangor was a precursor of interethnic ties which led to the formation of the Alliance government in 1957.

The wealth generated from tin, however, led to challenges to the traditional Malay authority structure. Rulers in tin-mining areas soon became wealthier than the sultans themselves, and competition for territory and revenue created opposing camps of Malay rulers and Chinese miners, supported by British merchants in the straits settlements.[18] Severe local conflict developed and, finally, virtual civil war —from 1868 onwards, the main tin mining areas were wracked by intermittent fighting. Economic activity in the adjacent straits settlements was affected and a number of prominent merchants who had been appointed to a newly created Legislative Council demanded that action be taken to contain the violence.[19]

The tin boom had, in the meantime, attracted individual wealthy British entrepreneurs who had courted Malay chiefs, offering to act as their agents and financial advisers. These individuals were frustrated in their desire to develop large-scale agriculture (to supplement mining) by the difficulty of establishing land ownership and the absence of formal contracts or the legal apparatus to sustain them. These individuals too demanded that the colonial authorities intervene in the independent Malay states.[20]

The relevant authorities (seated in Calcutta) were, however, committed to a policy of nonintervention in Malaya and ignored these entreaties. This led to demands for, and the eventual creation of, a separate crown colony named the Straits Settlements in 1868. Nevertheless, the Colonial Office, under whose jurisdiction the Straits Settlements now fell, was equally reluctant to interfere in the Malay states.[21]

British concern to secure existing holdings in Africa and Asia against inroads from competing European powers (particularly Germany) soon led, however, to a reconsideration of policy in Malaya, and "intervention" followed in Perak, Selangor, and Sungei Ujong (the mining district of Negri Sembilan) in 1874.[22] An agreement between the governor of the Straits Settlements and the ruler of Perak provided for the appointment of a British resident, "whose advice must be asked and acted upon on all questions other than those touching Malay religion and custom."[23] Under this "residential system," a State Council comprising Malay aristocrats and Chinese mining employers was created to advise the sultan. In practice, its members paid more attention to influencing the British resident, whose administrative measures came before the council.

The intervention "formula" applied to Perak was, however, unworkable. The traditional structure of rule in the state precluded the sultan from acting upon any "advice" the resident might offer, while the resident could not interfere with this structure without violating the terms of his residency. Moreover, the two sides expected quite different things from the agreement. The sultan anticipated British support in his struggles with newly wealthy district chiefs, but on terms that would buttress his traditional authority, while the British wanted to take over the ruler's role as collector of state revenues, thus threatening to undermine the very foundation of that authority. The arrangement soon collapsed, as it did when tried in Selangor and Sungei Ujong, and was replaced by one involving direct rule by the resident. This was subsequently extended to the remainder of Negri Sembilan and to Pahang after a decade or so.

Along with direct rule, the British introduced western political, legal, and administrative norms, including the principles of absolute private property and contractual obligation, and the physical infrastructure (roads and railroads) necessary for later large-scale capitalist development.[24] They established a new system of land ownership and replaced corvée and slave labor, traditionally owed to Malay rulers, with "free" wage labor.[25] British investors soon began entering the Malay states in increasing numbers to purchase tracts of now alienable land, possibly harboring tin. However, British tin-mining companies using European staff and expensive capital equipment had difficulty competing with the Chinese who used immigrant labor.[26] Some investors planted crops such as pepper, tea, gambia, sugar, and coffee. But many of these early experiments in agriculture failed—it was only with the later introduction of rubber that agriculture in Malaya became a large-scale commercial success.[27]

By the end of the nineteenth century, as British commercial activities and influence permeated most of central Malaya, the business community began to chafe at having to deal with separate state administrations in Perak, Selangor, Negri Sembilan, and Pahang. So the British in 1896 created the Federated Malay States (FMS) and thereafter administered the four states collectively.[28] In 1909, the British annexed four northern states previously ruled by Siam and, along with Johor, these became known as the Unfederated Malay States (UMS). Thus, at the onset of World War I, British colonial possessions in Malaya consisted of three Straits Settlements and nine Malay states.[29]

So far, I have focused on the effect of commercial exploitation of tin on the economy and society of central Malaya. There was, however, another product which was to have an even more important impact on Malay peasant life. The introduction of rubber to Malaya at the turn of the century brought many changes.[30] Malayan conditions proved ideally suited to the rubber tree, which was imported from South America (via London's Kew Gardens), and large-scale production proved feasible in the Malayan case because the British had access to extensive tracts of suitable land and to cheap labor.[31] Rubber plantation acreage expanded rapidly until rubber came to eclipse tin as the colony's highest export earner.[32] European (mainly British) enterprises dominated the plantation business—in 1940 they owned almost three-quarters of all rubber estate land.[33]

The introduction of rubber had a profound effect on Malay society, because it introduced the money economy to wide areas previously untouched by it. In land ownership, demands by British plantation companies for absolute ownership of their holdings led to a system of registered land titles—for the first time, every individual shareholding was entered into a local subdistrict register and permanent title granted to the owner. This severely disrupted traditional economic relations based on abundant land and poorly defined property rights. For example, Malay peasants now had to pay a perpetual quit-rent for the pleasure of holding title to land they had always occupied.[34] They were no longer free to clear and cultivate new land as the need arose; any use of land without reference to the Land Office was considered illegal occupation. They found that land could be confiscated arbitrarily for state use under minor pretexts, such as nonpayment of quit-rent, or absence of visible cultivation.

Traditional production patterns were also disrupted when Malay villagers, responding to high prices between 1910 and 1920, themselves began to plant rubber trees. Although colonial administrators tried to discourage this—the proper role of Malay cultivators, from their point of view, was the traditional, stable, but less profitable task of growing rice—smallholder rubber rapidly became the mainstay of the peasant economy in central and southern Malaya.

Adoption of rubber as a cash crop by Malay villagers affected the emerging pattern of land ownership. Land supporting trees with the potential to produce for several decades suddenly acquired considerable value and, under the new title system of land ownership, was permanently alienable; it could be, and was, sold to non-Malays who lived outside the village.[35] Colonial administrators expressed concern at the prospect of Malay ancestral land being converted to rubber cultivation and passing into the hands of non-Malays. They therefore introduced the Malay Reservations Act (1913), which specified that Malay reserve land could be sold only to Malays and that only a limited number of agencies could hold Malay reserve land as collateral for loans.[36] The act, however, because it limited the ability of landowners to mortgage their main asset (their reserve land), had the effect of limiting Malay access to capital. If Malays chose to sell their land, the price would be less than the market rate because of the restrictions on ownership. The act also encouraged Malays to stay in reserve areas, and this had implications for the emergence of a Malay commercial class because commercial opportunities in rural areas were relatively few as compared with those available in cities and towns.[37]

Other changes affecting economic relations in Malaya were also occurring at this time. By the end of the nineteenth century, foreign traders and laborers (Chinese in tin mining and Indians in rubber plantations) were forming large settled communities.[38] From South China, coolies had been recruited for the tin mines. Chinese traders and entrepreneurs had also come and, by the start of World War I, they dominated non-European commerce in towns and cities.[39] Punjabi traders, businessmen, and professionals had migrated and, from South India, peasants and lower-class Tamils and speakers of Telugu and Malayalam had come to labor on the rural estates of Johor and Negri Sembilan or on public works projects, such as those for the railroad.[40] Those transported from India not only provided manpower but also served the British purpose of trying to balance the immigrant communities. The following excerpt from a colonial dispatch indicates the official thinking in this regard:

> I am . . . anxious for political reasons that the great preponderance of the Chinese over any other races in these settlements, and to a less marked degree in some of the native states under our administration, should be counter-balanced as much as possible by the influx of Indian and other nationalities.[41]

The growth of these immigrant communities and their prominent role in non-European commerce was paralleled by increasing European dominance over the economy as a whole. Between 1900 and 1920, foreign (predominantly British) capital poured into Malaya, responding to the pull of tin and, specifically, the opportunities provided by the introduction of new, mechanized tin dredges, which yielded substantially higher profits and enabled British companies to wrest control of the industry from the Chinese.[42]

In the economy as a whole, Chinese business activities were generally overshadowed by those of the much larger European companies which had the advantage of access to large-scale sources of capital, political influence, and advanced technology. These European companies dominated the main sectors of the economy (the import-export trade, banking, shipping, plantations, and mining), while Chinese companies were typically engaged in retail trading and commodity dealing, some wholesaling activities, small-scale transportation, and a few minor industries such as food processing, saw milling, rice milling, tanneries, and ice factories (and, of course, tin mining, using labor-intensive methods).[43]

In importing and exporting, large European houses, partly through their control over trade credit, were preeminent.[44] In banking, three major British banks (Chartered, Hong Kong & Shanghai, and Mercantile), along with a number of smaller British and Dutch concerns, dominated the industry.[45] Such banks, however, were reluctant to make domestic loans (except where necessary to finance short-term trade credits) and preferred instead to transfer most of their local deposits abroad, to London.[46] Thus, although some small Chinese banks were established before World War II (the Overseas Chinese Banking Corporation was one), domestic investment capital was very hard to come by, especially for non-European investors.[47] The Malay or Indian entrepreneur had very limited access to formal sources of capital with which to establish or expand a business.[48]

In shipping, western steamers played the leading role in transporting goods and immigrant labor between China and Malaya from the mid-1870s onwards, and between India and Malaya beginning in the early twentieth century.[49] As trade expanded rapidly in the first half of the twentieth century, western shipping companies (mainly British and Dutch) formed freight conferences and monopolized the Malaya and Dutch East Indies trade with Europe and America. Furthermore, a limited number of British merchant houses in Singapore controlled agencies for most shipping and insurance companies in Europe. These houses therefore enjoyed strategic advantages as exporters; they could ensure priority shipping of their cargoes even in periods of booming trade, when shipping space was at a premium.[50]

In short, Malayan commerce, banking, and services were European-dominated. Moreover, these activities were also concentrated to an extraordinary degree in a very small number of large companies (Sime Darby and Guthries were two examples). The resulting oligopolies continued to dominate some sectors of the economy until as late as the early 1970s.[51]

The discussion so far has focused on the impact on indigenous society of economic changes associated with the imposition of colonial rule. But British administration also directly affected society, by changing traditional structures of authority.[52]

The British administration was hardly a model of coherence or efficiency—there were, in fact, three different styles of administration. The Straits Settlements were ruled directly from Singapore as a colony under a British governor, the indigenous rulers having long since been driven (or bought) off. Few vestiges of the traditional Malay state apparatus remained and the leading Malays were, in general, participants in the "modern" sector: journalists, teachers, and businessmen. There was an appointed Legislative Council, comprising official representatives from the colonial government and a smaller number of unofficial members drawn from the business community, some of them non-European. But European officials and business leaders rejected as dangerously radical the idea that some members be elected by popular vote. From their perspective, most non-European residents of the Straits Settlements were "aliens of different races who had little interest in the government of a territory in which they were only temporary sojourners."[53]

In contrast, each state of the FMS continued to be ruled in the name of its Malay ruler, but under the direction of the British resident who was the executive head of the state government (and was guided by directives from the federal capital, Kuala Lumpur). This arrangement enhanced the symbolic importance of the sultans while undermining their political power; the British adviser ruled and the Malay ruler advised, it was said.[54] Taxes once collected by the sultan were paid into a central colonial treasury under the control of the adviser. In effect, the colonial regime offered the ruler dignity and affluence while stripping him of authority over all but customary and religious matters. A Federal Council was established in 1909, comprised of the Malay rulers and British residents of each state, the British high-commissioner and chief secretary, and four appointed unofficial members, to enable the Malay rulers and the residents to express their views to the federal bureaucracy. The proceedings of the council were, however, soon dominated by discussions between European businessmen (the unofficial members) and colonial officials on a variety of commercial, fiscal and technical matters:

The four Malay Rulers, seated in lonely dignity on a raised dais, remained silent observors of these proceedings. They were unfamiliar with the matters under discussion and unable to join in a dialogue in English, since they were not fluent in that language.[55]

In 1927, the rulers finally withdrew, to be replaced by appointed unofficial members drawn from the Malay aristocracy. The size of the unofficial minority on the Federal Council was subsequently increased in stages until, on the eve of the Japanese invasion, it accounted for twelve of the twenty-eight seats (of the twelve, five were Europeans, four Malays, two Chinese, and one Indian).

A deep resentment on the part of the Malay ruling class at the emasculation of their power led the British to respond in a variety of ways: they retained some of the rulers in their traditional positions, supporting them on fixed colonial pensions;[56] they coopted the more prominent onto state councils to make policy recommendations;[57] and they inducted many into the Malayan Civil Service (MCS), the Malayan Administrative Service (MAS), the police force, or the army —that is, they turned them into civil servants.[58] In the case of those raised in the traditional ruling class, this last approach was not always successful, because they were unfamiliar with norms of bureaucratic behavior (nepotism and bribery, for example, were accepted elements of the traditional system of rule). So the British focused their efforts on educating the next generation in the English fashion. In 1905, a Malay College was established in Perak, a "Malay Eton" for those of aristocratic birth (a quota for commoners was later instituted), designed to train Malays for appointment to administrative positions in the colonial government. Only in the UMS did indigenous rulers have a substantive role in the colonial administration— elsewhere they were included pro forma in governing coucils designed to facilitate local political participation, but were in practice ignored.

Historian John Gullick has observed of the whole system of colonial rule in Malaya:

> Step by step a curious and ramshackle constitutional structure had been erected in what is now Peninsular Malaysia and Singapore.
>
> Ultimate control . . . by one man [the High Commissioner] and the supply of staff from a common pool made the system workable. But its absurdity and inefficiency had become obvious long before it was cruelly exposed in 1942.[59]

THE BRITISH COLONIAL ZENITH

During the first four decades of this century Malaya was counted as one of the brightest jewels in the British imperial crown. The income generated in the colony at times surpassed that of any other territory. As a senior colonial office official observed in 1928:

> The Government revenues of British Malaya . . . were roughly 20,000,000 [sterling] last year. The overseas imports of British Malaya as a whole for the year 1926 were valued at 117,000,000 [sterling] and the overseas exports at 147,000,000 [sterling] . . . . These remarkable totals exceed those of the total external trade of the whole of the rest of the Colonial dependencies put together. The value of exports per head of the population of British Malaya for the last two years has exceeded that of any other country in the world, and is higher even than the figure for New Zealand, which leads the self-governing Dominions in this respect.[60]

The objective of British colonial policy in Malaya during this period was to manage the economy in such a way as to enhance the prosperity of Britain. Two of the most important means used to achieve this end were the currency board system (CBS) and the system of taxation.[61]

The currency board system linked the value of Malayan currency (Straits dollars) to sterling at a fixed rate.[62] Its underlying principle was that Malayan currency should be backed 100 percent by currency board sterling assets.[63] The Currency Board thus operated somewhat like a central bank. When Malaya enjoyed a favorable trade balance, residents would accumulate pounds,[64] which they would change into local currency at local banks. The pounds would then be passed on to the Currency Board and would finally end up as board deposits or securities in London. The increase in Malayan currency received by the residents of Malaya was exactly matched by an increase in the board's sterling assets and this automatic mechanism thereby ensured the full sterling backing of every straits dollar in circulation.

The purpose of the currency board system was to secure British investments in Malaya against currency depreciation.[65] But it had the effect of prejudicing the long-run prosperity of the local Malayan economy. It exacerbated the economic instability inherent in Malaya's trade dependent economy, and discouraged internally gener-

ated economic growth. As Khor Kok Peng observes: "Internal instability of output, employment and living standards was the price paid
for the maintenance of balance of payments stability."[66] At the same
time, it precluded use of monetary policy instruments to moderate
the effects of these swings because the Currency Board had no ability
to control the size of the money supply; its function was simply to
satisfy the demand for local currency, not to regulate it.[67]

The system constrained domestic investment; any expansion of
the domestic economy which did not happen to coincide with an
external balance of payments surplus was stifled. Because it could
not accommodate increased demand for investable funds by increasing the money supply, the CBS led in such a situation to higher
interest rates that choked off the initial desire to invest.

Lastly, the CBS tied up scarce financial resources in low-interest
deposits in Britain while the colony had to borrow at high interest
whenever development funds were needed. Currency board reserves
in London thus represented financial resources foregone from the
point of view of the Malayan economy: "The 100/110 per cent reserve
in sterling was tantamount to an investment or an overflow of capital
from Malaya and Singapore to the United Kingdom and the Commonwealth countries."[68]

Taxation policy, like the CBS, was used in Malaya primarily for
the benefit of British firms and the British economy. Malaya was one
of Britain's largest revenue earners; in 1936, for example, of all British
colonies, the FMS provided the most public revenue per capita for
the empire.[69] The bulk of this revenue came not from the richly-
profitable European mining and plantation operations,[70] but from
consumption of "vices," specifically from excise duties on liquor,
tobacco, and opium. As the main consumers of these items were
Chinese laborers in the tin mines, this colonial taxation system per-
petuated the system used in the traditional Malay states where revenue was generated primarily from non-Malays.

The principal drawback of the colonial taxation system, from the
point of view of the local economy, was that fiscal surpluses were
not available to the Malayan economy but were repatriated and held
mostly in low-yielding sterling securities in London.[71] In 1928, for
example, of total assets of M$125.3 million, the FMS transferred
about half (M$64 million) to London. As in the case of other colonies,
these transfers represented domestic resources foregone.

ECONOMIC INSTABILITY AND THE DEPRESSION

One of the most important results of colonial policy in Malaya was the creation of an extremely trade-dependent economy. Rupert Emerson commented on "the amazingly high degree to which [Malaya's] economic eggs have been concentrated into the two baskets of rubber and tin."[72] After the turn of the century, while tin and rubber provided the bulk of exports, food and basic goods—once produced locally—were increasingly imported.[73] In 1931, 68 percent of total income (M$105 million out of M$154 million) in the FMS was generated in the rubber and tin industries alone, as compared with less than 2 percent (M$3 million) in rice production. Meanwhile, the ratio of exports to total production grew very rapidly during the interwar period. Malaya's heavy reliance on imports of foodstuffs, manufactured consumer items, and capital goods was illustrated in 1932, when 66 percent of the rice consumed in Malaya was imported. Among trade-dependent colonies, Malaya ranked as one of the *most* trade dependent.

This had implications for economic growth:

> The most dramatic and damaging effect of trade dependence in the colonial period was the great instability experienced by the economy as a result of very volatile fluctuations in the prices and demand for Malayan exports, fluctuations which followed the world trade cycle. As an economy with an export:import ratio of over half, colonial Malaya (especially the trade-centered Straits Settlements and the rubber and tin-centered Federated Malay States) was particularly susceptible to even slight changes in world market conditions. Trade instability had repercussions on several aspects of the economy: income, wage-rates, employment, government revenue and expenditure, profits and investments.[74]

Fluctuations in rubber prices had particularly far-reaching impacts on the economy as a whole. By the mid-1910s, rubber export income had outstripped that of tin, and for many years before World War II rubber earnings were more than twice those of tin.[75] But rubber prices reached their peak in 1909 and oscillated wildly in the following three decades. For example, the average rubber price that prevailed during the period 1935–1939 was only 14 percent of the average recorded during 1905–1909. Such fluctuations affected commodity export returns as a whole—while tin prices increased in each of the five-year periods from 1905–1909 to 1925–1929, the increases were insufficient to offset the precipitous decline in rubber returns.

The effect of fluctuating commodity returns on domestic economic development was particularly apparent during the Great Depression of 1929–1932 for, by 1932, the price of rubber stood at less than a quarter of its 1929 value, while that of tin had fallen by a third. The value of all exports had dropped to only 25 percent of its 1929 level.[76] As a result, both revenues and expenditures of the colonial administration in 1932 were less than half what they had been only four years earlier. Employment in plantations and mines alone declined by 196,000 (more than one half) in the same period. Between 1930 and 1933 there was a net repatriation of Indian laborers back to India of over 240,000. As Chinese laborers were not repatriated to the same extent, the level of unemployment in Malaya among the Chinese retrenched from mines and related industries, docks, and skilled crafts was very high (estimated at 450,000 in 1931). One consequence was the greatly increased number of Chinese who resorted to farming vacant land in an attempt to survive. Later, the presence of these Chinese squatters in rural areas would have important implications for the ability of Chinese communist guerillas to obtain material support in the countryside during the Malayan Emergency (1948–1960).[77]

The effects of the Depression were thus more seriously felt in Malaya than they were in less trade-dependent economies:

> It can . . . be said of the Federation [of Malaya] that foreign trade in rubber and tin furnishes the margin between life and death. When world trade, and particularly the American motor vehicle trade, flourishes, the F.M.S. flourishes with it, but when the world is poor the F.M.S. has nothing to fall back on but its accumulated surpluses.[78]

After the Depression, introduction of international commodity restriction schemes in the late 1930s slowed the recovery of both the rubber and tin industries and provided British companies an opportunity to further tighten their control of the primary export sector. By cornering official output quotas, they were able to reduce the already limited output shares of both Chinese tin miners and Malay rubber smallholders.[79]

JAPANESE OCCUPATION

The Japanese invasion of Malaya in 1941 ended the "golden years" of British colonial rule. It began with landings on the northern coast of the Malay Peninsula in December, and culminated in the capture of Singapore in early 1942. While the British were later able to return, important changes had occurred in their three-and-a-half-year absence that sowed seeds for Malayan independence a little over a decade later.

The first thing the Japanese did was to nurture Malay nationalism as a means of rallying popular support for the occupation. In doing so, their efforts built on earlier manifestations of nationalism that warrant a brief mention here.

In the 1920s, two institutions had been established in Malaya which later became important training grounds for Malay national-ists.[80] The first was the Sultan Idris Training College, established in 1922 to satisfy a burgeoning demand for village primary school teach-ers. Choosing its four hundred students by competitive examination from among peasant villagers throughout the Peninsula, the college soon became the center of Malay intellectual life: "It brought to-gether, from all parts of Malaya, young men, serious and intelligent, with a sense of vocation."[81] The second was the Singapore Malay Association (KMS), originally founded in 1926 to support the first Malay member appointed to the Legislative Council of the Straits Settlements. The KMS was the first Malay association with an avowedly political purpose and became a model for later nationalist movements in the Malay states.

Colonial policy, seeking to "preserve traditional Malay culture," had tried to keep Malays in comparative isolation, encouraging them to stay within the geographic limits of Malay agricultural settlement and within the occupational bounds of peasant farming and the government service. But the spread of rubber and other cash crops, the attendant social changes (especially after World War I), and the permanent settlement of large immigrant communities had led Ma-lays to become more politically aware. The creation of the KMS and the role of the Idris College were indicative of this increasing Malay political awareness in the 1920s. This trend was also reflected in the actions of four unofficial Malay members (each representing a state ruling family) appointed to the Federal Council of the FMS in 1927 who used their position to champion Malay concerns.

Malay dissatisfaction with their lot, especially in comparison with that of the British and the larger immigrant communities, grew in the 1930s with the effects of the Depression. This prompted two types of Malay nationalist response. The first was the product of efforts by English-educated Malays who had pursued careers in the administrative service. They formed Malay Associations, modeled on the KMS, to champion Malay interests with the colonial administration. In 1939, the first meeting of representatives of these associations was held in Kuala Lumpur, and within a year Malay Associations were set up in most of the Malay states as well as in Sarawak and Brunei. But for these associations to attract broad popular support, their leadership necessarily had to come from the aristocracy. Yet few Malay aristocrats were prepared to differ publicly, either with the Malay rulers or with British administrators. The extent to which the Malay Association movement was constrained by this obedience to established authority was illustrated at the second congress in 1940 when a majority of those in attendance voted to encourage Malays to support the British war effort.[82]

A different type of Malay response to British rule was that of a small group of Malay intellectuals, including graduates of the Idris College and some journalists, who formed the Young Malay Union (KMM) in 1937 to oppose colonial rule altogether. KMM leaders criticized the Malay aristocracy and Malay administrative officers for assisting British rule, and they advocated independence for Malaya in a union with Indonesia (its members were much impressed by the example of the Indonesian leader, Sukarno). Although small in size, the KMM was very influential during this formative period in the growth of Malay nationalist sentiment.

The arrival of the Japanese encouraged a growing political awareness in the Malay community. Japanese conquest of the Peninsula destroyed the aura the British had cultivated of colonial permanence and invincibility. The change in government and the general dislocation of society during the occupation period generated much greater political activity within the Malay community than had existed hitherto. The Japanese themselves fostered political involvement: mass demonstrations, slogan competitions, and lecturing contests were frequently held; pan-Malayan conferences and training programs were arranged; and all residents were encouraged to attend Japanese language classes. The object was to foster positive participation "in the Japanese spirit" at all levels of Malay society.[83]

The Japanese also encouraged certain nationalist organizations, notably the KMM.[84] KMM leaders had welcomed the Japanese advance because it promised to sweep aside European colonialism and the whole fabric of indigenous feudalism maintained by British rule. Some had made contact with Japanese agents in Singapore and near the Siamese border and had been detained during British sweeps against fifth-column elements. Many of those not detained worked in southern Siam under a Japanese intelligence officer, Major Fujiwara, to rally support from local Malay communities for the Japanese invasion.[85] Thus, when word began to spread among the retreating British forces that Malays were actively collaborating with the Japanese, the individuals involved were in fact members of the KMM. This collaboration had important repercussions—it marked the beginnings of a British disenchantment with the previously favored Malay community that grew when the sultans refused to flee with the British to the safety of Singapore and most Malay civil servants decided to stay at their posts (some were in fact promoted to positions higher than those they held under the British).[86] The result was that British military officials dealt almost exclusively with the Chinese during the occupation and, when they returned, British administrators arbitrarily imposed a new constitution that deprived Malay rulers of their sovereignty and stripped the Malays of many of their privileges.[87]

Although younger KMM members revelled in the novelty of being able to parade in celebration of the "liberation" of Asia and to condemn colonialism openly, KMM leaders soon found themselves dispersed by the Japanese throughout the Peninsula and in no position to influence the new regime.[88] The Japanese, concerned that indigenous politics not be allowed to impede the conduct of the war, manipulated the KMM primarily for propaganda purposes.[89] The influence of more radical KMM leaders was undermined by close supervision of their activities and limiting their freedom of movement. Their numbers were diluted by the addition of members recruited by the Japanese. Some of the KMM leaders became so disillusioned that they withdrew from political activity altogether and the

KMM itself became increasingly an instrument of the Japanese occupation. As Stockwell suggests: "It was perhaps more because of its futility than because of its potential danger that the Japanese disbanded the KMM in June 1942."[90]

In sum, "radical" Malay nationalists had adopted the Japanese cause at the beginning of the war in the hope that their independence objectives would be furthered by a Japanese victory. But the Japanese instead used the radicals to lead youth movements and publicity campaigns in pursuit of goals that assumed firm alien (Japanese) control of power.[91] This approach was consistent with Japanese policies elsewhere in the Co-Prosperity Sphere—the Japanese tended to favor local nationalists only in those occupied countries where there was already a strong nationalist movement. Burma, Siam, Indochina, and the Philippines, for example, all received nominal independence from the Japanese, whereas Malaya, with a relatively short Malay nationalist tradition, was kept under direct military rule, her nationalists largely ignored.[92]

This situation prevailed until nearly the end of the war. In July 1945, however, as the Japanese found their position in Southeast Asia under threat and in response advanced plans for Indonesian independence, they at the same time launched an eleventh-hour effort to develop a Malay nationalist movement based on the *Indonesia Raya* (Greater Indonesia) principle. A new nationalist organization, KRIS, was hastily organized by Ibrahim Yaacob, leader of the former KMM. But it was hamstrung from the outset by disagreements between the Japanese authorities and its Malay leaders over the objectives to be pursued. The movement collapsed with the Japanese surrender, its only meeting, scheduled for mid-August 1945, overshadowed by the dropping of the A-bomb.[93]

The different manner in which the major ethnic groups in Malaya responded to the Japanese occupation heightened ethnic antagonisms and influenced the way the British approached reestablishing their colonial administration once the war was over. The Malays for the most part cooperated with the Japanese, Malay officials and police (and the rulers) continuing in their previously assigned roles. In contrast, the Chinese were the principal source of resistance to the Japanese occupation. Chinese antipathy towards the conquerors, originally engendered by news of the Japanese invasion of China, but later fuelled by Japanese massacres of Chinese villagers in Malaya, led to strained relations with the collaborating Malay community and to violence directed against Malays during the weeks between the Japanese surrender and the return of the British.[94]

Armed resistance to the Japanese was organized by the Malayan Communist Party (MCP). Chinese society in Malaya was severely disrupted by the Japanese invasion and destabilized by fear arising from the subsequent massacres of Chinese.[95] As in the case of the KMM, the MCP saw in the Japanese invasion an opportunity to attract support. But, unlike the KMM which collaborated, the MCP focused its efforts on leading the anti-Japanese resistance. Most traditional Chinese leaders had either fled the country or been co-opted by the Japanese and thus were no longer able to fill their traditional role within the Chinese community of protecting their supporters. The MCP stepped into the vacuum and, by monopolizing the resistance, became by default the only organization capable of offering security to the threatened Chinese community.[96] But it viewed its anti-Japanese resistance effort as but a precursor to a much larger anti-colonial struggle soon to follow.

The MCP established both a guerrilla army and a supporting civilian organization that could be used to supply the guerrillas with food, money, recruits, and intelligence (the Malayan People's Anti-Japanese Army [MPAJA] and the Malayan People's Anti-Japanese Union [MPAJU], respectively). The MPAJA was almost exclusively Chinese,[97] its first units comprising trusted MCP cadres who had received training from the British at a guerrilla warfare and sabotage school hastily convened in Singapore during the weeks following Pearl Harbor.[98] The influence of the MCP over the MPAJA was clear, but there was little evidence of the MCP itself:

> Throughout the war years the party remained underground to such an extent that not even the members of the MPAJA could be sure who were the party members in their midst. It was, of course, recognized by all that the leadership ranks of the army were staffed by trusted party members, but there were also rank-and-file party members among the regular soldiers. . . . in the day-to-day camp activities, no attempt was made to hide the Communist coloration of the whole movement. Almost daily classes in political indoctrination were conducted; the clench-fist salute, the "International" and the "Red Flag Song," and all the other formal trappings of Communism had to be accepted by all. Most important, the members of the MPAJA and the MPAJU had

to recognize the absolute disciplinary power of the central headquarters.[99]

Despite its creation of the MPAJA, the MCP was not primarily interested in confronting the Japanese. In fact, the MCP sought to avoid drawing Japanese attention to the MPAJA and took relatively little aggressive action against the occupiers.[100] The MPAJA's function, from the point of view of the MCP, was to provide participants with the illusion that they were contributing to the defeat of the hated Japanese, without exposing them to the risks of actual fighting.[101] Recruits were subject to indoctrination, propaganda, and military camp routine, as a substitute for fighting. As Lucian Pye has observed:

> Not only did the men have to believe that they were warriors who had proved themselves in a struggle of great violence, but the entire Chinese community had to be convinced that the MPAJA was a champion of all loyal Chinese and a powerful force striking against the Japanese enemy.[102]

The MPAJU, while collecting money and provisions for the MPAJA with emotional appeals for Chinese racial unity (and threats as well), reinforced this illusion of power by holding open public meetings at the edge of the jungle at which anti-Japanese songs were sung and fully uniformed and armed soldiers of the "liberation army" presented. To the peasants in attendance, these soldiers were intended to represent a mighty army lying deep in the jungle. Such propaganda techniques appeared to work—the seven thousand guerrillas who came out of the jungle in 1945 convinced that it was their might which had defeated the enemy were met by significant numbers of civilians who shared that belief, welcoming them as heroes.[103]

The MPAJA conducted very few operations against the Japanese.[104] Even in terms of nuisance value, the MPAJA was such an insignificant threat to the Japanese that it in no way altered the plans of the Japanese army. The MPAJA, in fact, usually gave priority to catching and killing traitors, over guerrilla activity directed against the Japanese. Whereas total Japanese losses, killed and wounded, during the initial conquest and the subsequent occupation numbered 2,300, MPAJA executions of Malayans, mainly Chinese, numbered 2,542.[105]

The MPAJA guerrillas were however the principal recipients of

Allied military support, because they represented the only possible source of support for an anticipated Allied invasion (scheduled for late 1945). After a meeting between members of a British army liaison team (Force 136) and leaders of the MPAJA in the jungle in August 1944, Allied transport planes launched over one thousand sorties and supplied the MPAJA with one-and-a-half million pounds (weight) of equipment and supplies between December 1944 and June 1945. In addition, the British paid the MPAJA three thousand pounds per month and provided Allied military advisers—planes and submarines dropped a total of 510 men to join the MPAJA forces.[106] The British were well aware of the MCP's dominance of the MPAJA and its likely communist political objectives after the war. They were also aware of the limited impact that the MPAJA was having on the Japanese and of the probable diversion of Allied and captured Japanese weapons into stockpiles for future (anticolonial) struggles. Nevertheless, they chose to support the MPAJA for want of an alternative.[107]

In summary, the MCP used its monopoly of resistance to the Japanese to bolster its standing in the Chinese community and to garner material and organizational resources for a much more important struggle soon to follow. Once the Japanese surrendered, MPAJA guerrillas emerged from the jungle to bask in the glory of their reception as liberators and to confiscate property (arms) and punish "collaborators." The resulting executions, including not only Chinese who had opposed the MCP but also Malays and Indians, created a wave of fear and violence that had clear ethnic overtones:

> Since large numbers of Malays and Indians had worked for the Japanese and the majority of these peoples had not openly opposed the conquerors, the MPAJA's announced objective of punishing and even killing all who had assisted the recent enemy produced serious racial tensions. Fear of the MPAJA became fear of the Chinese and . . . many Malays lost sight of the distinction between Chinese who were Communists and Chinese in general. In some areas, shocking riots erupted;[108]

This interethnic violence was to have consequences for ethnic relations after the British colonial administration was reestablished in 1946, and for the Malay response to the Communist Emergency, which erupted in 1948.

MALAYAN INDEPENDENCE

When the British returned to Malaya after the war, they not only established new constitutional arrangements for governing the colony but also began preparing the ground for eventual independence. Efforts were made to cultivate Malays who might form the core of an independent government and to establish political and economic institutions that would shape the character of an independent Malaya. The internal hostilities of the Emergency (1948–1960), however, made this a long and slow process—the communist insurgency had to be decisively defeated before the British were prepared to grant independence.[109] This section describes the events which culminated in Malayan independence in 1957 and the political developments within Malayan society during the 1940s and 1950s that established the character of postindependence Malaya.

The first major British initiative was to unify the previously disparate state administrations in Malaya into a single entity, the Union of Malaya.[110] But Malayan Union became an extremely controversial issue and a two-year campaign waged against it by Malays (1946–1948) both mobilized moderate Malay opinion behind the idea of early independence and demonstrated the leadership potential of English-educated descendants of Malay ruling families who occupied "native" positions in the colonial civil service.[111]

Under the Union of Malaya, a centralized government was created to administer the Malay states and the former settlements of Penang and Malacca (Singapore remained a separate Crown Colony). The new arrangement was accompanied by constitutional changes which extended the political rights of non-Malays. A 1946 White Paper on Malayan Union justified these changes as follows: "All those who have made the country their homeland should have the opportunity of a due share in the country's political and cultural institutions."[112] Citizenship, for example, was to be extended for the first time to all persons born in Malaya or Singapore (or residing there for ten out of the previous fifteen years), while naturalized citizenship could be acquired after a residence of five years in Malaya or Singapore. Thus one of the British objectives in introducing the new constitution was to grant all who lived in Malaya equal treatment under the law.

Not surprisingly, most non-Malays supported this, as a majority of them for the first time would now qualify for citizenship. Malays, however, had serious misgivings about being deprived of their privileges as "native" dwellers. They felt in danger of being overrun by the non-Malay communities. They became even more concerned when it was learned that constitutional provisions affecting the Malay position were being drafted in secret, without Malay participation. When the content of these provisions was finally revealed, barely a month before the Union was established, a majority of the Malay rulers immediately voiced their strong objection.

The Malay response was a campaign of vigorous agitation that included mass demonstrations and rallies throughout the country and a boycott of the new constitution: none of the Malay rulers attended ceremonies installing the first British governor of the Malayan Union; Malay members refused to participate in the deliberations of the new Union Advisory Council; and all Malays wore white mourning bands for seven days after the Union was established.

Initially, the British were determined to force through the new constitutional scheme and the legal changes that conferred common citizenship on all residents. But, in the face of unanimous opposition from the rulers and increasing Malay violence directed against non-Malays, they were forced to back down.[113] They proposed, in 1946, that the constitution be renegotiated, and agreed to grant the Malay rulers and Malay civil servants the right to prepare the initial draft. The product of these deliberations was a proposal for a nine-state Federation of Malaya that strengthened the position of the Malay rulers as constitutional monarchs and included legal provisions more favorable to Malays than those incorporated in the Malayan Union. New citizenship requirements, for example, automatically granted Malays citizenship but required non-Malays to fulfil certain requirements of domicile, language, and birth before becoming citizens.

Adoption of the Federation of Malaya Constitution in 1948 reassured the Malay community. While the above-mentioned citizenship provisions were less restrictive than Malay leaders would have liked, Malays were nevertheless guaranteed constitutional privileges as a result of their indigenous status over other (immigrant) residents. And the new federal arrangement ensured Malay political dominance, since Malay politicians and civil servants dominated state government (Malays in general looked upon the states as their primary bulwark against the political demands of non-Malays).

What is most striking about the Malay campaign to oppose the

Union and the eventual creation of the Federation is the response of the British. When senior Malay civil servants on the Union Advisory Council boycotted the council's meetings, British administrators took no action. Moreover, civil servant members of UMNO, the principal organization formed to oppose the Union, were given permission to attend UMNO meetings during office hours, without loss of pay.[114]

This British toleration of civil servant opposition to what was in effect official policy was explained by the fact that:

> almost all the educated Malays of the time were civil servants or had civil service experience. To deny Malay civil servants the opportunity to participate in political activity would have been tantamount to excluding almost the entire potential Malay leadership from the political arena and risking the possibility of administrative sabotage.[115]

Furthermore, for all its opposition to the Union proposal, UMNO was basically pro-British and by no means left-wing. The British were preoccupied with countering other, more radical, Malay groups, such as the Malay Nationalist Party, and therefore toleration of UMNO seemed a sensible strategy. Moreover, the British saw in UMNO a strong political organization which could unite the Malay community and be used as a potent anticommunist weapon against the MPAJA and the MCP.[116]

In 1948, the MCP launched an anticolonial insurrection in the jungles of Malaya, to which the British responded by imposing emergency rule. Although the most serious hostilities were over by 1951, the Malayan Emergency officially lasted until 1960. During this time, the British portrayed the MCP as an external threat to Malaya, inspired by Peking or Moscow, and brought in thousands of troops from Britain and other possessions and former colonies to wage an anticommunist struggle against the guerrillas.[117] The MCP and other "leftist" organizations (including some Malay nationalist organizations) were banned and their members forced underground, the press was tightly controlled and the police granted extraordinary powers to search, detain without trial, impose curfews, and control movement. The death penalty was imposed for unlawful possession of weapons.[118]

Among the dominant Malay population of the countryside, memories of ethnic antagonisms during the war and MPAJA reprisals after the Japanese surrender were still fresh, so there was little sympathy for the MCP. The insurgents thus found themselves isolated from the majority of rural-dwellers. Another factor contributing to their defeat was the relatively advanced level of resource-related infrastructure development, and the deliberate construction of new roads into former guerrilla safe-areas.[119] The British also forcibly relocated nearly one million (mostly Chinese) rural-dwellers into more then six hundred resettlement projects:

> The major component of this massive reshuffling of the population was the establishment of so-called new villages which were self-contained and defensible, and which allowed the population to be efficiently cut off from communist insurgents, thereby robbing the insurgents of possible support and supplies.[120]

Many of the Chinese placed in the new villages had originally taken up farming on empty land when they lost their jobs in the tin mines and the cities during the Depression.

The MCP was in the end decisively defeated. Although the Emergency postponed Malayan independence, once the guerrillas were largely contained, British plans for granting independence were accelerated. By the mid-1950s, it was becoming increasingly apparent that pressures for independence were growing, especially among members of the Malay elite.[121] But the British were concerned that the rules of the economic game not change suddenly and that independence not disrupt the activities of British companies (especially their right to transfer capital and profits out of the country).[122]

The British therefore specified that they were prepared to hand over power but only under certain conditions—namely, that the new government embrace democratic elections and multiracialism.[123] The second condition appears at odds with simultaneous British encouragement of mono-ethnic parties such as UMNO and the Malayan Chinese Association.[124] But British support for moderate ethnic parties was designed to forestall the emergence of a class-based politics, which the British considered particularly threatening to their long-term interests.[125] At the same time, it offered the British an opportunity to use Chinese and Indian parties as levers to exact concessions from UMNO, which was increasingly insistent on the granting of immediate independence.[126]

As early as 1948, the British had created a Communities Liaison Committee comprising leaders of the major ethnic communities to

bargain on issues affecting them. This had two effects: class grievances had to be couched in ethnic terms and channeled through the
leaders of each community to be considered in this forum; and a
precedent was established for interethnic negotiations which later
produced the Federal Constitution of Malaya and the Alliance, which
formed the first independent government.[127]

The British demand that the new government of Malaya be chosen
by democratic elections was significant because there were no traditions within Malay society that would naturally have given rise to
democratic institutions and practices after independence. A more
authoritarian form of government would have buttressed the position of, and thus found favor with, the traditional Malay rulers. By
insisting on a democratic system, with the sultans retained as constitutional monarchs, the British strengthened the leaders of UMNO,
who themselves welcomed the arrangement because it allowed them
to exercise direct political power (independent of the rulers), while at
the same time exploiting their noble birth to win electoral support.[128]

There were significant differences within the Malay elite between
the traditional rulers, Arabic-educated religious reformers,[129] a largely
vernacular-educated radical intelligentsia strongly influenced by Indonesian nationalism, and the English-educated civil servants of aristocratic descent who founded UMNO. The British favored the UMNO
component because they believed that, with their close association
with the British administration, these civil servants could be relied
upon to stay the established course of political and economic development.[130] Leading Malay civil servants were actively encouraged to
adopt dual political and administrative roles. For example, when a
system of Malay "members" was introduced as a precursor to cabinet
government, the first three appointees were all civil servants, including Dato Onn, the member for home affairs, who was not only a
Johor state civil servant but also a former UMNO leader and president of the moderate Independence of Malaya Party.[131]

Differences within the Malay elite, however, especially those separating the civil servant-politicians and the sultans (whose approval
the British considered essential before an independence agreement
could be finalized), were rarely aired in public—to the Malay masses,
UMNO was presented as the party *defending* the rulers. An important
turning point had been reached, however, in the relationship between these two components, when in 1946 the rulers acquiesced to

the UMNO leadership's insistence that they boycott the official ceremony installing the new governor of the Malayan Union: "In those few hours the very basis of Malay political traditions had been subverted and the trend toward constitution [sic] monarchy had inexorably begun."[132]

Significant differences existed even within the ranks of English-educated Malay civil servants over the issue of how to organize the Malay community for political action and what sort of independence Malays should strive for. Dato Onn and his supporters wanted to transform UMNO into a multiracial party and, facing insurmountable opposition, left to form his own Independence of Malaya Party.[133] Subsequently, the leadership succeeding Onn responded to the British demand for multiracialism by forging an interracial coalition, the Alliance "party," with the mono-ethnic Malayan Chinese Association and Malayan Indian Congress (MIC). The Alliance agreement guaranteed Malay political and administrative hegemony in return for Malay agreement on citizenship rights for non-Malay residents and acceptance of non-Malay dominance of domestic commerce. Thus Chinese and Indian business interests were protected while Malay civil-servant politicians were free to consolidate their hold on government, without opposition from the non-Malays.

The contents of this Alliance agreement are important because they established a modus vivendi governing relations between the three main ethnic groups after independence. Under the agreement, Malays, as the "indigenous" people, were granted de jure social and economic privileges with which it was hoped to draw them into commerce and industry.[134] These privileges were thus justified in terms of an overriding national interest in promoting the economic advancement of the least advantaged in society (who happened to be disproportionately Malay). Special group rights for Malays were explicitly recognized and incorporated in the new constitution:

> Article 153 of the Malayan constitution requires the King . . . to safeguard the special position of the Malays and of the natives of Borneo. It is no longer a question of safeguarding a traditional way of life against intrusive change, but of recognizing the disadvantages which may have followed from doing so before. The indigenous communities have fallen behind in the economic progress of the country and this weakness is to be recognized and counterbalanced by securing to

them special rights, in the sphere of politics, the public service and educational opportunities.[135]

The measures assembled under section 153 of the constitution actually amounted to a rather mixed bag, reflecting an assortment of colonial measures originally introduced by the British to help the Malays. The emphasis was on particularistic benefits (those that helped individual Malays, rather than Malays as a whole): in the civil service, a hiring quota of 3:1 in favor of Malays was applied to some Division I appointments;[136] in education, Malay scholarships were created to boost the numbers of Malay students at universities; and, in business, Malays were given preferential access to licenses, such as those required to operate taxis, buses, and trucks.[137] While of great symbolic importance, and often the focus of non-Malay resentment, these sorts of benefits in fact had only limited effect on most Malays. Those favored were relatively few in number and the cumulative benefits they received were not great.[138] But there were also some provisions that benefited all Malays—encompassing access to reserved land, use of Malay as the national language (English was to be phased out by 1967), adoption of Islam as the national religion, and placing of a Malay sultan on the throne as the national monarch.

As a result of the Alliance agreement, the constitution included provision for non-Malays to be granted full political rights, in the form of citizenship on the basis of *jus soli*, that had previously been granted to only a few. This measure, providing non-Malays with security from deportation and conferring on them the right to vote, was in part a product of the Emergency (which was still officially in effect at the time of independence) and the struggle for Chinese allegiance waged between the colonial authorities and the MCP during the 1940s and 1950s.[139]

In terms of constitutional structure, it was agreed that Malaysia would take the form of a federation in which the states would retain substantial authority over local resources and customs. This was significant because it ensured continuity in Malay political dominance at the local level. At the center, the federation would be governed by a parliamentary democracy dominated by the Alliance.

In addition to these explicit constitutional provisions, the interethnic modus vivendi included certain informal understandings which later proved at least as important as the formal constitutional ones.[140]

It was agreed, for instance, that private (including foreign) capital would be allowed to continue its domination of the economy, while public sector development policy would focus on encouraging food production and providing the supporting infrastructure for economic development. Hence the Alliance bargain protected Chinese and Indian commercial activities from direct government intervention. Meanwhile, Malay traditional rulers would retain considerable political power in their states and enjoy a symbolic role as protectors of the (largely) rural Malay half of the population.

These, then were the conditions under which independence was granted. It was clear that, despite the decline of their empire, the British were prepared to leave Malaya only on condition that their substantial commercial interests were protected and that a viable Westminster-style democracy was left in place. With the formation of the Alliance and agreement over the constitution, these conditions were met, and on August 31, 1957, the British flag was lowered on the *padang* (square) of the capital Kuala Lumpur and the Federation of Malaya became formally independent.

CONCLUSION

This chapter has outlined those aspects of Malaya's colonial and precolonial history which have had important implications for economic policy-making since independence. A brief review of the main points is in order.

Precolonial Malaya was a land of lush abundance, with plentiful arable land that supported a relatively small population. In fact, a general "ethos of bountifulness," born of these favorable climatic and environmental conditions, has been a persistent theme in Malay culture, even during times of economic hardship. By encouraging the belief that nature will always provide, this ethos has discouraged savings and investment among Malays. Other aspects of traditional society have had the same result. The relationship between rulers and their subjects, for instance, discouraged accumulation because the latter wanted to be able to escape tyrannical rule by simply moving from the area. Agricultural improvements and material possessions restricted villagers' ability to flee in such a fashion and were therefore discouraged. Economic development policies in the post-independence era have to some extent been hamstrung by this traditional reluctance to invest among Malays.

Parts of Malay society have been in continuous contact with world trade and commerce since at least the eleventh century A.D. With the establishment of a regional trading center at Malacca in the fifteenth century, the sultan of Malacca presided over what was at that time "the crossroads of the East," *the* entrepot capital for trade passing by sea from China and the Spice Islands to India, Arabia, and beyond. So the reliance on trade, which has been a lasting characteristic of the economy of Malaysia, had early beginnings.

Trade brought foreign traders and entrepreneurs, mainly Chinese, but also Indians and others, whose increasingly lengthy visits to the Peninsula soon amounted to semipermanent residence. The resulting immigrant enclaves were precursors of the large non-Malay communities that have played an important role in the economic and political life of Malaya since independence. Agreements forged between Malay chiefs and rulers (the sultans) and Chinese commercial entrepreneurs seeking access to to the interior established early precedents for intercommunal agreements which later prepared the ground for independence. Such agreements also led to the practice, continued since independence, of taxing non-Malays to provide the bulk of state revenues (which, in turn, have been used largely to benefit Malays).

Trade also brought European traders. Malaya's colonial experience, though it included long periods of Portugese and Dutch influence, was primarily that of a British possession. The British did not see Malaya as a place suitable for English settlement (unlike Kenya or New Zealand). Rather, the primary goal of colonial administrators in Malaya was to extract resources and profits to be channeled back to Britain. To this end, systems of monetary management and taxation employed in Malaya (as elsewhere in the empire) were used to "milk" the colony of accumulated funds. Infrastructural and social development in the colony were warranted only to the extent that they facilitated the exploitation of resources. A relatively modest initial investment in administration and infrastructure proved hugely profitable, both for private companies and for the colonial administration, which was able to repatriate millions of pounds in surplus revenues to the Treasury in London. In short, the eighty years of colonial administration that preceded Malayan independence created a typically dependent economy, one in which frequent ups and downs in local economic conditions occurred, but where the British had no interest in fostering the long-run prosperity of the local economy. Thus the government after independence faced serious problems of economic imbalance (stemming from the dominance of the primary sector and the absence of any significant industrial capacity) and instability.

The two main resources which Malaya had to offer were tin and rubber. Their exploitation had the effect of commercializing much of Malay society, and of undermining traditional economic relations, landholding patterns, and systems of authority. Concerned that traditional Malay land was being rapidly alienated and that Malay food production was thus being disrupted, the British introduced "native" preferences favoring the Malays over other ethnic groups (as embodied in the Malay Reservations Act). These preferences, however, had the effect of discouraging Malay entrepreneurship, since they restricted Malay ability to capitalize on land ownership, which was their primary resource. Even when Malays ventured into small-scale business they found their activities constrained by trade and services monopolies controlled by a small number of European trading houses. Early in this century, Malay peasant farmers did embrace smallholder rubber as a cash crop, but they were discouraged from increasing the land area under cultivation and were never able to compete effectively with large-scale European estate companies.

So a traditional Malay reluctance to invest was reinforced by colonial policies designed to insulate Malays from broad economic changes produced by tin and rubber development. As a result, at independence Malays were barely represented at all in the business life of the country. One of the principal objectives of government policy since that time has been to redress this imbalance.

British rule altered the traditional structure of Malay society. The sultans were made much more visible but at the same time the colonial residency system effectively eroded their power (especially their ability to levy taxes). The sons and relatives of the Malay aristocracy were educated in the equivalent of English public schools and given administrative positions in the growing civil service. As a result, the civil servants who led the independence movement were linked by blood ties with the Malay rulers whose approval was required as a condition for British withdrawal. This colonial policy of elite co-optation thus established the foundation for a moderate alliance of traditional aristocrats and UMNO civil servants that dominated the politics of Malaysia after independence.

Meanwhile, the indenturing of large numbers of Chinese and Indian laborers to work the tin mines and rubber plantations in the late nineteenth and early twentieth centuries increased the size of the immigrant trading enclaves and established the ethnic mixture which remains a characteristic feature of Malaysian society. By taxing the Chinese and Indians through levies on opium, alcohol, and tobacco, the British continued the traditional practice of "milking" the wealthier non-Malay communities as a means of generating state revenues.

The advent of the Great Depression highlighted the extreme degree of trade dependence that Malaya's basically two-commodity economy exhibited. The Malayan economy was more seriously affected than most by dramatic declines in commodity prices and by the attendant social disruption. The movement of many Chinese from cities and tin-mining areas onto vacant land to raise food, for example, later provided a fertile source of support for communist guerrillas during the Malayan Emergency.

The Japanese invasion of Malaya soon after Pearl Harbor and their subsequent three-and-a-half-year military occupation of the colony had a number of effects that were consequential for post-independence Malaya. The differing responses of the three major ethnic communities to the Japanese presence (the Malays and Indians collaborated while the Chinese resisted) heightened ethnic antagonisms that the British had sought to contain. At war's end, an orgy of violence, resulting from the settling of ethnic scores, provided an abject lesson for community leaders of what might happen in the future if attention were not paid to managing ethnic group relations (only in 1969 was there violence on a comparable scale). The memory of these events helped motivate the Alliance agreement that set the stage for independence.

The Japanese occupation also had an important effect on the balance of radicals versus moderates in the Malay and Chinese communities. Radical Malay nationalist leaders (who advocated immediate independence from the British and creation of a greater Indonesian nation) were co-opted by the Japanese, dispersed throughout the peninsula, diluted by Japanese recruits, and compromised by their role as propaganda siphons. As a result, after the war, radical leaders were never able to regain the degree of influence they had wielded in the Malay community during the late 1930s. Moderate Malay civil servants—those who had championed Malay interests before the British but not gone so far as to call for complete independence—remained at their posts under the Japanese and survived the occupation with their stature intact.

Chinese radicals, in the form of the MCP, monopolized the armed resistance to the Japanese and used it as a stepping stone for the later guerrilla insurgency of the Malayan Emergency. But the guerrillas were almost exclusively Chinese and were unable to attract the support of Malay villagers who comprised the vast majority of rural dwellers. This, combined with occasional reprisals against Malays for assisting the British, sealed the fate of communist efforts to develop a base in the Malay community from which to organize politically after independence. The military defeat of the insurgency by the British meant that Chinese radicals, like their Malay counterparts, were no longer a major factor in politics by the time independence was granted.

Resuming their interrupted administration in late 1945, the British proposed a new constitutional scheme that, in granting non-Malays expanded rights and removing most Malay preferences, reflected a legacy of British disillusionment with the collaborating Malays and a concern, on the part of colonial administrators, to foster moderate Chinese leaders. The provisions of the Malayan Union constitution, however, heightened a Malay sense of insecurity that had been encouraged by the ethnic violence after the Japanese surrender (this sense of insecurity was later reflected in provisions of the independence agreement guaranteeing Malay political hegemony). The occupation had led members of all ethnic groups to become much more politically aware (they were all, for example, faced with the decision of whether or not to collaborate), but, in the case of the Malays, the subsequent two-year struggle to defeat the Malayan Union actually mobilized Malays for the first time. The British decision to abandon Malayan Union in favor of a federal arrangement reaffirmed the strength of the Malay moderate leadership. It solidified a Malay nationalist movement, led by English-educated members of aristocratic families who occupied civil service positions, whose influence was eventually to lead to the granting of independence. It also preserved the power of state governments which were seen by the

Malays as important bulwarks of Malay political power against challenges from the non-Malay communities.

The process of granting independence took over a decade, mainly because of the Emergency. The Emergency encouraged the British to preempt a broad-based, radical nationalist struggle (which could threaten the continuity of British policies and investments), by backing UMNO and sponsoring the moderate Malayan Chinese Association. British conditions for handing over power (democratic elections and a multiracial government) were influential in shaping the character of the coalition that has ruled Malaysia for the past thirty years. The obstacles encountered by the early UMNO leader, Dato Onn, in trying to turn UMNO into a multiracial party suggested to Malay leaders that the best way to meet the British condition of multiracialism was by forming a moderate Alliance of the three main ethnic parties, UMNO, the Malayan Chinese Association, and the MIC. A recent precedent for cooperation of this kind between the various ethnic leaderships had taken the form of the Communities Liaison Committee, a British creation designed to preempt class-based politics by channeling political forces through ethnic leaders. Such British manipulation of interethnic group relations was matched by the British favoring of one element of the Malay elite, namely the UMNO group, against others (such as the sultans) who preferred more authoritarian forms of government.

The agreement on which the Alliance was based, including special privileges for Malays, citizenship rights for Chinese, Malay political hegemony balanced by non-Malay economic preeminence, and a continuation of existing economic "rules of the game," established the terms of the interethnic settlement which has played a central role in the evolution of Malayan politics. It provided the basis on which disputes between the three major ethnic communities could be resolved and lasted virtually unchanged throughout the first decade of independence, at a time when intergroup conflicts in other communally divided, postcolonial societies, especially in Africa (the Congo and Nigeria are two examples), were leading to the rapid disintegration of their societies.

3

ETHNIC BARGAINING AND MARKET-LED DEVELOPMENT: EARLY INDUSTRIAL STRATEGY, 1957–1969

I have argued in chapter 1 that to understand the political sources of industrial strategy choice in Malaysia one must consider the role of political coalitions. But the important coalitions, in the case of Malaysia and some other Third World communal societies attempting to industrialize, are not those linking economic actors or intermediate associations, which have been the subject of recent scholarship. Rather, they are the coalitions that link major *communal* groups.

Communal alliances produce modae vivendi that govern relations between potentially antagonistic ethnic, religious, or linguistic groups. Communal alliances or coalitions also influence the course of a country's economic and industrial development. As relationships between groups within an alliance change, so too will approaches to economic policy-making and industrial strategy tend to change.

This chapter is the first of three dealing with Malaysian industrial strategy choice over successive decades. It shows how the market-led approach adopted during Malaysia's first decade was strongly influenced by the nature of the coalition linking Malay, Chinese, and Indian leaders which formed the Alliance government at independence. Subsequent chapters will trace the effect of changes in this inter-ethnic arrangement on government approaches to industrial development during the 1970s and 1980s.

The chapter begins with a brief overview of the economic situation confronting the government of newly independent Malaya. This is followed by a description of the industrial development strategy employed during the period 1957–1969 and an analysis of the political factors that contributed to the formulation and evolution of such a strategy. The chapter concludes with an evaluation of the results of this strategy, and a description of the state of the Malaysian economy immediately prior to the communal upheaval of 1969, described in chapter 4.

ECONOMY AT INDEPENDENCE

In the wake of World War II, colonial Malaya had experienced sporadic economic growth, with real GNP (in peninsular Malaya) rising at an average annual rate of 2.8 percent (1947–1958).[1] The economy at independence was dependent for its prosperity on exports and was vulnerable to price fluctuations affecting just one or two commodities; in 1955, for example, exports of tin and rubber accounted for 85 percent of gross export receipts which in turn contributed 48 percent of GDP.[2] Malaya's primary-product dependence was accompanied by foreign control over the production of major commodities. For example, in 1953, European companies owned 83 percent of the land under estates (mainly rubber, but including some oil palm and coconut estates) and these holdings were highly concentrated, with 92 percent of them in parcels of over one thousand acres.[3] In tin mining, three British companies alone accounted for 45 percent of total output in 1954, and European companies collectively produced 60 percent of all tin in that year. Foreigners (mainly the British) also controlled the most lucrative segments (60 to 70 percent) of the import-export trade, as well as other services such as shipping and insurance.[4] Three major British banks (Chartered, Hong Kong & Shanghai, and Mercantile) dominated Malayan banking; together with other smaller foreign banks, they controlled 75 percent of all bank deposits in 1955.[5]

The bulk of Malayan industry at independence was devoted to the processing of agricultural and mineral products (in fact, all of Malaya's major crops received some form of processing before they were exported). The largest such industry was that engaged in the smelting of tin. On a much smaller scale, light manufacturing industries produced import-substitutes like furniture, bricks, tiles, pottery, pewter, and silver. Of these industries, only foundries and ice and match factories employed workers in any numbers.[6]

The British had had little interest in fostering local industry because Malaya performed a useful role as a captive market for British manufacturers. Consequently, industry was not very important within the economy as a whole—industry and construction together accounted for only 11 percent of GNP in 1957. The industrial "sector" was represented by a total of five thousand manufacturing "shops," most of them "back-yard" operations. With an industrial workforce of just over sixty thousand, there were an average of only twelve workers per factory (including part-timers).[7]

Industry was concentrated geographically along the west coast of the Peninsula, adjacent to the entrepot ports of the Straits Settlements (Penang, Malacca, and Singapore), where the greatest numbers of people were to be found. It was also concentrated in the hands of the immigrant Chinese (and, to a lesser extent, immigrant Indians), rather than the native Malays.[8] Chinese firms, in particular, while small in scale compared with their European rivals, were significant in the areas of rubber dealing, small-scale tin mining, some import-export trade, shipping, banking, retail (stores and restaurants), and construction.[9] Malays, who made up approximately 50 percent of the population (the Chinese accounted for 37 percent and the Indians nearly all the remainder), in 1958 owned only 10 percent of the registered businesses, paid only 4 percent of the personal income tax, and owned only 1.5 percent of all share capital.[10]

In profile, then, the Malayan economy looked much like those of other newly independent nations in the 1950s. It was raw-material-dependent, foreign-dominated, lacking in diversity, and dualistic, a rural-urban dualism being compounded in the Malayan case by a native born/non-native born division. Malaya did, however, enjoy some advantages. For example, a 1955 World Bank report noted that Malaya possessed a relatively well-developed infrastructure, as a result of British efforts to provide access to exploitable natural resources and to isolate the communist guerrillas during the Emergency.[11] Malaya's formal education system was considered one of the best in the region.[12] And, when the British departed, they left in place an extensive and fully functioning public administration, staffed by civil servants many of whom had considerable experience in the affairs of state.[13]

In this context, the government of newly independent Malaya faced the challenge of developing a strategy to encourage industrial expansion. The result, during the period 1957–1969, was a largely market (i.e., company)-led approach to industrial development. The next two sections describe this market-led strategy and explain how and why such a policy came to be adopted.

INDUSTRIAL STRATEGY, 1957–1969

Government development efforts during Malaya's first decade focused primarily on the rural-agricultural sector.[14] We find this sectoral emphasis reflected in public development expenditures over the first Malaya five-year plan (the First Malaya Plan [1956–1960])[15]— while agriculture and rural development received 23 percent of the total, and infrastructural development 52 percent, industrial development received only 1.3 percent.[16] The pattern continued for the next decade. In the Second Malaya Plan (1961–1965) and the First Malaysia Plan (FMP, 1966–1970), industrial development accounted for just 2.5 and 3.3 percent of official development spending, respectively, while agricultural and rural development accounted for 17.6 percent during 1961–1965 and 26.3 percent during 1966–1970.[17]

The government's rural programs involved extensive direct government intervention to develop rural areas.[18] Infrastructural development (including drainage and irrigation, large-scale land development, and rubber replanting),[19] designed to increase agricultural output, was accompanied by efforts to increase Malay economic participation by assisting Malay entrepreneurs in such areas as transportation, construction, and the timber industry,[20] and by programs designed to improve living conditions in rural villages and towns (through rural electrification and the building of sanitary water supplies, new roads, community and health centers, and schools).[21]

The government's approach to commercial and industrial sector development was quite different from that employed in the agricultural sector. Here the government chose to rely on private sector initiative to generate investment and on the mechanism of the market to distribute resources.[22] It neither initiated industrial projects itself, nor did it attempt to direct private industry to produce certain products. Instead, industrial policy during the late 1950s and 1960s sought to encourage private sector development by means of nonselective inducements.[23] The state's role, according to then Minister of Commerce and Industry, Khir Johari, was simply "to create a favourable investment climate and to leave the projects to be undertaken entirely by private enterprises."[24] The end result, in the words of another senior government minister, Dr. Ismail bin Dato Abdul Rahman, was to be "modern capitalism," as practiced in the United States, for "that was the best system to advance living standards and the national economy."[25]

Thus, while the government provided basic services (transport, communications, power, etc.), developed new industrial sites, offered general financial inducements (incentives and subsidies in the form, for example, of tax relief), and to a limited extent protected existing industry from foreign competition,[26] these measures were all formulated with a view to preserving the predominantly free-enterprise character of the commercial economy.[27] The government's commitment to the virtues of free enterprise in commercial and industrial development was to remain a centerpiece of policy for more than a decade, until shaken and finally abandoned in the wake of the riots of 1969.[28]

Among the measures adopted by the government during this period were passage of the Pioneer Industries Ordinance (PIO), creation of Malayan Industrial Development Finance (MIDF), and the imposition of new tariffs. The Pioneer Industries (Relief from Income Tax) Ordinance of 1958[29] granted exemption from the 40 percent company tax to new industries deemed essential to Malaysian economic growth.[30] MIDF was established in 1960 to borrow funds from public and private sources and redistribute them through the purchase of debt or equity in promising private-sector industrial ventures.[31] To provide land for industrial plants, a subsidiary of MIDF, Malaysian Industrial Estates (MIE), was assigned the task of helping industries establish themselves on "industrial estates" developed by local development agencies.[32] Lastly, tariffs, which had been levied in colonial times primarily as a revenue-producing device, were now used in some cases as a means of fostering industry.[33] However, a Tariff Advisory Committee, established within the Ministry of Commerce and Industry in 1961 to recommend tariff changes favorable to the emergence of new industries, in practice advocated tariff *reductions* for imported industrial materials rather than tariff *increases* for finished products.[34] And powerful plantation and mercantile interests, fearing rising costs, were able to block extension of tariff protection to new industries.[35] Thus the tariff structure that prevailed during this period was quite mixed in its impact on industry.

Together, these government incentives to private sector industrial development (tax relief and provision of capital, land, and tariff assistance) embodied maximum entrepreneurial freedom and limited government regulation. Nevertheless the government did regulate to some degree. For example, in respect of policies fostering Malay entrepreneurship, the state clearly did act to favor some segments of industry (those that were Malay-owned) over others. Yet UMNO support for increased Malay economic participation was tempered by a commitment to a laissez-faire economy with the result that measures favoring Malay business ventures were essentially only piecemeal and ad hoc. The basic character of the free enterprise economy, from the perspective of UMNO leaders, was not to be infringed.[36] Thus, even when the government and UMNO found themselves faced with rising demands from Malays that something be done to improve their economic position relative to the non-Malay communities, the main institutions they established in response, the Majlis Amanah Rakyat, or Council of Trust for the Indigenous Peoples (MARA),[37] Bank Bumiputra,[38] and the Federal Agricultural Marketing Authority (FAMA),[39] were limited in their ability to intervene directly in economic transactions. Although the First Malaysia Plan (1966–1970) did sanction government establishment of small-scale industry in rural areas, the change came only as a result of a great deal of popular pressure and did not seriously challenge the free enterprise system.[40] In large measure, it was the market (and companies in the market), rather than state agencies, which determined the course of industrial development during Malaya's first decade.

The government did attempt to attract foreign industrial investment. But in this endeavor Malaya faced the twin obstacles that new foreign private investment was generally scarce in Asia in the 1960s (representing only 14 percent of total flows to the developing world, and about one-third of the amount flowing into Latin America) and that the country itself had a reputation for "riskiness" as a result of the country's experiences with the Emergency (1948–1960) and the Confrontation with Indonesia (1963).[41] For this reason, the main intended beneficiaries of measures such as the setting up of industrial estates and the passage of the PIO were foreign companies. And much of the investment in import-substituting industry during the 1960s was foreign rather than domestic in origin.[42]

To summarize the various strands of the industrial development strategy described so far, it has been argued that, while state development efforts focused on the rural-agricultural sector, the private sector was left to determine the course of development in commerce and industry. Government initiatives in this area involved regulation and the use of limited measures to encourage industry. But (with the exception of policies favoring Malays) they were essentially nonselective and did not reflect a predetermined state direction for industry. Moreover, their primary beneficiary was not the local industrial entrepreneur but rather the foreign (particularly British) investor.

How and why did such an essentially "market-led" strategy come to be adopted? What were the factors that led Malayan elites to pursue a predominantly "market-led," as opposed to a "state-led" or "mixed state-regulatory," approach to the development of industry?

There are several aspects that require investigation: why did the Malayan state take an active role in the rural-agricultural sector but leave industrial development largely to private enterprise, limiting its role in this area to that of regulator, facilitator, and nonselective encourager? Why did the state itself not become an active industrial entrepreneur in its own right during a period in which industry was so underdeveloped and when there was a widely recognized need for greater industrialization and when indigenous private-sector efforts were so manifestly feeble? Why were active state efforts in agriculture not mirrored in an industrial sector that seemed to cry out for state direction? Among state actions which did affect industry, why were macro-oriented policies and tax incentives favored over micro-oriented measures (such as tariff manipulation) which might have facilitated state targeting of industries that seemed particularly "ripe" for development? And why did efforts to attract foreign capital into an already foreign-dominated economy take precedence over measures to develop an indigenous industrial capacity?

EXPLAINING THE MARKET-LED STRATEGY

Among the political determinants of the 1960s market-led strategy, the nature of the political settlement between the major communities played a central role. This section will review the structure and character of communal relations during the 1950s and 1960s and describe the role these relations played in shaping economic policy.

Other factors that had a contributory (though I argue subsidiary) role will also be considered.

As we have seen in chapter 2, the British colonizers in the early 1950s faced the difficult problem of what to do about Malaya's extreme communal divisions which they, by deliberate colonial policy, had accentuated over the course of half a century. The three major communities were separated not only by ethnicity but also by religion and language. As one colonial administrator observed:

> Divided from each other in almost every respect, the peoples of Malaya have in common essentially only the fact that they live in the same country. In race, religion, culture, economic interests, and the other attributes usually associated with the existence of a nation their outstanding characteristics is [sic] not unity but profound diversity.[43]

A necessary condition for peaceful transition to independent rule, the British felt, was the existence of a political party to which the reins of power could be handed. They specified that such a party had to be committed both to democracy and to intercommunalism.[44]

This, as we saw in chapter 2, prompted the formation of the Alliance coalition. The three component parties successfully presented themselves as a unified front to the British, on the basis of a settlement reached after prolonged negotiation during the preparation of a submission to the British on the independence constitution. This settlement amounted to a series of compromises over controversial communal issues;[45] essentially, Chinese and Indian leaders accepted Malay political and cultural dominance,[46] and the inclusion of special rights and privileges for Malays in the Constitution, in return for Malay recognition of Chinese and Indian rights to full citizenship and to a voice in the government of independent Malaya.[47] It is useful at this point to expand upon the content of the settlement as it affected subsequent economic policy formulation.

Implicit in the Alliance framework was Malay acceptance (at least for a time) of the existing Chinese and Indian stranglehold over indigenous business activities of all kinds, including small-scale manufacturing, processing, construction, and finance.[48] UMNO leaders committed themselves to liberal economic policies that would enable non-Malays to continue these commercial and industrial activities without fear of confiscation or intervention.[49] This acceptance of the economic status quo, in return for MCA and MIC agreement not to challenge the political preeminence of UMNO,[50] was reflected in the composition of the cabinet. While the positions of Prime Minister and Deputy Prime Minister were reserved for Malays, the important finance and commerce and industry portfolios were assigned to leaders of the MCA.[51] Thus, despite their minority position in government, senior MCA leaders nevertheless wielded significant influence within the Alliance. This stemmed at least in part from the control they exercised over Chinese business contributions flowing through the MCA into the coffers of the Alliance.[52] Thus, for example, the MCA had veto power over cabinet appointments, as was illustrated in the case of UMNO representative, Khalid bin Awang Osman, who was transferred from his post as Assistant Minister of Commerce and Industry to an ambassadorship in West Germany in late 1965 as a result of MCA pressure.[53] The "package deal" satisfied the major claims of each community: in effect, the price to be paid by non-Malays for full participation in the activities of the Federation and for continued economic dominance was their acceptance of Malay cultural and political hegemony. Malays, most of them aristocratic, English-educated, present and former civil servants, held most of the senior positions in the civil service and government.[54] So, an essential part of the Alliance settlement was that the state apparatus was to be controlled largely by the Malay community.

Relations between the leaders of the different ethnic groups within the Alliance and the terms of their negotiated settlement help us explain why the industrial development strategy that emerged during Malaya's first decade took the form it did. Malay leaders, recognizing that Chinese and Indian political acceptance of UMNO hegemony was conditional on the state's not interfering in private commerce and industry, beyond the performance of its traditional regulatory functions,[55] were constrained from imposing any particular vision of Malaya's industrial future on the private sector. Moreover, all parties to the settlement shared a common interest in suppressing claims to special treatment (i.e., state promotion of particular manufacturing industries over others).[56]

A good illustration of how the interethnic settlement constrained UMNO tendencies to adopt statist economic policies deemed harmful to non-Malay commercial and industrial interests is provided by the experience of Abdul Aziz bin Ishak. In the early 1960s, Aziz, then Minister of Agriculture and Cooperatives and a leading member of

UMNO, launched a one-man crusade to transfer the ownership of rice mills from private Chinese entrepreneurs to Malay-dominated, government-funded rural cooperatives. To this end, he summarily revoked the licenses of some 350 Chinese rice millers in the state of Perak, prompting vehement protests from the affected Chinese. Soon MCA leaders became involved and, concerned that capitulation on the issue would result in a loss of confidence by Chinese business-men in their ability to protect Chinese economic interests, threatened to withdraw their support from the Alliance. Malay leaders, conclud-ing that the Minister had gone too far in displacing Chinese business interests, acquiesced to the MCA's demands; in late 1962, Aziz was dismissed from the Cabinet for "unconstitutional practices," namely, for violating the guarantee, under article 152 of the Constitution, that the government would protect the "legitimate interests" of non-Malays.[57]

The example is important in that it illustrates the Malay leaders' conviction that intercommunal cooperation was a necessary condi-tion for survival.[58] Thus, although politically dominant (and there-fore capable of arbitrarily imposing state policies on the private sec-tor), Malay leaders were prepared to make important concessions to non-Malay concerns, and to limit the extent to which government encroached on private sector economic activities, in the interests of preserving communal peace. The fact that the MCA leaders had their way on this issue, when the affected Chinese were particularly dis-liked by Malays for their role in exploiting Malay rice farmers, is indicative of the power of the ethnic settlement to constrain state incursion into the realm of private economic activities.[59]

This *dis*incentive to direct state involvement in the commercial and industrial sector had its reverse image in strong political *in*centives for the state to involve itself in the development of agriculture. The concentration of Malays in rural areas and UMNO's concern to estab-lish its legitimacy with them as *the* Malay political party in the face of challenges from competing parties (such as the Islamic party, PMIP) encouraged Malay leaders to focus state development efforts in the rural-agricultural sector.[60]

Summarizing my argument relating the choice of industrial devel-opment strategy during Malaya's early years to the nature of rela-tions between the three major ethnic groups, I have said that al-though there was general agreement on the necessity for industrial expansion, state development efforts were focused on the rural-agri-cultural sector. Direct state action to foster industrial development was precluded by the terms of the Alliance settlement that protected non-Malay economic interests from government encroachment. Moreover, industrial development policies entailed political costs for UMNO leaders—in the eyes of many Malays they suggested that the state was favoring urban commercial (predominantly non-Malay) in-terests.[61] These Malay political concerns of UMNO leaders also ex-plain why official measures affecting industry appeared to increase dependency by benefiting foreign capital, despite the fact that the Malaysian economy was already heavily foreign-dominated (espe-cially in the critical mining and plantation sectors).[62] The state en-couraged expansion of foreign-owned industry because this allowed it to strengthen the industrial sector while avoiding any appearance of showing favor towards domestic non-Malays. Thus the constraints inherent in the interethnic settlement and in the nature of political relations between ethnic groups militated against the Alliance gov-ernment adopting anything other than a market-led approach to industrial development.

This is not to say, however, that other factors were entirely with-out influence on policy choice in this area. For example, the historical legacy of colonial free-trade policies with respect to industrial imports had a continuing impact on the way the Alliance government ap-proached the task of developing industry,[63] and some specific poli-cies relating to industry (for example, the government's preference for measures involving tax relief, via the PIO, over trade restriction, via tariffs) mirrored colonial administration preferences. But it would be an exaggeration to suggest that these policies were motivated by nothing more than the weight of historical precedent. In the agricul-tural sector, after all, such precedent apparently counted for little— the government there embarked on interventions on a scale quite unprecedented in colonial times.

One colonial legacy that did have an impact on certain of the state's industrial policies was the preeminent position of foreign capital in the economy. Not only was the European (mainly British) presence substantial, but it was also highly concentrated in a limited number of large companies which controlled mining, plantations, and banks. Local (mainly Chinese) entrepreneurs had, by the late

1950s, created only limited concentrations of wealth to rival these heavily capitalized European operations.[64]

This foreign presence affected state development policies in two respects. Plantation and mining interests were able to capture a significant share of the expenditures allocated to infrastructure and rural development (a large share of government spending on agriculture went to plantation development, for example). And these same interests lobbied successfully against the use of tariffs as a primary means of encouraging local manufacturing, for fear that they would raise the landed cost of imported equipment. Thus pressure from foreign capital contributed to an existing reluctance on the part of the Alliance government to engage in micro-management (i.e., to favor particular industries selectively, using tariffs or other incentives).

A further external influence on policy was a World Bank report of 1955 which favored industrialization under the leadership of the private sector and recommended extensive measures to attract foreign investment.[65]

Some have argued that these factors (colonial precedent, pressure from the representatives of foreign capital, and the recommendations of the Bank) were largely irrelevant, for Malaya had little choice when it came to deciding on an industrial strategy. One variant of this argument suggests that Malaya's structural position within the international economy left the country little choice but to concentrate government expenditure on bolstering existing raw material production.[66] This view, which draws on theories of comparative advantage, fails to account for later Malaysian efforts to develop industry that were motivated *primarily* by a perception that the country could not afford to rely solely on those goods in which it had a comparative advantage. A second variant suggests that, whatever its preferences, the Malayan state did not yet have the institutional capability to take a direct role in fostering industry at this early stage. But this argument is contradicted by abundant evidence that the bureaucratic apparatus of the Malayan state was in fact quite well-equipped to formulate and implement an industrial policy: it had a colonial history of close administration, with wide powers and coverage;[67] its public officials were known for their relative integrity;[68] its leaders shared similar values and backgrounds to those held by the (Malay) political leadership;[69] and the administrative service was relatively well insulated from day-to-day societal pressures.[70] Rather than limiting the state's institutional capacity to implement a state-led industrial policy, these characteristics combined to make the Malayan state rather well-suited to the task.

In summary, I have argued that the market-led industrial strategy pursued by the Malayan government after independence was strongly influenced by both the nature of relations between the major ethnic groups and the complexion of the state (which was largely captured by one ethnic group). These factors encouraged the government in Malaya's early years to leave industrial development largely to the private sector while focusing state efforts on the rural-agricultural sector. I have suggested that other considerations, such as the precedent set by colonial policies and the continuing influence of foreign capital, may have influenced the approach to industry to some extent. But the overall shape of the strategy owed more to the internal dynamics of post-independence Malayan politics than to external factors.

The strategy was not a static one, however. The next section focuses on how policy toward industry evolved during the 1960s in response to changing domestic and international circumstances.

THE STRATEGY EVOLVES

In the mid-1960s, the withdrawal of Singapore from the Federation of Malaysia caused the loss of a significant proportion of the Federation's industry (this industry had been fostered by the Singaporean government on the island before unification with Malaya).[71] At about the same time, an influential World Bank report revealed that official estimates of the likely contribution of the growth of industry to overall economic growth were quite unrealistic, unless the government was prepared to undertake much more substantial and vigorous encouragement of industry than had been the case hitherto.[72]

Together, Singapore's departure and the Bank report resulted in more state attention being directed at industrial development. The Bank report advocated the creation of an autonomous industrial development agency to coordinate state efforts at industrial promotion[73] and, in response, the government announced the formation in 1965 of the Federal Industrial Development Authority (FIDA, renamed the

Malaysian Industrial Development Authority in 1968). FIDA was to undertake industrial feasibility studies, promote industry at home and abroad, coordinate industrial development activities, recommend specific industrial sites for development, direct the pioneer industries program, and make recommendations to the Minister of Trade and Industry on industrial development issues.[74]

On the face of it, the announcement of FIDA would seem to represent a major departure from the earlier market-led approach. In fact, state support for FIDA was rather tenuous: almost two years were to pass between the formal announcement of the agency and its actual creation, in April 1967.[75]

In 1968, new investment incentives in the form of an Investment Incentives Act, targeting foreign investment with tax concessions, new depreciation allowances, liberalized pioneer status conditions, and free trade zones, were introduced.[76] But the basic configuration of state policy towards industry remained largely unchanged. The private sector was still expected to take the initiative in developing the industrial sector and in responding to changing domestic and international economic circumstances. The basic decisions on what to produce and how to produce it were still left to the private entrepreneur. The state was not an active participant in industrial undertakings nor was it directing industrial change through use of micropolicies favoring particular industries (or particular companies) in pursuit of a long-run vision of industrial change. The new incentives were oriented marginally more towards export production than had been the case earlier in the decade. But they retained their nonselective character and were more concerned with attracting foreign investment than fostering a domestic industrial capacity. The basic nature of the market-led industrial adjustment strategy thus remained largely unchanged until the aftermath of the events of May 1969.

THE MALAYSIAN ECONOMY AND INDUSTRY IN 1969

The Malaysian economy during the 1960s recorded an average annual growth rate of over 5 percent (annual real GDP growth 1966–1970 was 6 percent).[77] Meanwhile, private sector investment, reflecting the success of government efforts to create a favorable investment environment, rose at an average annual rate of 7.3 percent.[78] In manufacturing, growth averaged 10.2 percent, far exceeding the performance of the economy as a whole (GDP grew at an average of 5.5 percent) and the share of manufacturing in GDP consequently rose from 8.5 percent in 1960 to 13 percent in 1970.[79] In value-added terms, manufacturing contributed 13.1 percent to GNP in 1970, as compared with 8.5 percent in 1960.[80] Most industry, however, was still confined to raw material processing and the production of import-substituting consumer goods.[81]

The leading industries in terms of value added at this time were food, wood products, raw material processing (rubber, coconut, and tea), chemicals and chemical products, and nonmetallic mineral products. Together these accounted for more than half of the total value added and about 44 percent of manufacturing employment.

On the other hand, the fastest growing industries at the end of the decade, in terms of output and employment, were the textiles, basic metals, electrical and nonelectrical machinery, and assembly of motor vehicle industries, which grew two to three times as rapidly as the next fastest growing.[82]

In the economy as a whole, despite government agricultural development efforts, rural-urban income inequalities persisted.[83] Malay participation in the modern commercial economy was still extremely limited in 1969. Progress in "Malayanization" of commerce, using preferences and incentives, had been painfully slow. Even those enterprises formally classified as Malay-owned were often in fact "Ali-Baba"-type arrangements, in which a Muslim Malay (Ali), to obtain Malay preferences, lent his name to an enterprise which was actually run and capitalized by a Chinese businessman (often a Baba —a descendant of traders from the Straits Settlements), who retained most of the profits.[84] Malay ownership of share capital in public limited companies in 1969 stood at only 1.5 percent, as compared with 23.7 percent for Chinese and Indians and 62.1 percent for foreigners.[85] Malay participation in manufacturing employment had improved during the decade, but still amounted to only 30 percent of the total (it was 27 percent in 1962 and 19 percent in 1957) and was considerably lower in higher-skilled jobs and managerial positions.[86]

The state's market-led approach to commerce and industry had had the effect of perpetuating this system of "separate but unequal" development for the different ethnic communities which had been fostered under colonial rule. Although state actions in rural areas, such as the creation of the Rural Industrial Development Authority (RIDA), had demonstrated official commitment to improving the lot of rural Malays, the results from the point of view of many of the putative beneficiaries were hard to discern.[87] The stresses resulting from continuing ethnic inequality prompted Malay assertions that the Chinese were the ones who had been the principal gainers from government economic policies and that independent Malaysia had simply opened up for Chinese businessmen "more and better avenues for the acquisition of unlimited wealth."[88]

The 1960s had seen the emergence of a handful of Malay entrepreneurs; preferential public procurement policies had helped several dozen well-connected Malays acquire wealth and economic influence. But Malay private sector wealth continued to be insignificant in comparison with that of Europeans and Chinese active in the Malaysian economy.[89] For example, whereas only 33 percent of Chinese households in 1970 earned an average monthly income of less than M$200 ($48), 74 percent of Malay households did.[90]

The market-led industrial strategy had extended the economic lead of the Chinese and it was increasingly apparent, as the 1960s progressed, that the Chinese stood poised economically to become the principal legatees of foreign owners as the latter gradually departed. Many Malays feared this "passing of the baton" from colonial to immigrant interests would presage the intolerable, namely a situation in which they would become like the native American Indians, an economically subordinated and depressed people in their own land.[91]

The social and economic tensions arising from these ethnic perceptions are widely believed to have been the source of the communal violence that broke out in the capital Kuala Lumpur on the afternoon of May 13, 1969, and came to threaten the very existence of the twelve-year Alliance between Malay, Chinese, and Indian leaders. It is to a discussion of the effects of this breakdown in communal peace that we turn in the next chapter.

4

THE SETTLEMENT CHALLENGED AND STATE INTERVENTION: MIXING MARKET AND REGULATION, 1970–1980

On May 13, 1969, following a general election that the Alliance coalition won (but with a bare majority) race riots broke out in Malaysia's capital, Kuala Lumpur.[1] The fighting, predominantly between Malays and Chinese, left 196 dead and 439 injured, according to official figures, with non-Malay deaths exceeding those of Malays by six to one. Army troops were brought in to quell the unrest, but these troops were largely Malay and their intervention, often on the Malay side, in fact exacerbated the situation in places. The government declared a state of emergency and authorized widespread arrests, twenty-four-hour curfews, censorship of radio, television, and newspapers, and a ban on all political activities. Parliament was suspended and did not reconvene until 1971.[2]

Violence of this intensity was without precedent in postcolonial Malaysia and the events of May 13 came to be seen as a watershed in the country's political history. They indicated the extent to which the intercommunal settlement, which had provided the underpinnings for Alliance government rule since independence in 1957, had been eroded as a result of ethnic antagonisms on both sides.

The results of the 1969 election were perceived by many in the Malay community as representing a non-Malay challenge to the political hegemony of their (UMNO-dominated) government. As a result of the "provocative acts" of Chinese opposition party supporters, who dared question the special political rights of Malays that had been part of the original communal settlement, and the vigorous responses of radical Malay nationalists, who called for non-Malays to be expelled from "Malay Malaysia," the previously even-handed approach toward the different ethnic communities practiced during the 1960s fell out of favor.

The Malay leaders most influential in the interim government which enjoyed emergency powers (notably Tun Razak, who was soon to succeed the Tunku as Prime Minister) no longer felt themselves bound by the original Malay pledge not to use their control of the state apparatus as a weapon to squeeze economic concessions from the non-Malay communities. Consequently, the previous official hands-off policy towards non-Malay commercial and industrial activities was abandoned after 1969 in favor of extensive state regulation of the economy to promote Malay economic participation, and the creation of numerous state-owned corporations to act as proxies for Malay economic enterprise in the economy (until such time as Malay entrepreneurs could themselves challenge non-Malay business). Although it still remained for the non-Malay private sector to determine *what* goods were to be produced, the state increasingly sought to influence decisions concerning *how* those goods were to be produced (whose capital, whose labor, etc.) and arrogated to itself a growing share of domestic economic activity. Non-Malays, especially the Chinese, saw this state intervention as infringing on their freedom to conduct business unimpeded by burdensome regulation, a freedom they believed guaranteed by the ethnic settlement underpinning communal relations. However, their resistance to state initiatives designed to enable Malays to participate more equitably in commercial and industrial activites served only to precipitate more aggressive state action on behalf of the Malay community.

This chapter is concerned with the political determinants of industrial policy during Malaysia's second decade. In it, I show that the change observed in state industrial development strategy after 1969, from a decade-long market-led strategy to one with a much greater interventionist component, was the product of a change in the coalition settlement between the major communal groups in Malaysian society. I characterize the base of agreement between these groups as "eroding" in the 1970s, in the sense that elements within each group took issue with some of the tenets of the original settlement that had guaranteed Malay political hegemony in return for assurance of the rights of non-Malays to conduct business unimpeded by state intervention. In fact, the settlement was perceived by each side to have been eroded by the other. Malays, for example, took offense at the actions of some within the Chinese opposition who had openly questioned whether Malay political dominance ought be allowed to continue. Malay leaders responded by adopting an economic policy which had the effect of challenging non-Malay economic dominance. Whereas the Malay-dominated state had earlier felt itself constrained by the prevailing modus vivendi from intervening in commerce and industry, we see in the 1970s a state that was increasingly assertive in furthering Malay interests in the commercial and industrial sector of the economy. As the previous (market-led) economic regime unraveled, it was possible to see emerging in the 1970s the lineaments of the full-fledged state-led industrial development strategy which was adopted after 1980.

The chapter begins with a description of the ethnic upheaval of 1969 and of the changes this wrought in the attitudes of the major ethnic groups. Next, the principal policy outcome of this change in ethnic relations, the New Economic Policy (NEP), is introduced, and its implications for official industrial development strategy analyzed. Increasing state efforts to codify and enforce NEP objectives in the industrial sector, as erosion of the ethnic bargain proceeded during the 1970s, are then detailed. The chapter concludes with an assessment of the impact of state policies designed to benefit Malays on the terms of the intercommunal bargain, on the level of state intervention in the economy, and on the overall approach to industrial development employed during the decade.

The riots of May 13, 1969, followed an election campaign dominated by communal issues, the final days of which have been described as "without restraints" and "vulgar and brutal."[3] In the vote, the governing Alliance coalition was re-elected with a substantially reduced majority and less than 50 percent of the popular vote. Most worrying to the leaders of UMNO was the poor showing of the Alliance's Chinese component, the MCA, against opposition Chinese parties. It appeared, from the election results, that the MCA no longer enjoyed the confidence of the largest non-Malay group, the Chinese—it had won just thirteen of the thirty-three seats it contested and most of these were in heavily Chinese areas, like Malacca and Penang.

The ethnic tension that had accompanied the campaign was heightened after the election results were announced. While supporters of UMNO were subdued, feeling cheated in their victory, non-Malay (especially Chinese) opposition supporters celebrated their gains. The leader of the largest opposition party welcomed the results as a real breakthrough: "On 10 May 1969, the forces of democracy received a great boost. After the results of the election there was a new mood for [sic] the country, one of renewed hope that democracy might work afterall."[4] In celebration, supporters of the Chinese opposition staged exuberant "victory" processions through the streets of the capital. These prompted retaliation by UMNO supporters and the resulting clashes provided the spark that ignited the first rioting on May 13.[5]

The riots were relatively concentrated in space and time, being confined to Kuala Lumpur and the surrounding urban areas of Selangor, and lasting just two or three days.[6] The reported casualties were relatively small (compared with, for example, the several hundred thousand murdered in the anticommunist bloodletting in Indonesia in 1965) and, within a week, the authorities were beginning to ease curfew restrictions. It needs to be explained, then, why such a relatively minor outbreak of urban violence should have led to watershed changes in relations between the communal groups in Malaysian society and in the government's whole approach to economic policy after 1969.

To begin with, although the numbers of reported casualties were small, Malaysia was a relatively small country and one unaccustomed to urban violence, so the unrest was of much more concern to the authorities than had it occurred, say, in Bombay or Calcutta. Kuala Lumpur had not seen violence on this scale since 1945. Moreover, official casualty figures are widely believed to underestimate in a systematic way the numbers actually killed and injured, especially among the Chinese (the reporting officials were overwhelmingly Malay). And numbers alone gave no sense of the brutality of many of the deaths, involving dismemberment and wholesale slaughter (in the case, for example, of Malay machine-gun attacks inside crowded Chinese movie theaters). In the absence of newspapers or radio reports, stories of the most gruesome of these deaths circulated quickly by word of mouth through each community, further fanning the flames of ethnic hatred.

The fact that the violence broke out in the capital was also important in accentuating the sense of imminent ethnic paroxysm that many observers recall. Government leaders, denied access to regular communications and unable to travel safely, even to their offices downtown, experienced the violence first-hand and therefore the task of containing the violence and of preventing its recurrence took on a special urgency from their perspective.[7]

The 1969 rioting must also be seen in the context of the state of heightened ethnic tensions that preceded the elections. The violence was not viewed as a minor aberration, as it might in another country, because it was widely interpreted as an outward expression (perhaps the tip of the iceberg) of the fear and mutual animosity felt between the Malay and non-Malay communities (they were roughly equal in size). Even before the campaign began, ethnic antagonisms were clearly in evidence (reflecting Malay resentment at non-Malay control of the economy and non-Malay resentment at the constitutional guarantee of Malay political power) as indicated by the level of ethnic vitriol witnessed early in 1969. Stories of religious desecration circulated with increased frequency in each community (for example, rumors that the Chinese were leading dogs and pigs into mosques). The process of personalization of ethnic hatred was thus already well advanced, even before political parties began to fan the flames with their election slogans. Against this background of latent ethnic hostility, the first word of violence was thus interpreted by all communities as a sign that at last action was to be taken to even the score and to give vent to the ethnic hatred that had been simmering for some time.

Thus, the seriousness with which the violence was viewed was the product of a feeling that it was an expression of deep-seated hatred and that, unless something was done in both the short and the long terms to diffuse that hatred, Malaysia would self-destruct in an orgy of ethnic violence. The actions of the Malay troops sent in to quell the violence, in attacking unarmed Chinese civilians, accentuated the sense of imminent disaster—it was by no means a given that civilian rule could be reestablished and that the army, which represented the only effective form of control, would refrain from using its weapons to systematically eliminate the non-Malays.[8] From the point of view of many Malays, their political leader, Tunku Abdul Rahman, had given too much away to placate the non-Malays and now only the army now stood between Malays forfeiting not only economic control of their country, but also political control, to non-Malays.

If we consider these factors together—the small size of the country, underreporting of casualties, the scale of brutality, the location, and the latent ethnic hostility to which the violence at last gave expression—they provide us with an explanation for why the rioting, which might have been considered of relatively minor significance had it occurred elsewhere, led to landmark changes in policy and also in ethnic relations in Malaysia.

For months after May 13, government leaders were preoccupied with determining the underlying causes of the riots. Among Malay leaders of the Alliance, there were differences of opinion. While some blamed proximate events, particularly provocations by radical individuals and communists seeking to create a situation of chaos,[9] two more popular views emphasized underlying political and economic forces at work. Among the political factors said to be important were Chinese opposition demands that Malay political pre-eminence be reevaluated. Lee Kuan Yew had been the first to do this publicly, when he called for a Malaysian (i.e., specifically not *Malay*) Malaysia, during Singapore's brief union with the Federation (1963–1965). In 1969, opposition statements were much more direct, attacking constitutional provisions that gave special rights to Malays and designated the Malay language, *bahasa melayu*, as the only official language. Their argument, that the interethnic settlement of 1957 should not be considered binding on future generations, is reflected in a statement by one of their leaders:

> The 1970 generation of Malaysians of all races is vastly different from the old 1957 generation. They constitute a majority. Their wants, their hopes, are also different; and the world they live in at home and abroad is no longer the same. No generation has the right to dictate to the future generation as yet unborn or not ready to vote what precisely their political destiny must be.[10]

The Malay community found statements of this kind very threatening. Later, when it became apparent from the election results just how tenuous support for the Alliance among non-Malays really was, many Malays became increasingly alarmed. This anxiety was then fueled by statements made by groups within the Malay community. Malay nationalists, for example, drew attention to the fact that many of the constitutional provisions favoring Malays, then under attack from the Chinese opposition, were not in fact being implemented, and Malay student leaders argued that Malay accommodation with non-Malays should cease altogether. Of the latter, the Tunku observed: "These people only want Malay rule. I asked them: 'Can you really do this? Can you really do without the other races?' And they replied: 'We don't care.' "[11]

A number of senior UMNO leaders who subscribed to a political interpretation of events concluded that the riots were the product of an overt challenge by the Chinese opposition to the established terms of the intercommunal settlement. They felt that the best way to respond was by insulating the terms of the bargain from political pressures by embedding them more explicitly in the Constitution.

A contrasting economic view attributed the riots to Malay frustration at continuing economic inferiority (that is, to the fact that the economic power of the Malay community was not commensurate with its political power). In 1969, for example, Malays owned only 1.5 percent of corporate equity, in comparison with the 22.5 percent share of the less numerous Chinese, and the 62.1 percent share owned by foreigners.[12] Special Malay rights enshrined in the Constitution and subsequent "affirmative action" efforts undertaken by the Alliance government had been insufficient to avert a growing feeling of economic insecurity in the Malay community.[13] The remedy that was suggested by, among others, Tun Razak, was increasing state economic intervention to promote ethnic Malay economic activities.[14]

The interpretation of events that was eventually to take on the mantle of "official wisdom" combined both political and economic explanations. It suggested that Malay resentment toward non-Malays (especially the Chinese) had been rising steadily since independence, as a result of the concessions to Chinese concerns on language and educational issues, and also because measures designed to help Malays economically were not working (or not working fast enough). The situation was tolerable so long as Malay political hegemony was assured. When non-Malays began questioning whether Malays should receive special help *at all*, however, and whether they had any right to dominate the apparatus of the state (i.e., whether the intercommunal bargain ought to apply any longer), ordinary Malays were frightened into taking to the streets.

The changes adopted after 1969 should be seen as the product of this particular version of events. On the political side, UMNO leaders concluded that provision had to be made in the Constitution to ensure that the principles embodied in the ethnic settlement (specifically those protecting Malay political power) were placed beyond question. Subsequently, the scope of political debate was narrowed by constitutional amendment to exclude those issues which had been exploited so effectively by non-Malay opposition leaders and which had so inflamed Malays as to lead them to violence.[15]

UMNO leaders also decided to expand the Alliance to include a broader range of Chinese and Malay parties (the coalition was re-named the National Front). By boosting its parliamentary majority to more than the two-thirds majority required for constitutional amend-ment, the National Front reassured the Malay community that Malay political dominance would continue. Henceforth, it was almost in-conceivable that a non-Malay-dominated party or coalition could cap-ture enough seats to form a government and challenge the terms of the ethnic bargain.[16]

In economic terms, the perception that Malays continued to be disadvantaged prompted Malay leaders to formulate the NEP with the goal of improving the economic position of Malays on a broad front.[17] Using an "expanding pie" metaphor for economic growth, they argued that, so long as economic growth continued, the abso-lute size of each community's "slice" could be protected, even as the Malay "slice" was made larger. In effect, while accusing non-Malays of precipitating the riots by challenging the terms of the ethnic bar-gain, the Malay leadership itself, by introducing the NEP, threatened the bargain by questioning the economic position of non-Malays.[18]

CHANGING THE RULES: THE NEW ECONOMIC POLICY

The government's principal response to the riots took the form of the NEP.[19] Under the NEP, economic progress was no longer to be measured simply in terms of economic growth but also in terms of advances in the economic well-being of the have-nots in Malaysian society.[20] While "national unity" was an important goal of govern-ment policy, the NEP argued that such unity was

> unattainable without greater equity and balance among Malaysia's social and ethnic groups in their participation in the development of the country and in the sharing of the benefits from modernization and economic growth. [It] cannot be fostered if vast sections of the popu-lation remain poor and if sufficient productive employment opportu-nities are not created for the expanding labour force.[21]

As stated by a Malay leader who helped formulate the NEP:

> The justification for Malaysia's NEP goes beyond principle and beyond moral values . . . . It is our conviction that a more equitable distribution of wealth and a more balanced participation of all [of] Malaysia's communities in the modern, fast-advancing sectors of the Malaysian economy is a sine qua non, an indispensible condition for a united Malaysian nation in the longer run and an essential requisite for political survival and stability in the shorter term.[22]

NEP objectives were relevant not just to national unity but also to economic expansion. The present Prime Minister, Mahathir, has observed that:

> [the NEP's] formulation was made necessary by the economic needs of the nation as much as its politico-social needs. There can be no economic stability without political and social stability. Thus the NEP is also a formula for economic growth.[23]

Justifying the NEP as a basically non-partisan, noncommunal response to the economic needs of the country, government leaders presented the policy as their contribution "to reduc[ing] and eventually eradicat[ing] poverty, by raising income levels and increasing employment opportunities for all Malaysians, irrespective of race."[24] But since Malays dominated the ranks of the poor,[25] it was clear that the Malay community stood to benefit disproportionately from the poverty eradication measures embodied in the NEP. It soon became apparent that the primary thrust of the NEP lay elsewhere, namely in:

> accelerating the process of restructuring Malaysian society to correct economic imbalance, so as to reduce and eventually eliminate the identification of race with economic function. This process involves the modernization of rural life, a rapid and balanced growth of urban activities and the creation of a Malay commercial and industrial community in all categories and at all levels of operation, so that Malays and other indigenous people will become full partners in all aspects of the economic life of the nation.[26]

This, then was the policy's "second prong."

Despite government efforts to emphasize its poverty-related aspects, the NEP was principally a Malay response to the changed relations that existed between the Malay and non-Malay communities after 1969.

To review, non-Malays, by advocating termination of special political and economic rights for Malays, had, in the eyes of the Malay community, challenged the existing structure of the ethnic settlement. The Malay response had two components. The government amended the Constitution to strengthen the *political* position of Malays and to place the issue of Malay political dominance beyond the realm of public discourse. At the same time, it launched a challenge to non-Malay (especially Chinese) *economic* dominance that took the form of the NEP. In the NEP, we find the rationale for a greatly expanded state role in the economy, one that was henceforth increasingly communal.

In a sense, the NEP represented a kind of Third World indigenous economic nationalism, but in the Malaysian case the principal antagonist was not foreign. Instead, the indigenous (but non-Malay) capitalist became the target for state measures designed to bolster the economic status of the politically dominant Malay community.[27]

Government measures designed to empower the Malay community economically focused on developing Malay entrepreneurship and providing Malay businessmen with the finance, expertise and facilities necessary for success. Programs were set up to help Malay entrepreneurs by providing the skills and fostering the attitudes considered appropriate to the modern industrial economy. New state institutions were created to act in the economy as agents for the Malay community.[28] Commercial development in rural areas was encouraged as a means of bringing commercial and industrial opportunities within reach of rural Malays. The government also exerted pressure on non-Malay and foreign commercial and industrial enterprises to provide novice Malay businessmen with technical assistance, marketing and purchasing cooperation, and generous financial terms.[29]

Not all of this was "new." As we saw in chapter 3, economic measures to assist Malays (especially in rural areas) had been adopted on a piecemeal basis during the decade preceding the riots. But the NEP now established a coherent framework and rationale for policies targeted specifically at Malays, and they were supported by a much more determined government effort at implementation.[30] The NEP introduced new initiatives, but also established specific targets. For example, Malay employment in the industrial sector was to be increased until it reflected, at every level, the ethnic composition of the population at large (of which, at that time, 54 percent were Malay).[31] Similar goals were established for Malay ownership and management:

> Within two decades at least 30% of the total commercial and industrial activites in all categories and scales of operation should have participation by Malays and other indigenous people in terms of ownership and management. The objective is to create over a period of time a viable and thriving Malay industrial and commercial community which will operate on a par and in effective partnership with non-Malays in the modern sector.[32]

Non-Malay leaders were not opposed to the NEP in principle, but were very concerned at the impact that its implementation might have on their economic position. The government sought to assuage these anxieties by arguing that NEP goals could be achieved within the context of overall economic growth (the "expanding pie"). In other words, the proposed increase in the Malay share in the economy could be generated as a product of efforts to involve more Malays in the commercial and industrial economy, and need not deprive economically powerful groups (i.e., the Chinese) of their accumulated economic wealth.[33] Thus Malay leaders tried to preempt non-Malay opposition by arguing that policies benefiting the Malay community were designed at the same time to benefit all Malaysians. As stated in the Second Malaysia Plan:

> The New Economic Policy is based upon a rapidly expanding economy which offers increasing opportunities for all Malaysians as well as additional resources for development. Thus, in the implementation of this Policy, the Government will ensure that no particular group will experience loss or feel any sense of deprivation.[34]

The broad reorientation of economic policy embodied in the NEP had important implications for the industrial development strategy employed in Malaysia during the 1970s.

INDUSTRIAL STRATEGY UNDER THE NEP

The NEP represented a significant change in government economic policy emphasis, both in communal and in sectoral terms.

During the 1960s, agricultural programs had been the principal focus of government intervention efforts.[35] These included large land development and irrigation schemes under the auspices of FELDA, and programs generated by government agencies such as the Malaysian Agricultural Research and Development Institute (MARDI), the Rubber Industry Smallholder Development Authority (RISDA), Bank Bumiputra, and Bank Pertanian (Agricultural Bank) to boost agricultural production.[36]

In the 1970s, these efforts were eclipsed by stepped-up government efforts to develop the commercial and industrial sector. By 1975, the industrial sector had more than doubled its share of GDP over its 1961 level (17 percent versus 8 percent), while the agricultural share had declined by nearly a third, from 34 percent to 24 percent.[37] The general shift in policy emphasis towards industry was accompanied by a change in the strategy applied to industrial development. The earlier market-led approach—which had left decisions in the industrial sector (about what was to be produced, by whom, and in what manner) to the private sector—was superseded by a strategy embodying unprecedented levels of state intervention.

Malay leaders, in the wake of the 1969 riots, no longer felt the need to be as cautious as they had in wielding their considerable political power (they had effective control over all branches of the state apparatus) to advance Malay economic interests. It was clear from the events of May that the previous arrangement, whereby the economic dominance of the non-Malay communities was insulated from state interference, was considered so irksome to the majority of Malays that it could no longer be sustained. The riots had caused a change in attitude among UMNO leaders toward relations with the non-Malay communities—they no longer felt as constrained by the ethnic settlement as they had in the 1960s.[38]

The new active state role was welcomed by Malays such as Tan Sri Jaafar Albar who, in 1968, at a conference of Malay businessmen (the Second Bumiputra Economic Congress), had been outspoken in denouncing the concept of free enterprise. From their perspective, economic growth under a free-market system inevitably disadvantaged the Malay community. If the goals of the NEP were to be met, they argued, it was essential that the prevailing market-led industrial strategy be replaced by one allowing for direct state intervention on behalf of Malay economic interests.[39]

State economic intervention after 1970, therefore, was motivated by a Malay desire to create a "viable commercial and industrial Malay business community" to challenge the Chinese and Indian dominance of economic activity in Malaysia.[40] Initially, it took the form of substantially increased allocations for industrial development in the government's development budget, and attempts by government leaders to cajole existing businesses into changing their management, ownership, and employment practices to accommodate Malays. When this failed, the state imposed increased regulation on private business, creating a system of sanctions and inducements designed to open opportunities for Malays.[41] Government pressure was necessary because most non-Malay employers were reluctant to hire Malays, whom they claimed were inexperienced, and therefore a drain on profitability. To counter this, any firm seeking state support (e.g., a tax holiday or import protection) had to undertake to employ at least 30 percent Malays *at all levels*.[42] At the same time, regulations were promulgated reserving a proportion of certain economic activities (government contracts, for example) for Malays and Malay-owned firms.[43]

Not content with regulation, the state, in "a significant departure from past practice," also embarked upon a policy of "participat[ing] more directly in the establishment and operation of a wide range of productive enterprises through wholly owned enterprises and joint ventures with the private sector."[44] It established numerous new public corporations and extended the range of operations of existing ones in an attempt to create proxies for Malay business that would eventually be transferred to private sector (Malay) ownership.[45]

In effect, the state, while still embracing company-led growth, now became a significant economic actor in its own right. The extent of this increased state commitment to involvement in the economy can be gauged from the ten-fold rise in official allocations for government corporations recorded in the Second Malaysia Plan (SMP, 1971–1975) over the First Malaysia Plan (FMP, 1966–1970).[46] The communal motivation for this change in the state's role was quite explicit; it arose, according to the SMP, "from the aims . . . of creating a Malay commercial and industrial community."[47] In effect, state enterprises were to operate on behalf of the Malay community until such time as individual Malay entrepreneurs were experienced enough and numerous enough to present a real challenge to Chinese, Indian, and foreign entrepreneurs in the marketplace.[48]

Given the poorly developed nature of Malay entrepreneurship in 1970, this approach had much to recommend it. Large state corporations, such as MARA, PERNAS (Perbadanan Nasional—a state investment holding corporation charged with promoting Malay participation in business), and the State Economic Development Corporations (SEDCs), enjoyed numerous advantages associated with their size and official status. Companies they spawned could act as competitive "umbrellas" for small Malay entrepreneurs. A PERNAS subsidiary, for example, might distribute wholesale goods to Malays otherwise denied supplies for lack of credit from non-Malay suppliers.[49]

It is worthwhile considering, for a moment, the nature and functions of some of these newly created (or greatly expanded) public enterprises. MARA, PERNAS, the UDA (Urban Development Authority) and the thirteen SEDCs were the most active of these semi-autonomous government agencies, providing employment, business services, advice, training, and loans to Malays, and sometimes themselves undertaking joint ventures with local or foreign firms.[50] To give a sense of scale, PERNAS in late 1975 employed about four thousand people and operated eight subsidiaries engaged in a wide range of activities, from trade and mining to property development and securities trading. The UDA at the same time had the principal responsibility of supplying Malays in business with office space and other premises in urban areas. SEDC activities, like those of PERNAS, were wide-ranging, encompassing agriculture, manufacturing, the provision of business and office premises, and wholesale and retail trading.[51]

Institutions such as these helped Malays by supplying the wherewithal to compete on an equal footing with non-Malay capital. For example, to prepare more Malays for skilled jobs in manufacturing and commerce, many agencies offered training facilities (the MARA Institute of Technology [ITM] produced nearly three thousand graduates between 1966 and 1975).[52] MARA, Bank Bumiputra (and, since 1974, its subsidiary, Bank Pembangunan—the Development Bank), and to a lesser extent Malaysian Industrial Development Finance (MIDF), extended credit to Malay businessmen at concessionary rates.

In addition, after 1972, a Credit Guarantee Corporation (CGC) made commercial bank credit easier to obtain by guaranteeing commercial loans to small-scale enterprises. Business advising and consultancy services were also made available through MARA, the National Productivity Centre, and the Ministry of Trade and Industry's Bumiputra Participation Division, which developed programs for novice Malay entrepreneurs.[53]

For Malays interested in investing, but not inclined to start their own business, MARA established several unit-trusts. Malays generally had only a small amount to invest, had little experience of buying shares (stocks) and showed a clear preference for buying government-issued certificates, rather than shares in limited companies. Thus MARA's unit-trusts, and similar schemes provided through Kompleks Kewangan (the Financial Center—a financial consortium that began as a MARA subsidiary) and the Tabung Haji, the institution through which Muslims save for their pilgrimage to Mecca, were all designed to help Malays meet the NEP's 30 percent Malay ownership target.[54]

The use of public enterprises to bolster Malay shareholding was assisted by restrictions placed on all public share offerings, requiring that they designate a certain proportion of the shares for Malays only. Few Malays, however, were sufficiently wealthly to participate: between 1971 and August 1974 only about M$200 million of the M$500 million in reserved shares were in fact taken up by Malays.[55] As a result, large public enterprises, such as PERNAS or the SEDCs, were compelled to step in with public funds to buy reserved shares for later distribution to Malay individuals. Thus public enterprises not only helped Malay entrepreneurs get started and launched state-run businesses for later transfer to Malay ownership, but also acted as holding companies for a small but significant proportion of Malaysian corporate equity.

So far, I have characterized expanded state intervention in the economy under the NEP as taking two forms: a) regulation and b) direct institutional involvement, by means of newly created or expanded public enterprises. It is worth noting, however, that state efforts to bolster Malay economic participation were not limited to regulatory and institutional initiatives. Malays themselves were called upon to adopt new attitudes more in keeping with a modern industrial economy. Prime Minister Tun Razak, for example, challenged

Malays to become more economically minded and to embrace science and technology,[56] while Senu Abdul Rahman proposed a "mental revolution" to spread modern ideas throughout the Malay community.[57] These statements were significant because they revealed a conviction that even extensive state involvement would not be sufficient to loosen the non-Malay stranglehold on the commercial and industrial sector unless Malays at the same time absorbed cultural lessons from the successful Chinese and Indians.

By 1975, results of the government's dramatic reorientation in economic policy were already apparent. The Malay share of manufacturing jobs had increased from 25 percent in 1970 to 32 percent, while one survey suggested that Malays comprised 17 percent of managers (compared with 11 percent in 1971). The Malay share of institutional credit was now almost 30 percent, up from 14 percent in 1971. And Malay ownership of all capital stood at 8 percent rather than the 2.4 percent of 1970.[58]

Despite these achievements, though, the NEP was a source of frustration, both to the UMNO leadership, which had instituted the policy, and to the non-Malay communities which had accepted it, with reservations, in the wake of the 1969 riots. Certainly Malay entrepreneurs were more in evidence than they had been in the 1960s, but in many cases their participation was limited to Ali-Baba-type ventures, which afforded non-Malay participants access to Malay quotas (in government contracts, for example) but rarely provided Malay partners with actual management experience.[59] Thus, increasing economic opportunity for Malays under the NEP was not necessarily being translated into increased business acumen. Moreover, filling 30 percent of management positions with Malays was proving difficult because there was a shortage of experienced Malay managers. Some companies claimed that while the government chided them for not employing Malays at senior levels, exhaustive recruitment efforts had turned up few prospects. Meanwhile, the government's own public enterprises were apparently "head-hunting" staff from each other and from government departments.[60] And some ambitious and qualified Malays were taking advantage of the situation by changing jobs frequently in response to a bidding war in salaries.[61]

This points to the difficulty of coordinating a strategy for Malay advancement. In an attempt to give coherence to this multiplicity of public agencies and programs, the Ministry for Coordination of Public Enterprises was created in 1974, charged with countering dishonesty, inefficiency, and waste in public enterprises, especially in the SEDCs. It was clear that, despite their designated role of promoting Malay competence in management, many public enterprises themselves had been unable to attract sufficient good Malay managers to run their own programs effectively.[62]

By the mid-1970s, then, the new strategy was not proceeding quite as well as expected. The Malay-dominated state, with the tacit acceptance of the other communities, had expanded its involvement in the economy. Through government regulation and the activities of a plethora of new and expanded state institutions, it had expanded opportunities for Malay employment, management, and ownership participation in existing businesses, and had even itself established businesses in the name of the Malay community. But these efforts had been constrained by a commitment to allow private-sector actors to make their own decisions (i.e., to allow market-led growth). While public enterprises trained, financed, and provided facilities for Malay entrepreneurs, accumulated capital on behalf of Malays, and even launched business ventures to be later transferred to private Malay entrepreneurs, the state was not prepared to *impose* NEP goals on the private sector, nor to direct industrial change using the MITI-style approach employed in postwar Japan.

By 1975, however, some Malay leaders were beginning to doubt whether these state efforts would be sufficient to enable Malays to meet NEP economic targets. The course advocated by people like Razaleigh Hamzah and Ghafar Baba combined economic modernism and Malay (communal) nationalism in a strongly statist approach to development. Citing the failure of Malays and "Malay interests" (i.e., government bodies acting on behalf of the Malay community) to achieve the 9 percent ownership target set by the SMP for 1975 (actual ownership was 7.8 percent), they called for a significant expansion in the use of state agencies as instruments for the achievement of Malay NEP goals.[63]

Their views were reflected in the Third Malaysia Plan (TMP, 1976–1980). The TMP emphasized the role of "Malay interests," rather than of Malay individuals, as the primary agencies for accumulating Malay ownership shares (new corporate share issues were to be purchased by "interests" and Malay individuals in the ratio of three to one), and the role of a new state-run investment fund, the Bumiputra Investment Fund, which was to "selectively acquire the reserved [Malay] shares in enterprises with high growth potential, for subsequent sale to Malays and other indigenous people."[64]

Advocates of this statist strategy explained slow progress towards NEP goals in communal terms; at root, the reluctance of non-Malay business to abide by NEP guidelines was to blame. Therefore, they argued, UMNO had to take a much tougher line with the non-Malay private sector and start enforcing, rather than simply advocating, the numerical quotas for employment and ownership specified in the NEP.[65]

But considerations of intra-Malay politics encouraged some Malay leaders to take a harder line on pro-Malay state intervention than others, and dictated the timing of new measures to impose NEP guidelines on the private sector. The UMNO General Assembly was to meet on June 21, 1975, to hold triennial elections for places on the party's influential Supreme Council. Attention was focused particularly on competition for three vice-presidential positions that ranked immediately below those of Party President and Deputy President (which were held by the Prime Minister and the Deputy Prime Minister, repectively) because it was widely believed that the winners would represent the future leadership of the party.[66] Among those prominent in calling for increased state intervention were two of the candidates for these positions: Tengku Razaleigh who, as chairman of the state oil company (Petronas) had enhanced his political reputation by adopting an intransigent position with respect to foreign oil firms; and Datuk Hamzah Aby Samah (whose candidacy, unlike Razaleigh's, was unsuccessful).[67] Razaleigh, for example, was a strong advocate not only of increased regulation but of the use of large state-run organizations to provide institutional help for would-be Malay businessmen—without the use of such organizations, he claimed, state efforts to get Malays into business would be a nonstarter.[68]

In embracing this economic "statist" position, Razaleigh and Hamzah chose to ally themselves with the old stalwarts of UMNO, as represented by Tunku Abdul Rahman (the first Prime Minister), Datuk Senu Abdul Rahman (the party's Secretary General) and Tan Sri Jaafâr Albar (former Secretary General and the one ranking UMNO leader who had openly demanded an end to the unregulated competitive capitalism that in his view obstructed Malay participation in business).[69] This is significant because Razaleigh usually joined Prime Minister Tun Razak on the opposite side of the table from the stalwarts when battle-lines were drawn in the political infighting that characterized UMNO at that time. It suggests that the timing of the Malay statist response to a perception of non-Malay obstructionism towards the goals of the NEP (i.e., why it came in 1975, and not earlier or later) had a lot to do with politics within UMNO and particularly with the maneuvering that preceded the party elections of 1975.[70]

The statist perspective of Razaleigh was by no means universally shared among UMNO leaders, however. Mahathir and Musa Hitam (the Primary Industries Minister), for example, who held impeccable Malay nationalist credentials,[71] were concerned at the effect that a heavily statist strategy might have on foreign investment. They favored free enterprise as the primary vehicle for Malay economic advancement, arguing that strengthening the private sector was the best way to open opportunities for Malays.[72]

But the views of those within UMNO favoring a statist strategy and a hard line with Chinese and Indian business prevailed with the introduction, by Minister of Finance Razaleigh, of the Industrial Coordination Act of 1975 (ICA). The ICA, for the first time, gave the state "teeth" to enforce NEP targets.[73] It made it mandatory for all industries to provide opportunities for Malays in employment, management, and ownership. Not surprisingly, its primary impact was felt by Chinese businesses which typically had maintained family-based employment and ownership structures, often dating back to colonial times.[74]

THE INDUSTRIAL COORDINATION ACT

The ICA, which took effect in May, 1976, created a system of licensing for industry in Malaysia. Its key provision made granting of licenses conditional on compliance with NEP guidelines. The act was without precedent, both because of its blanket coverage (apart from small-scale businesses, all industries were included, whether or not they sought taxation relief or other government assistance) and because of the extraordinary powers it vested in the Minister of Trade and Industry to direct and control the development of manufacturing industry.[75]

The act's principal proponent, Tengku Razaleigh (who became Finance Minister in the cabinet of Prime Minister Hussein Onn in March of 1976), justified it as necessary for the coordination and orderly development of manufacturing industry.[76] He suggested that only about 10 percent of Malaysian industries were "properly controlled" by the government, the rest being "quite free to do as they like as there are no existing regulations to control them." The new legislation, he said, sought "to streamline industrial procedures and growth, to keep pace with Government's economic policy, and to reduce unhealthy competition among manufacturers."[77] Subsequently, at official ICA seminars for manufacturers, the act was presented, variously, as a logical extension of existing legislation that had limited enforcement of NEP targets to firms seeking government assistance (for example, under the Industrial Investment Act of 1968), as a vehicle for collecting information about existing industry, and as a means of preventing industrial over-supply.[78]

But Chinese and Indian businessmen rejected the "regulation of oversupply" argument as a red herring: oversupply would not prevent a well-connected Malay entrepreneur from obtaining a license to produce; undersupply would not help a Chinese manufacturer about to lose his license (for failure to meet NEP goals). They saw the primary motivation for the legislation as communal and expressed alarm at the implied threat to the freedom of the marketplace.

Adoption of the ICA in 1976 represented another step in the erosion of the communal settlement that had prevailed since 1957. By making the very right of non-Malays to do business conditional upon their acceptance of UMNO priorities in the area of Malay economic advancement, the Malay state was clearly interfering with economic prerogatives which non-Malays felt were rightfully theirs, according to the terms of the settlement. This explains why the act was so controversial and why non-Malays were so vociferous in their opposition to it.

The Associated Chinese Chambers of Commerce and Industry (ACCCIM), the largest and most influential of Malaysia's business organizations, challenged each of the official rationales used for the act, in a well-publicized memo to the government.[79] It argued that the present level of state supervision of manufacturing was entirely appropriate; that industrial development thus far had not been haphazard nor had it suffered from lack of coordination; that the discre-

tionary powers accorded the Minister under the act were unaccepta-
bly broad;[80] that compulsion was not the best way of meeting the
restructuring targets of the NEP; and that the act would discourage
private-sector investment that was essential to expanding the "pie"
from which Malays would obtain a larger "slice" (without disadvan-
taging non-Malays). The memo demanded that the act be with-
drawn:

> [The ACCCIM] considers that the ICA is like a sword hanging over
> the private sector. As government leadership may change over time,
> the ICA, if it remains, will constitute a continuing threat to the private
> sector.

Not mentioned was the widely held view of both non-Malay opponents and Malay supporters, that the ICA represented a mandate
for the Minister to grant monopoly rights to well-placed Malays.[81]
Through its licensing arrangements, the act enabled the Minister to
discriminate in favor of Malays in general, but also of certain Malays
in particular. It was thus possible for the desired "Malay commercial
and industrial community"[82] to be defined, in practice, in terms of a
limited number of individuals and companies who had access to
licenses denied others.[83]

The government responded to strong opposition from the private
sector by establishing a cabinet-level Committee on Investment charged
with administering the NEP (and ICA) more "realistically." Chaired
by Deputy Prime Minister Mahathir (who was considered more fa-
vorably disposed towards the private sector than Razaleigh), the
committee was to "have a second or third look at some of the interpretations of policies [e.g., the ICA] which have given rise to complaints and consequently closed the investment climate." With the
help of committee oversight, Mahathir said, "the investment climate
should improve and the traditional confidence that the private sector
has had in the economy of this nation [will] be maintained if not
enhanced."[84]

At the same time, UMNO leaders tried to appear flexible in their
interpretation of the NEP. For example, they stated that targets for
Malay employment and equity participation were "global," and
therefore not necessarily binding on any specific sector or enterprise,[85] and that targets for Malay ownership might be allowed to
vary with the nature of the enterprise.[86] These reassurances, how-

ever, were targeted more at the foreign than the domestic business community. Local non-Malay entrepreneurs continued to register their opposition to the ICA in the form of numerous submissions to the Cabinet.[87]

The UMNO leadership, divided internally over how best to increase Malay economic power within the context of a basically company-led strategy, was clearly not prepared to enforce the ICA in the face of almost universal protest by the local business community. As early as September 1976, barely five months after the act took effect, Deputy Prime Minister Mahathir suggested that the government might consider altering certain clauses "to remove any misunderstandings that may have arisen in the minds of investors about the act's objectives."[88] Subsequently, in March 1977, amendments were indeed adopted, introducing consultation with the private sector on conditions that would be required for licenses, creating an appeals procedure and exempting a wider range of enterprises from the act's provisions.[89]

These modifications, however, were still considered unsatisfactory by non-Malay businessmen who claimed they did not reduce the broad application of the act to all branches of industry, nor did they alter the retroactive enforcement of licensing provisions to established industries. In the words of one observer,

> despite the Amendments, the ICA . . . continue[s] to be a 'disincentive' factor by creating a climate of uncertainty and unsolicited intrusion into what has always been regarded as the investor's prerogative of running his own business in a manner he best knows how, without any supervision by administrative bodies.[90]

The government had not responded to "fair and reasonable" complaints:

> After all the promises of important changes to improve the investment climate, the Amendments . . . have been somewhat of a letdown. An examination of the Amendments will not bear out the assertion that the Government "are just short of throwing out the entire Act." The Amendments are purely cosmetic and [in]consequential. They do not remove the difficulties and make no significant concession to the private sector.[91]

Businesses accommodated themselves in different ways to the ICA. Larger Chinese entrepreneurs sought partnership with Malays or resorted to bribery to circumvent the restrictions imposed by the act. Other Chinese investors, apprehensive over the implementation of the licensing scheme and concerned at the likely inflexibility and ethnic chauvinism of Malay civil servants charged with administering the act, invested in land or financial assets (such as government securities) rather than in productive enterprise.[92] As a result, by 1977, despite very high levels of liquidity in the economy, domestic private investment in commercial and industrial enterprise had declined sharply, and was well short of the M\$22 billion target projected for that year by the TMP.[93]

THE ICA AND INDUSTRIAL DEVELOPMENT: THE LATE 1970S

We have seen that changes in the terms of the settlement between ethnic communities in Malaysia prompted changes in the state's approach to economic development after 1970. Chapter 3 showed how, during the years between 1957 and 1969, the intercommunal bargain constrained the state from playing an active role in the modern commercial sector. Following the 1969 riots, however, the state began increasingly to intervene, with measures designed to strengthen the economic position of Malays in relation to that of non-Malays. By creating a licensing system to regulate non-Malay businesses, by imposing employment and ownership restrictions on them, and by creating numerous state institutions whose primary function was to work on behalf of Malays, the state in the 1970s became a much more active player in the economic "game." What were the implications of this pro-Malay economic activism for the course of industrial development in Malaysia?

The state, in trying to promote Malay economic enterprise and at the same time expand the industrial sector, faced several dilemmas. Non-Malay investors, responding to the NEP and the introduction of the ICA's business licensing scheme, cut back their investment in industry, at the time when government development plans, specifically the TMP, called for greatly increased dependence on private investment:

> Private investment is projected to provide the major source of capital formation during the 1976–80 period in contrast to the experience in

the Second Malaysia Plan when the main role was played by public investment. With public sector investment planned to increase by only 6.2% per annum or much slower than in the Second Malaysia Plan, the capacity required by the economy for its future growth depends significantly on high levels of private investment.[94]

At a 1977 Malaysian Chinese Economic Conference organized by the ACCCIM,[95] delegates pointed the finger at the NEP and the uncertainty it had caused as the source of this reduction in private sector investment, and again called for the repeal of the ICA.[96]

Government leaders were well aware of the difficulties they faced in sustaining levels of industrial investment. As they maneuvered to create a Malay entrepreneurial community, and thus to challenge non-Malay business control, they knew that the success of this strategy was dependent upon cooperation from the non-Malay private sector itself, in the form of investment for continued economic growth. Deputy Prime Minister Mahathir, addressing a seminar of the largely non-Malay Federation of Malaysian Manufacturers on the TMP, in 1976, acknowledged that doubts about the NEP may have affected decisions to invest:

> A number of problems and issues surfaced during the implementation of the [NEP]. . . . These problems were also probably responsible for the slight under achievement of the targets of the Second Plan. The problems and issues which arose during the course of implementation of the policy may have given cause for doubts in the minds of private investors.[97]

With private investment by jittery Chinese and Indian investors falling off, the state was forced to rely increasingly on foreign capital. This led to a second dilemma, for one of the ICA's unintended consequences was hesitance on the part of foreign investors to invest in Malaysia. Malaysia had hitherto been considered a good site for foreign investment.[98] But foreign developments that paralleled the ICA, including world recession in the wake of the first oil shock and regional instability following the communist victories in Indochina, now made foreign investors wary of committing themselves in the region.

Such wariness was encouraged in the Malaysian case by the effects of an earlier measure, the Petroleum Development (Amendment) Act (PDA), which had threatened to nationalize foreign investments in oil exploration and production.[99] The PDA, which was adopted in 1975 with almost no prior consultation with the affected foreign oil companies, extended the control of state-owned oil company, Petronas, over all marketing and distribution of Malaysian oil, and mandated Petronas majority ownership shares in all petroleum projects (they were to be managed as joint ventures with foreign oil companies). While controversial, these provisions were overshadowed by a third, specifying that Petronas was to acquire this majority ownership in all production, transportation and refining of Malaysian oil and gas by way of "management shares" carrying voting rights equal to those of five hundred ordinary shares.[100] Existing owners were given little choice but to issue such management shares.

The PDA unsettled foreign investors, both because of its arbitrariness and because it amounted in their eyes to a form of nationalization. The oil companies vociferously opposed it, some threatening to withdraw altogether, and eventually the government was forced to back down and to strike the most objectionable sections from the law, including those concerning management shares.[101]

So, with introduction of the ICA coming in the midst of this PDA dispute, many foreign investors looking at Malaysia decided that they should hold back on new spending. The result was a level of foreign investment growth well below that called for in the government's plans. In 1976, for example, foreign investment grew by a mere 3 percent, short of the 10 percent projected by the government.[102]

Government leaders did what they could to reassure foreign companies in the wake of the PDA debacle and the introduction of the ICA. Dato Onn, in a speech made soon after he became Prime Minister in 1976, was at pains to emphasize his government's open-arms policy towards foreign investment.[103] Campaigns were launched to publicize investment incentives, a "one stop" agency for investment approval was established at FIDA, and "pump-priming" mechanisms like highway construction programs were expanded.[104]

The government also stepped up its encouragement of export-oriented industries, such as those producing electrical goods and electronics components. This export orientation had its origins in 1968, with the Investment Incentives Act, but now received a higher profile, at least in part because of the perception shared by Malay leaders that export industry employment had the potential to pull

Malays into the modern sector faster (and to make them competitive with non-Malays quicker) than any other type of industry. Thus, in a speech delivered in August 1977, Razaleigh (then Minister of Trade and Industry) announced that foreign concerns manufacturing for export would be exempt from the provisions of the ICA:

> I understand that some manufacturers, especially those in export-oriented industries, are hesitant to expand or diversify because of the unwarranted apprehension that if they apply to expand or diversify their existing production units, the Government under the ICA will insist on changes in their equity conditions. Let me assure you that this apprehension is totally unjustified. The Government has not and will not take action to amend equity conditions of export-oriented operations wishing to expand or diversify their operations. It is only domestic-oriented industries that are required to ensure that the expanded portion of investment . . . will have to reflect increasing Malaysian and bumiputra participation.[105]

The government also tried to make local conditions more attractive to foreign investors. Labor laws that might discourage foreign investment went unenforced. For example, Intel, an exporter of semiconductors, reportedly required workers to perform up to eight hours compulsory "shift overlap" (i.e., a sixteen hour workday), in violation of the voluntary overtime provisions of the Employment Ordinance that the Labour Department chose not to enforce.[106] And measures were taken to exclude unions from key export industries, such as electronics, through the exercise of the Registrar of Trade Unions' discretionary powers to withhold registration from particular unions.[107]

Despite these measures, a shortfall in (domestic and foreign) private investment in commerce and industry forced the state to take up some of the slack. The low income of Malays and their correspondingly low propensity to save meant that many of the share offerings of private companies reserved for Malays had gone undersubscribed. So statutory bodies, such as PERNAS, MARA, and PNB, had to step in to purchase the shares. Their role as repositories for capital held in trust for the Malay community expanded well beyond that originally envisioned by Malay leaders. But this rapid accumulation of wealth in the hands of state agencies acting on behalf of Malays, and the scale of bodies like PERNAS, accentuated the anxieties already felt by non-Malay businessmen and thus further discouraged long-term private sector investment.[108]

Some Malays expressed dismay at the increasingly dominant role of state agencies. There were complaints that agencies such as MARA were crowding out novice Malay businessmen, a view encapsulated in the observation "first it was Ali-Baba, now it is becoming Ali-MARA, soon it will be all MARA and no Ali."[109] And there were allegations that, while income inequality overall was improving, inequality *within* the Malay community, between those rich enough to purchase shares reserved for Malay individuals (the "hundred millionaires") and the remainder of the Malay community, was worsening.[110] Malay leaders rejected these criticisms. Mahathir, for example, at the Bumiputra Economic Congress of March 1978, attacked the myth of a handful of extremely wealthy Malays and defended his government's policy of allocating corporate stock to those Malays who might use it most efficiently, rather than distributing small amounts of stock to all Malays.[111]

In conclusion, it should be emphasized that the effects of the NEP and the ICA were by no means limited to the economy. Among the most important were changes resulting from the NEP in the structure and role of the civil service. The bureaucratic structure inherited from the British, while suitable for administering a colony, was inadequate to tasks such as that of managing the vast investment stocks of a holding company like PERNAS. The centralized and strictly hierarchical model on which Malaysian public administration was built was poorly suited to operating businesses for profit.[112] So new structures, represented by semi-autonomous agencies like Petronas, had to be created to meet these new challenges. At the same time, the role assigned civil servants in implementing the NEP (and particularly the ICA) changed the character of the civil service itself.[113] As the foremost scholar of Malaysian public administration observed,

> in the past it was possible for the civil service to maintain some degree of impartiality and neutrality while at the same time giving extra benefits and privileges to one group, the Malays. Although the NEP has not substantially changed this arrangement, there has been a shift in emphasis in the implementation of the policy so that it is generally regarded as a policy aimed at benefiting Malays only. This not only means a larger political involvement of the bureaucracy, but a likeli-

hood of intensification of conflicts between the ethnic groups within the civil service.[114]

CONCLUSION

This chapter has traced the evolution of government commercial and industrial development strategy in response to political events during the second decade of Malaysia's post-independence history. The ethnic riots of 1969 led Malay political leaders to respond by reinforcing existing Malay dominance of the *political* realm; the rights of the Malay community were secured by placing them beyond the realm of legitimate political discourse, and the political position of UMNO as the leading party in the government was shored up by a reorganization of the coalition. At the same time UMNO launched a challenge to the non-Malay dominance of domestic *economic* activities by introducing the NEP to expand Malay economic power relative to that of the other ethnic communities.

Thus, the primary source of stability in Malaysia's multi-ethnic society (namely the communal settlement) began to erode, first as a result of the Chinese challenge to established Malay political hegemony and, subsequently, as a result of the Malay response to this challenge. I have shown how this erosion in the ethnic settlement became an important political determinant of the change in government industrial development strategy after 1970.

In essence, it led to changes in government development strategy away from rural toward commercial and industrial development; away from a policy of relative evenhanded official treatment of the different ethnic groups towards one explicitly favoring the Malay community; away from a relatively laissez-faire approach to industrial development towards one which' forced private sector businesses to adopt government employment and ownership quotas for Malays; and away from a basically passive state to one actively involved, through a wide range of public enterprises, in capital accumulation. The resulting approach to economic development may still be characterized as market-led (in the sense that the basic decisions over how to respond to changing domestic and international economic incentives remained in the hands of the private sector), but it was heavily modified by extensive state economic regulation and direct intervention to promote the interests of the Malay community.

By 1980, however, many Malays were increasingly frustrated that even the unprecedented levels of government intervention witnessed during the 1970s were insufficient to transfer to the Malay community the economic power they considered commensurate with their dominant political status in Malaysian society. Persuading or even forcing the non-Malay private sector to offer a certain proportion of jobs and ownership shares to Malays was clearly not working as a means of satisfying Malay economic aspirations. Even with these measures, Chinese and Indian businessmen appeared adept at protecting their economic position and at denying Malays a fair share of the economic wealth of the country. Meanwhile, foreign investment, especially in export-oriented industries, was contributing to industrial expansion, but did not appear to be benefiting Malays much except in the area of low-level employment.

This frustration on the part of the Malay community (and sense that existing industrial growth had reached its limits) contributed to the emergence in 1980 of a full-fledged state-led policy of industrial development, to which we turn in the next chapter.

5

INDUSTRIAL ASPIRATIONS FOR A DIVIDED SOCIETY: STATE-LED INDUSTRIALIZATION AND THE 1980s

In November 1980, Dr. Mahathir Mohamad, Malaysia's Minister of Trade and Industry, announced a dramatic new strategy for the development of Malaysian industry over the next two decades. The heavy industries policy was designed to give state agencies the leading role in establishing and operating a new stratum of large-scale, capital-intensive, import-substituting industries which would make use of indigenous resources, particularly cheap energy (oil, natural gas, and hydroelectricity) to produce intermediate industrial goods and consumer durables for the domestic market.[1] These state-run industries were to provide a foundation of key industries which could then support a range of private sector intermediate and consumer goods industries.[2]

Under the direction of the Prime Minister's Economic Planning Unit,[3] the Heavy Industries Corporation of Malaysia (HICOM) was set up "to plan, identify, initiate, invest [in], implement and manage projects in the field of heavy industries."[4] A "nucleus" of critical industries, including iron and steel, automobiles, cement, and internal combustion engines, was chosen and HICOM then began to explore joint venture arrangements with private (largely foreign) capital to develop them.[5] The extent of the government's commitment to these new heavy industries is indicated by the fact that total public-sector investment in heavy industrial projects was slated to reach between six and eight billion Malaysian dollars during the period 1981–1986, an amount roughly comparable to the entire government development budget for all social programs, including education, health, welfare, and housing.[6]

This chapter is concerned with identifying and explaining the political factors that lay behind the decision to adopt this heavy industries policy. In particular, it is concerned with explaining the abandonment of a basically market-led industrial strategy in favor of one in which the state took a leading role.

We saw in chapter 3 that during the first decade or so of Malaysia's independence the Malaysian state's approach to industrial development had been relatively "hands-off" in character. Industrial development, while considered a desirable goal, was thought properly the domain of private sector entrepreneurs by the government of the time. With ethnic rioting in 1969 and adoption of the NEP shortly thereafter, chapter 4 revealed a state increasingly determined to assert itself in the commercial and industrial realm in an attempt to reduce inequalities between the politically dominant Malay community and the economically dominant Chinese and Indian communities. The state began to tell producers, in effect, *how* to produce (who they should employ, what their ownership structures should look like, etc.), and was at the same time itself establishing public enterprises to operate on behalf of Malays. But it was not yet ready to dictate *what* was to be produced—industrial development remained largely the product of decisions made by private sector entrepreneurs responding to market incentives.

Both the market-led strategy of the 1960s and the modified market-led/state-regulatory strategy of the 1970s reflected the politics of relations between the major social groups in Malaysian society. Specifically, they were a product of the nature and evolution of the interethnic settlement that linked communal leaders in the governing interethnic coalition. In essence, the Malay-dominated state showed itself less and less willing to abide by the constraints implied by the original settlement and began to intervene in the economy and to impinge directly upon the interests of domestic (non-Malay) business.

Adoption of the heavy industries policy, the focus of this chapter, signaled a further stage in the evolution of the state's role in industry, for now the state was clearly carving out for itself a much more active role in shaping industrial change. In effect, it began to tell private sector industry both *what* Malaysian industry should produce and *how* it should be produced.

The heavy industries policy was formulated as a means of achieving two not very compatible goals, those of accelerating the pace of industrial growth and at the same time improving the economic position of Malays relative to those of the other resident communities in Malaysia. The policy was not simply an economic development policy, it was also a recipe for political change, and among the principal political factors motivating the new initiative was the changing nature of the communal settlement in Malaysian society. The erosion of this societal modus vivendi is central to explaining why the government chose to introduce a dramatic new initiative on the scale it did, when it did, and why this new policy took the form of heavily statist interventions to effect industrial change.

THE MALAYSIAN HEAVY INDUSTRIES POLICY

Mahathir's heavy industries policy embodied developments unprecedented in both scope and scale. In auto manufacture, the planned Proton Saga, Malaysia's "national car," was conceived as a concrete example of what Malaysia could achieve in the industrial realm given state leadership. To this end, HICOM joined with Mitsubishi in forming Proton (Perusahaan Otomobil Nasional Sdn Bhd—the National Automobile Corporation) to manufacture a vehicle based on a late model Mitsubishi subcompact.[7]

Production began in August 1985 at an annual rate of just 5,000 units, but output of the 1.3– and 1.6–liter Sagas was expected to expand quickly, to the initial plant capacity of 80,000 units a year (and later to 120,000). Although Proton's was the country's twelfth auto plant, it was the first in the country to undertake auto manufacture (the rest simply assembled vehicles manufactured elsewhere). It was projected to employ up to 3,200 workers and to cost an estimated M$560 million upon completion.[8]

Mahathir himself played a major role in negotiating with representatives of Mitsubishi; in overseeing the layout of the Proton plant; and in promoting the Proton Saga to Malaysian consumers. For example, during the celebrations marking completion of the thirteen-and-a-half-kilometer-long bridge linking the island of Penang with the mainland, the first car across the span was a Saga, driven by the Prime Minister.[9]

The Proton project was the most prominent, but by no means the only, major industrial initiative undertaken by HICOM. On the East Coast of the Malay Peninsula, where oil and gas were discovered in the early 1970s, a major iron and steel plant was planned as the nucleus of a modern steel industry in the state of Trengganu. The turnkey project, eventually completed in 1985, was to be gas-fired, with the capability of producing 510,000 metric tons of hot briquetted iron (HBI) by means of state-of-the-art "direct reduction" steel technology, and would feed an adjoining steel melt shop which would, in turn, produce steel billets for private rolling mills.[10] HICOM also envisioned the subsequent development of its own rolling mill, as part of a 2.3 million-metric-ton-capacity, fully integrated, steel complex, and the downstream development of, among others, a plant to produce spiral-welded pipes.[11]

A second iron plant, run by Sabah Gas Industries, was to be developed in association with the government of the state of Sabah and sited on Labuan Island off the coast of East Malaysia. This 660,000-metric-ton facility, like the HICOM plant in Trengganu, was to employ natural gas to process imported iron ore, with the finished product in this case destined for export, under marketing arrangements with the Austrian builder of the plant, Voest Alpine.[12]

In addition to developments in autos and steel, HICOM planned a major expansion of Malaysia's cement industry with the commissioning of a plant on Langkawi Island (off the West Coast state of Kedah). Although several private-sector cement operations already existed (the largest producer, Associated Pan-Malaysian Cement, had just doubled its capacity with a new, one-million-metric-ton, clinker facility), the hectic pace of Malaysian housing and highrise construction in 1980 suggested that the size of the cement market (then 2.5 million metric tons) would double in the space of just five years. The HICOM Kedah Cement plant, costing M$180 million and boasting an annual capacity of 1.2 million metric tons, opened in July 1984 as domestic demand for clinker was peaking at four million metric tons per annum, outstripping the available supply (3.8 million) and causing domestic cement prices to rise precipitously.[13]

In a fourth area, motorcycle and general use engines up to 200 c.c., HICOM initially sought a joint venture with a single Japanese partner. Ultimately, however, agreements were signed in 1983 with three partners (Honda, Suzuki, and Yamaha), each involving a 30 percent HICOM share in investments in the M$8–10 million range.[14]

Beyond these initial developments, HICOM plans called for future investments in aluminum die casting, pulp and paper production, and petrochemical (methanol and ethylene) manufacture.

The heavy industries initiative involved a number of other government agencies besides HICOM. Two of the largest projects undertaken at this time, the ASEAN/Malaysia ammonia-urea fertilizer project in Sarawak, and production facilities for the processing and export of natural gas, were built by Petronas, the state-owned oil company. Petronas was also active in expanding existing oil and gas refining capacity in both East and West Malaysia. Public projects to generate more electricity and to transport natural gas across the Peninsula were also launched to accommodate the dramatic expansion in private-sector activity expected to follow from the establishment of the government's new heavy industrial plants.[15]

Paralleling these state industrial initiatives were a series of high-profile campaigns launched by the administration in an attempt to encourage institutional innovations and new attitudes which would contribute to the state's industrial goals. Mahathir used these campaigns to bully, persuade, and cajole Malaysians (particularly Malays) into accepting his vision of Malaysia's industrial future.[16] He promulgated "Clean, Efficient, and Trustworthy," "Look East," "Malaysia Incorporated," "Privatization," and "Leadership By Example," so as (in his words) "to help Malaysians realize certain things and guide them toward certain objectives."[17]

For example, even before becoming Prime Minister, Mahathir identified "clean, efficient, and trustworthy government" as a sine qua non for industrialization, stating that "Corruption and the establishment of an efficient, modern and high technology society are incompatible."[18] But this did not mean that Malaysians had to embrace *western* norms. Rather, they were to be encouraged to turn away from the post-technological West, characterized by worker-employer strife, declining productivity, and general decadence (Britain was used as an example of this trend) and instead to "Look East":

> We see a competition between the Japanese and the Western method. And in the contest, we see the Japanese have made headway while the West has not only not made headway, but appears to be regressing. So in order for Malaysia to progress, we have to learn from the better example and the better example is the Japanese example. That is why we now want to look East where before we were looking West.[19]
>
> If we emulate them [the West] we will land ourselves in the same

quagmire they are in. . . . Japan, however, has already reached a developed stage and is still developing vigorously.[20]

Already Malaysia enjoyed significant trade and investment ties with East Asia. Japan, for example, accounted for about one quarter of Malaysian trade and one fifth of Malaysian direct foreign investment in 1981. But Malaysians were now encouraged to study and selectively emulate the cultural traits which appeared to have contributed to the successful industrialization of Japan and South Korea (including diligent work habits, harmonious social practices, and discipline).[21] Adoption of an "industrial culture" was considered a necessary precondition for successful industrialization in Malaysia.[22] As then Deputy Prime Minister Musa Hitam observed:

> Our government believes that the best deterrent against the international recession is increased productivity, hard work and financial discipline. This, indeed is the essence of our Look East policy; to delve within the culture of our neighbors and ourselves for the sources of independence and strength to protect us, so to speak, from the cold north wind.[23]

Mahathir directed the "Look East" campaign primarily at the Malay community, whose indolence and lack of drive he compared unfavorably with the productivity and industriousness of the Japanese:[24]

> What I say may not make me popular. Hard work is not popular, but it is for our own good.[25]
>
> Malays must get rid of their indolent image. . . . I want people to say that Malays, if given a task, are able to complete it.[26]
>
> It is not just skills we are after, but more importantly, the correct attitude toward work, including the sense of belonging which breeds loyalty.[27]

In encouraging attitudes appropriate to an industrializing country, Mahathir framed his appeals in terms familiar to Muslim Malays by referring to appropriate precepts of Islam.[28] This not only made his message intelligible to most Malays but also defused demands by leaders of the fundamentalist PAS that Malaysia turn neither East nor West but rather to Mecca, for appropriate values.[29]

How do we explain this enthusiastic embrace of "The East?" One important contributing factor was Mahathir's personal antipathy toward continuing neo-colonial influence in Malaysia. Although he claimed not to be anti-West, it is revealing that Mahathir's formulation of "Look East" paralleled bitter disputes with the British government over increased fees for foreign students, the sale of major British plantations in Malaysia to Chinese (rather than Malay) interests, and the reaction of the London Stock Exchange to the unfriendly takeover of a major British company with extensive interests in Malaysia by the Malaysian government.[30]

A further factor commending the East was the perception that countries like Japan and South Korea had industrialized without compromising their national culture or moral values. Thus, while the western model of development brought with it unacceptable cultural "baggage," Japan and Korea suggested development paths less threatening to traditional Malay culture.[31]

Japan and Korea also offered specific institutional innovations, such as "quality-control circles," enterprise (rather than British-style, craft-based) unions and Japanese-style *sogoshosha*.[32] The 1982 and 1983 Malaysian budgets included generous tax writeoffs for locally initiated *sogoshosha* and, by 1984, most of Malaysia's major trading firms participated in at least one such corporation.[33]

Among other campaigns tied to "Look East" was one promoting "Malaysia Incorporated" (following "Japan Incorporated"), the idea "that the private and public sectors [should] see themselves as sharing the same fate and destiny as partners, shareholders, and workers in the same corporation, which . . . is the nation."[34] "Privatization" was also made a prominent theme after 1983, as Mahathir campaigned to raise public sector efficiency, in keeping with his "Look East" emphasis on discipline and hard work and his professed dislike for inefficiency and the "subsidy mentality."[35] The apparent inconsistency between Mahathir's advocacy of privatization and his unprecedented expansion of direct state participation in industry was glossed over by the Prime Minister—state enterprises, he said, would all be privatized eventually, just as soon as they were profitable.[36]

These campaigns were highly controversial and drew a barrage of criticism. Critics ridiculed Mahathir's fawning emulation of the Japanese and pointed to aspects of Japanese society that were inappropriate or undesirable for Malaysia. They suggested, for example, that the Japanese subordination of women and strictly hierarchical system of labor-management relations were incompatible with both Islam and the egalitarian principles embodied in Malaysia's NEP.[37] They also warned of the dangers inherent in dependence on the dominant economic power in the region, one allegedly intent on militarism and expansionism.[38] Dr. Chandra Muzzafar, a prominent social critic, provides some of the flavor of the opposition to "Look East":

> Even if it were possible, should we emulate Japan? Japan is in essence a huge economic machine obsessed with growth, with the conquest of markets. Its astounding success as a producer and distributor . . . has blinded us . . . . The economy, for all its dynamism, is dominated by powerful companies and their elites. Social disparities are significant . . . . How can we choose as a model . . . a nation whose economic imperialism is an established truth? In trade, investments, technology transfers and aid, Japan's exploitative tendencies are quite apparent. This is . . . the saddest aspect of the whole Look East policy. For it legitimizes—even unwittingly—Japan's overwhelming economic power vis-a-vis Malaysia. It lends credence to its economic imperialism.[39]

The Prime Minister's response was to emphasize selectivity: "We want only to emulate the good values of the Japanese, such as their capacity for hard work and integrity, and not their bad habits."[40]

Some within the Malay community resented Mahathir's comparison of "indolent" Malays with the "hardworking" Japanese. But many Chinese also rejected "Look East" because of residual fears of Japanese domination, rooted in memories of anti-Chinese atrocities committed in Malaya during the wartime Japanese occupation. Many British-educated professionals from all ethnic groups, rejected "Look East" because of its implicit anglophobia.[41] Some, in a more cynical vein, portrayed "Look East" as simply a smokescreen for official favoritism shown Japanese companies in the awarding of lucrative contracts.[42]

Other Mahathir campaigns were also criticized. Economists predicted the failure of Malaysian *sogoshosha* because they lacked the one component critical to the success of the original, namely noncompetitive division of markets among firms,[43] and the privatization of viable public agencies was portrayed as the "selling of the family silver."[44]

Even within UMNO there was unease regarding Mahathir's campaigns. For example, Musa Hitam was careful to avoid becoming too closely associated with some of the more controversial of the Prime

Minister's "conceptual initiatives" during the time that he was Deputy Prime Minister.[45]

Taken together, the various components of the new industrial initiative—the HICOM heavy industrial projects, the attendant energy and infrastructure projects, and the official campaigns—represented intervention by the state in industrial development on a scale without precedent in Malaysia's history. In effect, the relatively laissez-faire strategy that allowed private-sector decisions to determine the direction of industrial development during the late 1950s and 1960s, and the limited regulatory approach adopted in the 1970s to pressure the private sector (i.e., non-Malay businessmen) into making room for Malay participation in commerce and industry, had been rejected. The state was now "taking the bull by the horns" and injecting itself (in partnership with foreign capital) directly into the industrial process in order to achieve its central economic and political goals.

How can this decision to embark on a state-led strategy after more than twenty years of laissez-faire policies be explained? While the principal concerned here is with the *political* factors that underlie policy change, in the first instance it is useful to review the government's own explanation for the new policy, which relies heavily on the disembodied "logic" of rational economic development. It suggests that the decision to pursue state-led rather than market-led industrialization was rational and technical, reflecting the economic imperatives of the stage of development at which Malaysia found itself by the early 1980s.

ECONOMICS AND THE HEAVY INDUSTRIES POLICY

Dr. Mahathir argued, in introducing the heavy industries Policy, that development of second-stage import-substituting industry was the logical next step in the evolution of Malaysian industry. Rapid expansion in manufacturing, which had begun in the late 1960s, was expected to continue through the 1990s, with manufacturing replacing agriculture, forestry, and fishing as the single most important sector of the economy.[46] This growth had been accompanied by changes in the composition of output, as Malaysian industry evolved from the simple assembly of imported components, to the manufacture of labor-intensive import substitutes and the processing of raw materials such as rubber for export.[47]

By the end of the 1970s, however, Malaysian industry appeared to some to have reached a plateau (manufacturing in fact grew at a rate of only 3.25 percent during the period 1980–1982). Despite rapid expansion, Malaysian manufacturing remained narrowly based, reliant on electronics and textiles as its main sources of growth. Large-scale, capital-intensive industry was almost nonexistent.[48] Only wood-related and (to a lesser extent) electronic and electrical industries were judged to have good future prospects. It was doubtful that manufacturing could reach the 24 percent of GNP target set by the Fourth Malaysia Plan (4MP, 1981–1985) by 1985.[49] In the words of the Malaysian Industrial Development Authority chairman, Tan Sri Jamil Jan:

> Our process of industrialization has now reached a stage where it will be difficult for us to maintain a rapid pace of development unless we set up some of the heavy industries ourselves. These industries are not only necessary but also feasible and viable.[50]

The administration believed that the direction of change was dictated to some extent by the fact that Malaysia's economy no longer resembled those of most Third World countries. In seeking external referents, Mahathir, who had expressed great admiration for the "Japanese economic miracle" and the achievements of South Korea under Park Chung Hee, argued that Malaysia ought to look to Japan and the NICs of East Asia.[51] The Prime Minister's enthusiasm for the Korean "model," in particular, is reflected in some aspects of the Malaysian heavy industries policy, especially its initial emphasis on import-substitution in preference to manufacturing for export. Korea appealed, not just because of its record of industrial success, but also because it was the only NIC whose people were not ethnically Chinese. In championing a non-Chinese example of industrial success, Mahathir was able to embrace a NIC "model" while avoiding accusations that he was perpetuating Chinese dominance in the Malaysian economy.[52]

Korean industrial "deepening" was state-led, rather than the product of private sector initiative. Malaysia's experience of industrialization in the 1960s and 1970s suggested the need for a direct state role in the establishment of industrial projects. Mahathir and senior government economists argued that domestic investors could not (or would not) amass the financial, technical, and entrepreneurial resources necessary to undertake large-scale projects with long gestation periods and rather unattractive commercial rates of return.[53] They pointed, in this regard, to the failure of commercial cost-benefit calculations to reflect the true social rate of return of industrial investments,[54] whereas state-initiated developments could be explicitly based on estimates of true social costs and then could pave the way for later private sector efforts.[55] Such developments could, at the same time, serve other national goals, such as those of reducing regional economic imbalances or encouraging efficient use of scarce resources by concentrating them where they were most needed.[56]

In summary, then, the main arguments used by Mahathir and his advisers to justify the heavy industries policy were economic ones—Malaysian industry appeared to have reached a turning point and a new state-led push, patterned after that of a nearby referent (Korea), was best suited to the economic needs of the country.

But this "logic" was challenged by private sector economists (as indicated by comments made at a seminar in August 1983 on the new policy) who asserted that the policymakers were poorly informed and that the policy itself was shallow, shortsighted and foolhardy.[57] For example, while HICOM internal memos were predicting average annual growth rates in car sales of 8 percent through the 1980s, industry experts were pessimistic about the future state of the market.[58] Total sales of 96,200 in 1983, the year the Proton project was actually launched, in fact proved somewhat of a high point. This level of sales of all sizes and models of vehicles, which has yet to be exceeded, amounted to just 20 percent more than the capacity of the Proton plant alone, which was to produce only sub-compacts.[59]

Many economists argued that the depressed economy could ill-afford such projects as the multi-million-dollar Japanese-built steel plant sited in an isolated area of Trengganu.[60] The state's proposed large capital-intensive plants would have a negligible effect on employment, divert public investment funds from more pressing uses, substantially increase foreign borrowing, and contribute to both budget and balance-of-payments deficits.[61] Although intended to produce goods which would substitute for imports, opponents argued that the planned industries were initially likely to be themselves highly import-dependent. Any savings in foreign exchange realised over the life-times of the projects would likely be exceeded by the heavy drain on foreign exchange reserves accompanying initially large investments in imported capital equipment.[62]

In terms of economies of scale, it made no sense, critics suggested, to establish plants designed to serve only the domestic market if the minimum viable capacities of those plants would never be reached simply by selling locally.[63] For example, in the case of Proton, the maximum productive capacity of the plant amounted to only 40 percent of the estimated 200,000-unit-a-year minimum necessary for economic viability of the typical world auto plant.[64] Any use of subsidies and tariff protection to ensure the profitability of such plants would result in inflated prices for intermediate and investment goods, which in turn would reduce economic growth overall and hurt Malaysian exporters' ability to compete abroad.[65]

The government's retort, that basic industries should be promoted regardless of profitability to ensure "balanced" development, was thus challenged by the argument that uneconomic large-scale projects producing uncompetitive intermediate products would eventually stymie, not stimulate, industrial growth.[66]

In terms of the eventual potential of the plants to produce exports, one prominent Malaysian economist observed,

> it is . . . widely understood that the process of industrialization cannot be sustained indefinitely if based on the local market alone. Though there is still scope for import-substituting industries Malaysia has to look to foreign markets for sustained industrialization.[67]

From this perspective, the viability of Malaysia's heavy industries depended on their looking beyond import-substitution to export production. Even among those who supported the adoption of a state-led industrial strategy, there were some who rejected the government's *choice* of industries because it failed to take into account future export potential. At a time when the government was contemplating massive investments in steel, cement, refining, and petrochemicals, for example, these industries faced huge surpluses and depressed prices abroad.[68] HICOM's cement plant, with an estimated break-even price of M$220–230 per metric ton, was begun when the protected local cement industry was receiving only M$180 and the world price was considerably lower, with large international stock-piles.[69]

In essence, according to critics, the government's heavy industries policy was tantamount to practicing "development by intuition"—that is, formulating economic policy initiatives without careful cost-benefit analyses of the likely economic outcomes.

POLITICS AND THE HEAVY INDUSTRIES POLICY

But economic calculations were not the only ones behind the dramatic reorientation in state industrial development strategy witnessed in 1980. What appear in most societies to be economic choices (over how best to develop industry and which industries to favor), are invariably at the same time political choices, over which groups are to derive the most benefit from the type of industrial growth proposed. As Peter Hall has observed:

> In most nations . . . , economic problems are also always political problems. Contemporary economic difficulties and the attempts to find solutions to them cannot be analysed in isolation from associated political dilemmas. To be pursued effectively, any policy must be politically, as well as economically, viable.[70]

Malaysia is no exception. The need to revitalize a flagging domestic industrial sector weighed down by faltering import-substituting industries accounts for neither the extent nor the direction of change that occurred in state-private sector relations beginning in 1980.

This was not the first time that Malaysian manufacturing had been in apparent dire need of revitalization. In 1968, for example, many economists and business leaders called on the state to rescue Malaysian industry from its entrapment in first stage, import-substituting production for the limited domestic market. This resulted in legislative change—the Investment Incentives Act created new incentives for investment in export-processing industries—but this fell far short of the dramatic initiatives witnessed under the heavy industries policy after 1980.

What sets the two eras apart is the relative salience of political factors for industrial choice. In the former case, while there was some pressure from within the small Malay business community for more state action to curb the economic power of the Chinese in commerce and industry, the government of Tunku Abdul Rahman was firmly committed to a basically laissez-faire approach toward non-Malay enterprise, and felt constrained not to "rock the [ethnic] boat" by directly challenging non-Malay business.

In contrast, by 1980, the leadership of UMNO was under considerable political pressure from the Malay community to meet NEP objectives by using direct state action to overcome business intransigence. Thus, to understand why the government turned away from a laissez-faire to a state-led strategy in 1980 (when similar economic pressures led in 1968 to relatively little change), we need to look beyond economic factors to political considerations. As one senior official observed of the new heavy industries: "The projects we're going into aren't purely economic projects. They have quasi-political, economic and strategic considerations."[71]

Mahathir's ability to implement the heavy industries policy, once it had been formulated, also reflected the importance of political considerations. When it appeared that non-Malay business was not prepared to support the goals of the government's NEP, Mahathir was prepared to abandon what was left of the implicit Malay commitment not to use the state apparatus as a weapon in the economy against the interests of non-Malays, because he incurred few political costs in doing so. The Malay-dominated National Front governing coalition enjoyed a solid base of support in predominantly Malay rural areas and sufficient continuing support from among urban Chinese voters not to fear electoral challenge.[72] Given its ethnic profile, the state was therefore effectively autonomous from those groups which in any other society might have been able to obstruct economic initiatives such as those of the heavy industries policy.

The Malaysian state had apparently no desire per se to project itself into the economic realm. The principal political objective of direct state participation in the economy was to benefit the Malay community and to escalate the challenge to non-Malay economic dominance that began with the formulation of the NEP in 1970. Pura has written of the motivations behind the heavy industries projects that they were not simply economic:

> Some powerful political considerations play a role, too. The government's involvement in the projects will help Kuala Lumpur meet its New Economic Policy goal of restructuring the national economy to increase the participation of Malaysia's bumiputras, or indigenous ethnic groups. The government-sponsored plants—notably the car, cement and steel plants—will erode the domination of ethnic Chinese

entrepreneurs in those industries and serve as training grounds for a new class of bumiputra industrial manager and skilled blue-collar workers.[73]

By the end of the 1970s, progress towards the NEP's ownership goals appeared to many Malays to be coming too slowly, with Malay holdings of corporate wealth standing at just 12.4 percent by 1980 (compared with 4.3 percent in 1970). At this rate, the target of 30 percent Malay ownership by 1990 seemed beyond reach. Most of the existing Malay shareholding was not really owned by Malays in any case, but instead by "Malay interests," government-sponsored agencies that had purchased equity on behalf of the Malay community (PERNAS was one example).[74] Without state intervention to marginalize the non-Malay private sector, it appeared that Malays would never themselves be able to challenge non-Malay economic dominance. The adoption of a state-led policy thus reflected the Malay response to failure of government industrial strategy to make sufficient progress in the 1970s towards its political goal, that of advancing the economic interests of Malays.

These political pressures for adoption of a state-led policy favoring Malays did not emerge all of a sudden—we may find clear parallels in an earlier era of Malaysian politics (the late 1960s) when many Malays called on the government of Tunku Abdul Rahman to be less evenhanded with the non-Malays (and the Tunku's reluctance to accede was said to have contributed to the 1969 riots). The government responded after 1969 with the NEP, which itself, as was shown in chapter 4, embodied a greatly expanded role for the state in commerce and industry, both by way of regulation and in the form of new state institutions designed to represent Malay economic interests. But (and this deserves emphasis) it took ten years of this intermediate regulatory-state institutions stage, and a perception that nothing had really changed as a result of it (or that change was occurring too slowly to satisfy Malay expectations), before UMNO leaders were prepared to embark on a full-fledged state-centered industrial development strategy.

POLICY IMPLEMENTATION AND DR. MAHATHIR

While the direction that industrial change took in the early 1980s—towards state-led growth—was a product of the evolving political relationship between competing communal groups, the particular manner in which this state-led strategy was manifest in the Malaysian context (for example, the emphasis on large-scale rather than medium-scale undertakings; the decision to develop joint ventures with foreign, especially Japanese, multinationals rather than use only state capital; and the prominence given to auto manufacture and the backwards linkage effects expected to derive therefrom) reflected the influence and style of its formulator. With his aggressive, "can-do" approach to policy-making, Mahathir stands in stark contrast to the three Malaysian prime ministers who preceded him. There is little question that he is an extraordinary figure in Malaysian post-independence politics.

Born in 1925, the ninth child of a Kedah schoolteacher, Mahathir was the first prime minister without links to the traditional Malay aristocracy, from which Britain drew the bulk of its colonial civil service in Malaya.[75] His mother was a Malay, but his father was the son of an Indian (Kerala) Muslim and a Malay woman.[76] Popular Malaysian political "wisdom" has it that Mahathir derives from this Indian heredity, in addition to his name, his (supposedly uncharacteristic, for Malays) aggressive approach to problem-solving and his obvious impatience with traditional consensus-building.

Although his family was not aristocratic, Mahathir enjoyed a comfortable upbringing in the provincial town of Alor Star where his father was a well-regarded English teacher. He was educated first at a Malay school and later at the elite English Sultan Abdul Hamid College in Alor Star, from which he was awarded a Kedah state government scholarship to attend university.[77] His predilection to pursue law in England (a calling pursued by each of the men who preceded him as Prime Minister) was stymied by a state government determination that Malaysia had lawyers aplenty and needed instead doctors.[78] Mahathir therefore entered the colony's medical college in Singapore in 1947 and thus was to become the first Malaysian Prime Minister who had not traveled to Britain for his higher education.[79] He qualified in 1953, worked as an intern for four years, and then set up the first private medical clinic run by a Malay in his hometown.

Mahathir's involvement in politics began when he was just twenty and coincided with the establishment of UMNO. He had formed and registered the *Kesatuan Melayu Kedah* (Kedah Malay Association) in 1945, while still at high-school, and therefore became one of the earliest members of UMNO when the state-level Malay Associations merged with the new Malay political party in 1946.[80] After independence in 1957, Mahathir was asked to consider standing for parliament for UMNO. His national level political career began in 1964 with his election as a member of the national legislature.

In his first years as an UMNO "back-bencher," Mahathir developed a reputation for being both active and voluble. He was considered fearless with a tendency toward bluntness.[81] His style was thus considerably at odds with the cautious, consensus-building, behind-the-scenes politics that characterized UMNO under the leadership of the venerated first prime minister, Tunku Abdul Rahman.

In policy terms, Mahathir chose to make his mark as a vocal supporter of Malay rights. Joining a small band of second-generation UMNO backbenchers—inevitably dubbed "Young Turks"—who demanded of the leadership dramatic social change in favor of the Malay community, he became known as a Malay "ultra," or racial chauvinist, in Malaysian political parlance. The "ultras" in effect gave vent to the sentiments of growing numbers of Malays who had acquired a higher education and aspired to be part of the new Malay middle class, but who felt that the state, ostensibly in the hands of the UMNO-led Alliance, was not doing enough for them.[82]

In 1969, however, Mahathir fell victim, like many other UMNO parliamentarians, to the declining electoral fortunes of the Alliance Coalition (of which UMNO was the principal component) in the general election that immediately preceded the interethnic riots of May of that year, and found himself once again a private citizen.

He was not out of politics, though. In fact, Mahathir first won national name-recognition following his circulation of a letter addressed to the Prime Minister in the aftermath of the riots, in which he identified the root causes of inequality between the Chinese and Malays in Malaysia and criticized the government's failure to respond to legitimate Malay grievances. He accused the Tunku of kowtowing to Chinese interests at the expense of the Malay birthright, blamed the Tunku for UMNO's electoral setbacks and for the riots, and called for his resignation.[83] In giving voice to views often privately shared but rarely publicly aired, Mahathir established himself as the de facto leader of that new breed of Malay politicians who were well-educated, outspoken, and bold in challenging the leadership and who staked their claim to political ascendancy on unblemished records as defenders of Malay nationalism (rather than on their ability to represent and work with all national communities).[84] For his troubles, Mahathir found his letter officially banned and himself expelled from the party, threatened for a time with arrest and imprisonment without trial under the draconian Internal Security Act.[85]

The significance of Mahathir's open confrontation with the Tunku in the wake of the riots ought not be underestimated. It illustrates both Mahathir's combativeness, even in the face of powerful opponents, and his rejection of the established Malay "rules of the game," especially the tradition that "[a] misdemeanor or excesses may be tolerated, but never a challenge or defiance of the leader."[86] In both respects Mahathir may be clearly distinguished from the majority of post-independence Malay politicians.

For the next two years, during rule by emergency powers and the slow easing out of power of the Tunku by his deputy, Tun Abdul Razak, Mahathir practiced medicine in Alor Star. He also wrote a book which was to prove the most controversial analysis of communal relations ever written in Malaysia.

The Malay Dilemma laid out Mahathir's views on the root causes of the Malay plight and incorporated an elloquent plea for Malays to confront and do something about their economically inferior position before it was to late:

> Malays seem to be teetering between the desire to assert their rights and arrogate to themselves what they consider to be theirs, and the overwhelming desire to be polite, courteous and thoughtful of the rights and demands of others. Deep within them is a conviction that no matter what they decide or do, things will continue to slip from their control; that slowly but surely they are becoming the dispossessed in their own land.[87]

The book was also highly critical of UMNO's failure to adequately represent Malay interests in the Alliance coalition government, castigating the Tunku for his apparent unwillingness to act to protect Malays from Chinese economic domination:

> The dilemma of the Malays is that not only is there little effort made to right the economic wrongs from which they suffer, but it is also wrong to even mention that economic wrongs exist at all. The whole idea seems to be that the less they talk about this the more the country will benefit from the economic stability built on Chinese economic

domination. What is more important, Malays are told, is that Malaysia must prosper as a nation, and amateurs like them in business are not likely to contribute to this prosperity.[88]

Even more controversial were sections of *The Malay Dilemma* asserting that heredity and environment conspired together to keep Malays backward. Citing, for example, the retarding effects of the traditional Malay abhorrence of celibacy, Mahathir observed:

> The result is that whether a person is fit or unfit for marriage, he or she still marries and reproduces. An idiot or a simpleton is often married off to an old widower, ostensibly to take care of him in his old age. If this is not possible, backward relatives are paired off in marriage. These people survive, reproduce and propagate their species. The cumulative effect of this can be left to the imagination.[89]

Other contributing factors to Malay inferiority, according to Mahathir, included family, specifically cousin, inbreeding ("the result is the propagation of the poorer characteristics . . . originally found in the brothers or sisters who were parents of the married couple"),[90] the lack of interracial marriages, and the practice of marrying early:

> It was, and still is, common to see married couples of thirteen or fourteen. These early marriages mean reproduction takes place before full maturity of the parents. The effects on both parents and children are well-known . . . . In this sort of society, enterprise and independence are unknown. The upbringing of children is distorted by the well-known excessive indulgence of grandparents and the incapacity of the parents to take care of their children. The long term effect on community and race is disastrous.[91]

These excerpts from *The Dilemma* suggest an image of the author as someone impatient with the backwardness of his own kind and disdainful of the existing Malay leadership. Not surprisingly, Mahathir's broadside at the Tunku and his highly contentious theories of racial superiority and inferiority proved too much for the UMNO leaders to swallow. Upon publication, *The Malay Dilemma* was immediately banned under rules forbidding the public airing of controversial communal issues.[92]

Despite the book, however, Mahathir's banishment from the Kuala Lumpur political stage turned out to be comparatively short-lived. In 1972, at the behest of new Prime Minister Razak, he was readmitted to the party and shortly thereafter appointed to the UMNO Supreme Council. His subsequent rapid rise through party ranks may be attributed less to personal popularity at the grass-roots level than to his ability to deliver a powerful sectional interest (Kedah UMNO) and the support he enjoyed from powerful sponsors, notably Razak, who was particularly adept at coopting potential political challengers.[93] In short succession, Mahathir was appointed a senator (1973) and given the task of rescuing an ailing publicly owned corporation (Food Industries of Malaysia—FIMA); elected to a safe seat in parliament in the 1974 general elections and appointed Minister of Education in the new Razak Cabinet; elected as one of UMNO's three vice-presidents (1975); chosen as Deputy to the new Prime Minister, Hussein Onn, on the death of Razak in 1976; appointed Trade and Industry Minister (1978); and made Prime Minister at fifty-five years of age in 1981.[94]

The leadership which took power in that year (Datuk Musa Hitam, another former "Young Turk" was named Deputy Prime Minister) heralded, for many local observers, the beginning of a new era in Malaysian politics. Prime Minister Mahathir was characterized as an idealist who had gained power without making the usual political compromises; a commoner of modest socioeconomic roots who had risen to the top while thumbing his nose at accepted Malay political styles.[95]

But it was apparent from his statements and actions during the 1970s that Mahathir was less a Malay chauvinist than a Malay modernist. Despite the controversial nature of his 1970 book, he was not anti-Chinese but, rather, pro-Malay self-help. He advocated state initiatives to build up a core of top Malay executives in business and instill in them responsibility for assisting in creating opportunities for other Malay businessmen.[96] Concerning the dilemma of lack of opportunities and capital for Malays, he observed:

> I feel strongly that capital and opportunities are important, but the most important thing is the ability to manage business, big or small, and an understanding of business. This is much more important . . . so it is the inability to manage business which is affecting the Malays most at the moment; and there is a need for them to learn business and management before they launch into business. Those Malays who have learnt have done well.[97]

As Minister of Trade and Industry and Deputy Prime Minister, Mahathir had rejected the notion of nationalizing Chinese business interests on behalf of Malays, and had demonstrated an ability to work with rising Chinese businessmen—even to the extent of holding up a Chinese auto executive, Eric Chia, in 1979 as an example of a successful Malaysian industrialist who deserved recognition for venturing boldly into new fields and succeeding.[98]

Mahathir's modernism is reflected in his preoccupation with formulating a grand vision of Malaysia's economic future (in contrast to the economic gradualism of his predecessors) and his impatience with administrative details and what he sees as traditional Malay obstacles to progress.[99] He has few peers willing to seriously challenge him on economic policy matters within the Cabinet, and thus there has usually been minimal prior consultation before new initiatives are announced.[100] He is widely read, with a preference for "visionaries" such as Milton Friedman and Kenichi Ohmae,[101] and is known to espouse populist, eclectic (and sometimes intellectually inconsistent) economic theories.[102]

From this brief portrait, then, Mahathir emerges as a man with a mission, impatient with the cautious gradualism of previous UMNO policy-making, whose preference was for ambitious, large-scale projects that could demonstrate to Malays and others what Malays were truly capable of. It was not surprising, then, that state-led industrialization under Mahathir's leadership became manifest in the *form* of highly visible, technologically sophisticated (by Malaysian standards), capital-intensive projects combining large amounts of state and foreign capital under Malay management.

State-led industrialization was an alternative, and more direct, means of achieving Malay ownership and employment goals than the persuasion and regulation practiced with limited success during the 1970s.[103] The state could mandate that the new public enterprises employ ethnic Malays in disproportionately large numbers. These enterprises could also provide an avenue for Malay recruitment to management positions that avoided the existing stiff competition from ethnic Chinese for private sector managerial positions. High-level appointments to state agencies such as HICOM provided the government with an opportunity to nurture a corps of industrial managers in the public sector who might go on to expand the ranks of Malay entrepreneurs.[104] If the new strategy worked as planned, it would also have the effect of expanding the economic "pie" at a rate sufficient to achieve the goals of the NEP and, according to some, "resolv[e] the communal problem once and for all."[105]

Mahathir's championing of the NIC "model," and his encouragement to "Look East," played an important role in justifying the heavy industries plans. In effect, these campaigns turned what might have been a debate over the communal implications of the new policy into one over the economic merits of the changes proposed. By appealing to external *economic* referents Mahathir was able to justify sweeping changes in the state-private sector relationship without having to address their *political* implications. The heavy industries policy was more than an attempt to re-create the economic successes of Japan and the NICs; it had the additional political goal of using Malay-controlled state enterprises to usurp the Chinese (and Indian) position in the economy and thus to align Malay economic power more closely with Malay political hegemony. The NICs thus provided convenient referents that could be used to justify and legitimate a state-led challenge to the existing communal balance.

THE POLITICS OF THE MALAYSIAN NATIONAL CAR

The political factors at work behind the heavy industries initiative are revealed most clearly in the case of the Proton auto manufacturing joint venture. Proton is an illuminating example because it illustrates how the state-led heavy industries initiative was intended not merely to deepen Malaysian industry but also to do so in ways that circumvented non-Malay (Chinese) entrepreneurs and strengthened the economic position of Malays.[106]

Proton represented Southeast Asia's most ambitious automotive industrialization project when it was launched in 1983. Malaysia was to be the first country in the region in which the government sought to displace existing private sector auto assemblers from a major segment of the market (four-seater, 1.3- to 1.6-liter sedans) and to put in their place a state-backed "national champion" auto firm in their stead. Among these existing assembly operations, apart from those foreign owned (27 percent), Chinese firms predominated over Malay firms (43 percent to 30 percent).[107]

The original idea for the national car project was first floated in

1980 when Mahathir requested a study of the possibilities for a made-in-Malaysia vehicle. Without the knowledge of local assemblers and parts manufacturers, whose combined experience over more than a decade of operation represented a significant source of expertise, the government began negotiating first with Daihatsu and then with Mitsubishi, about establishing a plant in Malaysia. The result was a secret agreement announced in 1982 to form a HICOM-Mitsubishi (70–30) joint venture to manufacture the Proton Saga, beginning in 1986.[108]

By ordering that the Proton agreement be reached in secrecy (and in haste), however, Mahathir denied HICOM access to the only domestic expertise available on auto manufacture, namely that of those who already made (or, strictly speaking, assembled) cars in Malaysia. Private sector representatives were deliberately kept in the dark over these negotiations. For example, Eric Chia, a leading Chinese industrialist and government-appointed member of the HICOM board, invested M$160 million to acquire the Toyota franchise in 1981, unaware that future sales of Toyotas were in considerable jeopardy as a result of the Proton negotiations then going on (the Saga would compete directly with Toyota and it was unlikely that the government would allow the Saga to emerge the loser).[109] Chia was not alone—even some civil servants within HICOM itself were unaware of the negotiations.[110]

The result was an agreement so full of loopholes that, as details leaked out, it came to be considered a virtual sellout to the Japanese by many both within and outside government. Among the loopholes was failure to specify a schedule for model changes, vagueness over how deletion allowances for locally sourced components would be calculated and how disagreements over the quality of those components would be worked out, and lack of detail concerning progress towards increasing local content. According to one study by the United Nations Industrial Development Organization (UNIDO):

> The probabilities of gain appear far more secure for Japan and Mitsubishi than for Malaysia. For the former the sun may continue to rise but for the latter, first light could still turn to darkness.[111]

With regard to existing private sector auto capabilities, a decision was made (reportedly by Mahathir himself) to ignore existing assembly facilities and not to involve existing component firms in supplying the local content of the Proton Saga.[112]

There were some advantages to denying private sector input and ignoring existing capabilities. For one, as Doner points out, the negotiators avoided the intervention of established foreign and domestic players who elsewhere in the region had proven themselves eminently capable of "unraveling" agreements already signed and sealed, by exerting pressure on governments at the eleventh hour.[113]

But the costs were high. State negotiators were deprived of auto-specific expertise and it is suspected that their initial investigations of the project's viability were limited.[114] Officials within the Malaysian Industrial Development Authority (MIDA) and private sector executives were experienced in such issues as how to calculate the value of items deleted from auto "packs," how to negotiate the terms of transfer of technology and how to evaluate local content.[115] How then do we explain the state's failure to avail itself of this knowledge?

Partly we may attribute it to a sense of urgency; the state rushed the negotiation process to avoid attracting the attention of other parties, especially those with a vested interest in killing the project. It wished to avoid a barrage of criticism by simply getting on with the project, and allowing the results then to speak for themselves. Partly we can attribute it to a desire not to foster rifts within the Malay leadership (both in UMNO and the civil service). As already noted, Deputy Prime Minister Musa was conspicuous in keeping his distance from this and others of Mahathir's heavy industries initiatives.

But relations between the Malay and non-Malay communities are also important in providing a rationale for ignoring existing expertise. Chinese dominance of the private sector, and a perception that Chinese entrepreneurs were able to exert considerable influence with MIDA, led Mahathir to freeze out both MIDA and the private sector when negotiating on the Proton with Mitsubishi. Given that, in the face of slow progress towards meeting NEP goals, the state had decided to take the lead in establishing industries that had the potential to displace Chinese operations, it made no sense, in the process, to rely on existing expertise, or to build on existing capabilities, because these were predominantly Chinese. To do so would have served to alert the Chinese to the imminent threat to their auto interests and would have enabled them to perhaps deflect the challenge in directions least damaging to their interests. It would simultaneously have further strengthened the Chinese dominance in industry, the reverse of what was intended by the heavy industries policy.

The formulation of the "national car" project thus shows us two things: behind the heavy industries strategy there was a conviction that, to effect economic changes on the scale envisioned, state initiative was essential; but beyond that, the extensive and unprecedented state intervention in industrial development, and the way it was carried out, reflected political factors relating to the state of relations between the Malay and non-Malay communities at the beginning of this decade. The state was prepared to forgo obvious sources of expertise (not only outside, but also inside government), that would have enabled it to negotiate on a more equal footing with the Japanese and might perhaps have contributed to more successful production and marketing of the Saga, because it was intent on achieving not only economic objectives but political ones as well.

OUTCOMES

Although the principal concern of this chapter has been to explain how and why the heavy industries policy came to be adopted in 1980 and 1981, the outcomes of the policy are relevant because they bear on the industrial problems which face the administration at the turn of the decade.

Economic conditions in Malaysia during the 1980s were, for the most part, far from conducive to the success of an expensive, state-sponsored program of second-stage import-substituting industrialization. As the heavy industries strategy was being formulated in 1980, a world economic slowdown caused the prices for most of Malaysia's major commodities to decline in real terms to their lowest levels in thirty years. As export- and income-tax yields declined, government revenues fell while expenditures continued to rise (to 58 percent of GNP in 1982). Consequently, the federal deficit grew to over five times its 1975 level (to 19 percent of GNP, one of the highest such percentages in the world at the time).[116]

The government responded with austerity measures at home and heavy borrowing abroad.[117] It took careful steps, however, to insulate HICOM allocations from the budget cuts instituted in 1982 and, as a result, HICOM was able to continue planning and building the new heavy industries with only slight rephasing.[118]

The economic climate appeared to moderate in 1984 and 1985, just as the first heavy industry projects were about to bear fruit.[119] Nevertheless, the Malaysian economy's vulnerability to sudden fluctuations in commodity prices,[120] was again manifest when, in late 1985, it was hit by yet another, even more debilitating, commodities slump, resulting in an overall economic contraction of 1 percent for the year (it grew by 1.2 percent in 1986).[121]

The new state-owned heavy industries were badly hit by this second recession, the worst in the country's thirty-year history. Indeed, the much-publicized industrial aspirations of the Mahathir administration appeared mocked by the record of the struggling state-run industries. HICOM's financial report for the year ending March 31, 1987, included after-tax losses of M$117.8 (US$47.3) million (an increase of 13 percent over the previous year). With virtually every major unit of the company, from its auto-making division (Proton), to its steel subsidiary (Perwaja Trengganu), and its cement operation (Kedah Cement) reporting a deficit, operating losses increased 71 percent (to M$249.6 [US$100] million).[122]

At Proton, net losses of M$39 (US$15.6) million in 1986–1987 and M$58.5 million (U.S. $23.4) in 1987–1988 were recorded.[123] In terms of both production and sales, the state-run automaker was falling well short of expectations. As one report put it, "for Proton, . . . the decline in passenger car demand has been nothing short of catastrophic."[124] Although the first Sagas initially sold well, with the benefit of heavy state support, a deep slump in domestic car sales occurred in late 1985. The downturn was particularly bad for Proton since it came at a time when the company was attempting to build up production to the full 80,000-unit capacity of its plant (sales of all makes and models totalled 68,000 units for 1985, barely 50 percent of the level forecast). While Proton was able to capture 66 percent of the passenger car market in 1987, the market itself was contracting rapidly, with combined sales of all producers and assemblers falling to a decade low of 38,200 units (compared with 96,200 in 1983).[125]

HICOM's M$1.2 billion (US$462 million) steel plant in Trengganu was in still worse shape.[126] Following after-tax losses for 1986–1987 of M$158 (US$63) million, it finally closed its state-of-the-art direct reduction steel furnace for sponge iron in April, 1987.[127] The official reason given was the failure of the plant to meet performance specifications (the Nippon Steel Corporation paid compensation totalling M$485 [US$200] million). But the decision not to persevere with the debt-ridden furnace was encouraged by movement in the relative price of raw materials—it was by that time cheaper to use scrap iron, rather than that produced by the furnace, to feed the adjoining melt shop.[128]

HICOM's cement joint venture, Kedah Cement, reported a loss of M$68 (US$25) million in 1987–1988.[129] Weighed down by a heavy debt burden incurred to finance plant construction and to cover an uninterrupted stream of losses, its prospects were dimmed by continuing depressed conditions in the domestic construction industry (construction shrank by 14 percent in 1986 and by a further 6.5 percent in 1987) and over-capacity among local cement producers.[130] An additional 3.4 million metric tons of capacity had been brought on stream during 1984–1987, but domestic demand had shrunk to 2.7 million metric tons. Only prohibitive tariffs on imports and fixed domestic prices kept the industry from collapse.[131]

The heavy industries projects, once trumpeted as the key to Malaysia's future economic prosperity, had by 1987 fallen on hard times and saddled the state with heavy debts. In a speech of October 23, 1987, announcing the budget for 1988, Finance Minister Daim revealed for the first time the full extent of the government's exposure to loss-making state-owned heavy and energy industries. He reported liabilities of M$5.5 (US$2.2) billion, of which M$3.7 (US$1.5) billion took the form of contingent liabilities relating to government-backed foreign loans incurred by public enterprises. Thirty-seven percent, or M$15.3 (US$6.1) billion of the total public-sector debt of M$41.6 (US$16.7) billion, was attributable to these public enterprise loans.[132]

In the face of HICOM's dire straits, it was decided that urgent steps needed to be taken to prevent the state's heavy industries from becoming embarrassing white elephants. Finance Minister Daim Zainuddin signalled, in a speech of June 23, 1988, that the Mahathir administration was reconsidering its eight-year-old commitment to the vanguard role of Malay industrial managers. He characterized (Malay) civil servants running the state's heavy industries as ineffective and, asked whether it had been a mistake to expect that civil servants would be able to run businesses successfully, he was quoted in the *Business Times* daily as replying: "Some are good . . . one or two."[133] He subsequently announced—in a dramatic change in policy—that the government had decided to hand over the management of its heavy-industries projects to private sector (local and foreign) managers.

In just a few months, Malay managers heading the major HICOM subsidiaries found themselves supplanted by non-Malays. For example, within twenty-four hours of Daim's speech, Proton Deputy Chairman Mohamad Saufi Abdullah had resigned and soon Executive Director Datuk Wan Nik Ismail followed suit. They were replaced by Japanese executives of Mitsubishi Motors Corporation (MMC). Kenji Iwabuchi, former Managing Director of MMC, became Executive Director and Kyo Fujioka, another MMC manager, was made head of a new corporate planning division at Proton.[134]

In a similar fashion, HICOM's steel billet-making subsidiary, Perwaja Trengganu, was passed from Director and General Manager Haji Razali Haji Ismail to Eric Chia, the private sector ethnic Chinese magnate of United Motor Works (and unknowing purchaser of the Toyota franchise during the original Proton negotiations). Meanwhile, Malaysian Chinese entrepreneur Heng Keah Yong was named manager of HICOM's 35 percent owned Kedah Cement.[135]

This management shake-up represented to many a "sell-off" of prestige government projects to Japanese and local Chinese interests, and a slap in the face to ethnic Malay pride (the top management of HICOM was previously entirely Malay, as was most of the plant workforce).[136] While they were the most controversial, these changes were by no means the only steps the government initiated at this time in an apparent attempt to back away from its earlier commitment to state-led industrialization in the face of mounting losses in state-run industries. Earlier, Daim had announced a list of sixty public enterprises which the government was evaluating, to determine (in his words) whether they should be "closed down, rehabilitated or privatized." Subsequent developments have demonstrated that Daim was serious in this intent.

In early 1989, HICOM was relieved of its perpetual loss-maker, Perwaja Trengganu. The transaction, clearly designed to ease the debt-related financial pressure on HICOM, involved the sale of the steel-maker to Ministry of Finance Incorporated, a private company

controlled by the ministry, as a possible precursor to the dismemberment of the company.[137]

Meanwhile another HICOM operation plagued by massive loans
and accumulated losses, Kedah Cement, is the subject of sale talks
between the government and private sector companies. In September 1988, the Secretary General of Finance announced that Malaysia's
largest cement producer, Associated Pan-Malaysian Cement (APMC),
had offered to take over Kedah Cement and another state govern-
ment-run producer, Perak-Hanjoong. The offer, still outstanding,
would give APMC 65 percent of the domestic market, but is conditional on the government's willingness to shoulder the majority of
the two companies' heavy debts.[138]

Among non-HICOM state-run heavy industries established since
1980, the East Malaysia steel mill of Sabah Gas Industries (SGI) was
included among those on Daim's list to be turned around, closed, or
sold.[139] SGI, along with Sabah Energy Corporation, comprise the
Sabah Gas Utilization Project of the Sabah state government, located
on the federal territory of Labuan Island. The project as a whole,
which involved an initial investment of M$2.3 billion (at 1985 prices)
and loans of M$1.5 billion, now has accumulated losses and loans
estimated at M$1.8 billion (US$664 million), much of this attributable
to foreign exchange losses on M$1 billion of yen-denominated loans.[140]
The federal government and the SGI board are presently considering
a confidential Price, Waterhouse report that recommends the sale of
the company, for a return estimated to just cover existing losses and
loans.[141]

Like the projects themselves, the campaigns associated with Mahathir's heavy industries initiative have shown limited results. "Look
East" has brought closer ties with Japan (and, to a lesser extent, with
South Korea and Taiwan) but these have been controversial.[142] For
example, labor relations on joint ventures linking Malaysian and
Japanese or South Korean firms have sometimes been acrimonious,
and the technology transferred to Malaysian partners has often been
less sophisticated than that originally promised by the foreign partner.[143] And Malaysian companies, especially in construction, have
sometimes found themselves unhappily displaced by firms such as
Shimizu, Takenaka Komuten, Kumagai, Kensetsu, Taisei, Hazami-
gumi, and Sumitomo of Japan, and Hyundai of South Korea. Why,

their principals ask, are the Japanese being accorded preferential access to Malaysian contracts when Japan has maintained high tariff barriers against Malaysian products, failed to give preference to Malaysian exports, and obstructed the national airline's attempts to obtain routes to the United States through Tokyo?[144]

Rising dissatisfaction with the Japanese, reflected in the oft-repeated but unsubstantiated allegation that "Look East" was simply a cover for favoring the Japanese (in return for certain quid pro quos) encouraged Mahathir to tone down the campaign after 1985. In fact, in a speech of September 1985, he even went so far as to compare modern-day Japanese exploitation with that practiced under the wartime Greater East Asian Co-prosperity Sphere (1941–1945). Clearly, by the mid-1980s, the "Look East" campaign was becoming a political liability rather than an asset to his administration.[145]

The slogan "Clean, Efficient, and Trustworthy" is today rarely heard, except when used by critics to draw an invidious contrast between the original promise of the Mahathir's administration and a variety of allegations that have been made of high-level misuse of public funds in the construction and financing of projects such as the Penang Bridge, the Dayabumi Complex and the buildings housing the UMNO party headquarters and the Putra World Trade Centre, and in the Bumiputra Malaysia Finance (BMF) affair (in which Malaysian taxpayers lost M$2.26 billion [US$859.5 million] as a result of unsecured property speculation loans made in Hong Kong by a subsidiary of a government-owned bank).[146]

"Privatization" remains in vogue. But while originally advanced as a means to effect fundamental change in the public-private sector relationship in Malaysia, privatization thus far has simply entailed the piecemeal and ad hoc selling of portions of the public sector to stem losses and reduce the public debt.[147] In most cases, despite forfeiting ownership stakes of 50 percent or more, the state has preserved its control over the "privatized" concerns, often by sale of equity to quasi-state entities such as Petronas or the central bank (Bank Negara). For example, when 30 percent of Malaysian Airlines was sold on the Kuala Lumpur Stock Exchange in October 1985,[148] and a further 15 percent on the London exchange in 1986, majority state ownership was maintained. Subsequently the state's remaining (direct) stake of 52 percent was sold to the central bank in a transaction designed to raise cash for foreign debt repayment. Neither the public listings in Kuala Lumpur and London nor the transfer to Bank Negara altered the reality of effective government control over the operations of the national airline.[149]

Similarly, the March 1986 privatization of the container terminal at Port Klang (the capital's port), involving a joint venture of Permodalan Nasional Berhad (PNB) and the Australian P&O Company, had limited impact. The Malaysian partner, PNB, is wholly state-owned and the PNB/P&O-managed terminal is part of a larger port complex which is completely state-owned.[150]

In January 1986, the Malaysian International Shipping Corporation (MISC) was privatized with an offering of 57 million shares on the Kuala Lumpur Stock Exchange. The government in this case retained a 29.4 percent stake, which was sufficient to enable it to exercise continued control over the operations of the company. Subsequently, as in the case of Malaysian Airlines, the government stake was sold in 1988 to the central bank.[151]

The much-trumpeted, but much-delayed, "privatization" of the government's department for telecommunications (Jabatan Telekoms) has got only as far as the transfer of telecommunications functions to a public corporation, Syarikat Telekom Malaysia (STM), wholly owned by the Ministry of Finance.[152] STM took over from Jabatan Telekoms in January 1987 and is to remain tax exempt through 1991. The former department, with a much reduced staff, now acts as the government's regulatory authority for telecommunications.[153]

Opponents of privatization, responding to secret negotiations, the paucity of subsequent disclosure, and the granting of lucrative contracts to those with close links to the Mahathir administration and to the country's dominant political party, UMNO, accuse the government of nepotism.[154] The beneficiaries, they assert, are able to exploit state-mandated monopolies relatively free from state oversight. UMNO, in particular, has apparently profited hugely from its privileged access to such monopolies. For example, in 1986 Finance Minister Daim ordered one of the country's largest private banks, the United Malayan Banking Corporation (UMBC), to provide guarantees for a loan that enabled an UMNO-controlled company, Hatibudi, to acquire United Engineers (Malaysia). United Engineers was subsequently the controversial recipient of one of the largest public works contruction contracts in Malaysia's history, that for the construction, maintenance, and operation of the North-South Expressway.[155]

In all, after some five years of privatization, only twenty-two government operations have been reclassified as "private." However, some of these have been relatively small in scale (a lottery and a television station, for example), others involve essentially fixed-term construction or management contracts, and included among the "privatized" are operations simply transferred to wholly-owned government corporations, or those in which the state retains a controlling stake.[156]

Since their introduction, Malaysian *sogoshosha* have fared poorly. The first and largest, Malaysian Overseas Investment Corporation (MOIC)(whose shareholders included many of Malaysia's largest corporations), went bankrupt in July 1986 with liabilities representing twenty-eight times the value of the company's equity. MOIC never once recorded a profit, and its managing director, Mohammed Abdullah Ang, has since been convicted of criminal breach of trust involving approximately M$400,000.[157]

In sum, Mahathir's state-led heavy industry initiatives have fallen short of expectations, while the associated campaigns have had limited impact on the course of Malaysia's industrial development. In spite of this, however, the economy, and private-sector industry in particular, have done rather well over the past two years.

RECENT DEVELOPMENTS

After two years of deep recession (1985–1986), the Malaysian economy has recently seen a resurgence in activity. The turnaround began in 1987, with GDP growth in real terms of 5.2 percent, and by 1988 the economy was expanding at an annual rate of 8.7 percent (the highest of the decade).[158]

The main catalyst for this recovery has been a surge in export earnings resulting from firming demand for Malaysian manufactured products abroad (especially for electrical and electronic goods and textiles) and from higher prices for Malaysian commodities. Exports of manufactured goods grew by 28.9 percent in 1988 and the manufacturing sector as a whole grew 15.5 percent (growth in 1989 is estimated at 10.5 percent).[159]

The prices for all of Malaysia's major export commodities—rubber, palm oil, timber, cocoa, tin, and petroleum—recovered in 1988, contributing to a revival of private sector consumer spending (up 15.5 percent, compared with 2.6 percent growth in 1987). The effect of increased returns from commodity exports was less marked, however, than it might have been ten years earlier. Whereas in 1978 commodity exports accounted for 61 percent of total export earnings (compared with 20 percent for manufacturing), in 1988 they represented only 27 percent of the total (49 percent were manufactures). Although prices for some commodities, such as palm oil and tin, retreated in 1989 from their earlier highs, preliminary estimates still suggest GDP growth in the year past of about 7.6 percent. For 1990 the government's budget foresees a growth rate of 6.5 percent.[160]

With the leveling off of export growth, there are signs that domestic investment demand is taking over as the driving force behind the continuing recovery. Encouraged by a liberalized regulatory regime introduced by the government in 1986 in the depths of the recession, private-sector (including foreign) investment has increased sharply in the past year or so.[161] The liberalization encompassed a simplification of bureaucratic procedures, the granting of exemption from NEP equity restructuring requirements to companies worth less than M$25 million and employing less than 75 full-time workers, and allowing foreign companies to own up to 100 percent of any new ventures, providing at least 50 percent of the output is exported and the remainder does not compete with goods already manufactured locally. In addition, the corporate tax rate was reduced by 5 percent (to 35 percent in 1989) and a 5 percent development tax formerly levied on all companies was rescinded.[162]

Foreign investment applications approved by the Malaysian Industrial Development Authority (MIDA) for the first five months of 1989 increased by 129 percent over the same period in 1988 and those for all of 1988 were 127 percent higher than in 1987.[163] Similarly, investments approved for Malaysia-domiciled concerns increased from M$1.874 billion in 1987 to M$4.216 billion in 1988. Overall, private-sector investment rose 17.9 percent in real terms in 1988 (compared with 5.7 percent in 1987).[164]

Among foreign investors, Japanese, Taiwanese, Hong Kong, and South Korean companies have been prominent, together accounting for 46 percent of foreign manufacturing investment applications in

1988. There is apparently growing interest among NIC investors in using Malaysia as a back door to the main export markets of the developed world and in taking advantage of Malaysia's well-educated, productive, and relatively cheap workers (one Taiwanese electronics company pays wages of US$4.60 per day, compared with US$20 in Taiwan) and the country's well-developed infrastructure, with industrial estates not yet suffering the same bottlenecks as those in Thailand. In addition, the declining value of the Malaysian ringgit against the yen and the dollar has made Malaysia an increasingly attractive export platform in comparison to Taiwan, for example, where export competitiveness is being hurt by the effects of a strong currency.[165]

Most foreign interest in the manufacturing sector has focused on the electronics industry whose exports in 1988 comprised the largest single export item, valued at M$14.7 billion (US$5.5 billion), and accounted for 56 percent of all manufactured exports.[166] The current state of this industry is worthy of brief consideration because at the present time it represents the fastest-growing segment of the manufacturing sector and because, in contrast to the heavy industries, its development is almost exclusively the product of private (mainly foreign) initiative.

Malaysia is now the world's largest exporter of semiconductor devices and the world's largest producer, outside the United States and Japan. Among the major electronics and electrical appliance manufacturers operating plants in Malaysia are National Semiconductor, Motorola, and Intel from the United States, West Germany's Grundig and BASF, France's Thomson-CSF, Japan's Sony, Hitachi, Matsushita and Sharp, and Canada's Northern Telecom.[167] In some cases, these companies' largest plants are to be found in Malaysia. National's Penang semiconductor factory, for example, with the relocation of some production from Singapore in 1989, has become the company's premier production site world-wide and is expected to produce 100 million (mainly logic) chips per month in 1990 for export to the United States and Europe. National has invested over M$420 (US$155) million in Malaysia thus far.[168]

While the manufacture of semiconductors dominates the electronics industry in Malaysia, there are signs that backwards and forwards linkages are developing. For example, Motorola and National Semiconductor have begun to encompass in their operations not just assembly and testing procedures but also wafer fabrication—the making of the actual silicon chips from which semiconductor integrated circuits are built.[169]

On the downstream side, Malaysia has seen recent expansion in the manufacture of consumer electronics and the entry of small- and medium-scale firms from the NICs. Matsushita and Sharp (Japan's second-largest electronics manufacturer) each have recently identified their Malaysian plant as one of four worldwide production centers for the manufacture of color television sets. In addition, Matsushita, with eight factories in Malaysia already, announced plans in August 1989 for a new M$100 million air-conditioner plant to export 300,000 units a year back to Japan. The company also plans to expand its existing M$900 (US$332) million investment to produce and export electrical goods formerly made in Japan, such as gas cookers, water heaters and vacuum cleaners.[170]

Similarly, Sony Mechatronic Products, when it begins production in Malaysia in 1990, will be the first plant outside Japan to make micro-sized computer floppy-disk drives. Like Matsushita, Sony has made Malaysia its biggest manufacturing base in Southeast Asia and is using Malaysia as a key export production platform for consumer electronics exports such as televisions, audio products, and video cassette recorders destined for the Japanese, North American, and Asian markets.[171]

Smaller electronics firms from Taiwan have also begun moving capacity to Malaysian plants, often securing their first beachhead for offshore production in Malaysia. This influx is most apparent in Penang, with its majority ethnic Chinese population, where 20 of 41 land-purchase agreements signed in the first six months of 1989 by the Penang Development Corporation (PDC—the management company for the Penang free-trade zone) were with Taiwanese firms.[172]

Despite this generally rosy picture, however, the ascendant electronics industry is not without its problems. The industry employs a large proportion of Malaysia's skilled and semiskilled industrial workers (more than thirty-five thousand work for the sixteen United States-owned plants), yet has been subject over the past ten years to wild swings in market conditions. Growth in electronics therefore does little to alleviate the country's traditional dependence on a few major exports (hitherto commodities) with oscillating prices.[173]

Furthermore, the industry remains almost exclusively the domain of foreign companies. The director for electrical and electronics industries at MIDA, Mardziah Aziz, has attributed this to a lack of familiarity with the industry and an inclination among local investors to cling to more traditional investments in commodity production and processing.[174] The result has been that there are few local producers or end-users of microchips. In fact this absence of a big end-users market in Malaysia or nearby countries—unlike in Taiwan or South Korea, where there high-volume production of computers and other office automation equipment provides a ready market for burgeoning chip producers—remains a key stumbling block to further deepening of the industry.[175]

The fact, then, that electronics manufacturing is leading the current recovery must be seen as somewhat of a mixed blessing because most of Malaysia's industrial export "eggs" then lie in just one "basket," because those "eggs" are subject to the same market instability that has characterized Malaysia's traditional commodity exports, and because the industry has a very small domestic component and therefore cannot be counted as much of a success for indigenous industry.

Turning to the government's heavy-industrial sector, recent developments worthy of note include modest success by Proton in selling the Saga on the United Kingdom market.[176] Since 1986, Proton has responded to the slump in domestic sales by turning to exports, pursuing sales in countries as diverse as Britain, the United States, Cyprus, Pakistan, Sri Lanka, and China.[177] Exports to Britain began in March 1989 and estimated sales for the year of nine thousand units were 50 percent higher than Proton's original target.

However, while higher plant utilization accompanying export sales undoubtedly helps Proton amortize its fixed costs more quickly, the company is actually losing money with every sale. To be even marginally competitive in the United Kingdom, the exported Saga, at seven thousand British pounds (US$11,326), has had to be sold at a lower price than in Malaysia.[178] Yet it incorporates modifications in body shape and control configuration required by British safety standards that mean that it is more expensive to produce than the domestic version.

It is unlikely that Proton will be able to export its way out of financial trouble with a car that was designed mainly for the Malaysian market. As predicted by critics of the project from the outset, a principal stumbling block is the very size of the domestic market, which precludes the realization of economies of scale which could lower the unit-cost of the Saga. Proton is also hamstrung by the high cost of the imported Mitsubishi packs that form the core of the Saga. Mitsubishi has little incentive to trim the considerable profit it earns from selling these packs, (along with additional components and manufacturing machinery) to Proton, merely to enhance the international competitiveness of a vehicle that is in direct competition with Mitsubishi autos in the 1.3– and 1.6–liter range produced in Japan, Thailand, and elsewhere.[179] Efforts to have more of the Mitsubishi parts replaced by those manufactured in Malaysia have yielded mixed results. While Mitsubishi apparently agreed in general terms in the original joint-venture agreement to the principle of increasing the local content of the Saga, in practice it has been reluctant to accept local components, labeling them "inferior" (even though some of them are used as replacement parts by other Japanese auto-makers selling in Malaysia), and has offering limited deletion allowances for the components that are accepted.[180]

Lastly, Proton can expect to make little profit on export sales because of expensive engineering changes needed before its product will meet foreign safety requirements. This is especially true in the all-important United States market, where conversion to left-hand drive would be required. Plans for United States sales, initially involving a distribution agreement with Malcolm Bricklin, the original franchise-holder for the ill-fated Yugo, fell through in 1989 amidst recriminations and lawsuits.

On the home front, with consumer spending picking up, auto sales have rebounded from the low of 38,200 in 1987 to 58,000 in 1988 and an estimated 67,000 for 1989. Proton has about 75 percent of the market (42,300 cars in 1988), and has responded to the turnaround by adding 600 workers and starting a two-shift operation an August 1989. The dominance of the company in terms of market share, however, ought not be interpreted as a resounding vote of consumer confidence in the Saga but rather a reflection of the unbeatable price advantage (about M$4,000 for the M$32,000 vehicle) that the car enjoys over its competitors Nissan and Toyota, as a result of the exemption granted Proton from the 40 percent tax on imported auto packs.[181]

This tax exemption and the changing nature of the relationship between Proton and its distributor, Edaran Otomobil Nasional (EON), have to be considered when evaluating Proton's latest results. Carrying accumulated losses of M$133 (US$49) million from 1985–1988, Proton announced a first-time profit, for the year ending March 1989, of M$32.5 (US$12) million on revenues of M$820 (US$303) million.[182] But in 1988–1989, the formerly semi-independent EON was placed more firmly under government control (state shareholding increased from 45 to 70 percent) and was forced to pay a higher price for the showroom stock it purchased from Proton. Thus Proton's profit, heralded as a dramatic about-face for the previous loss-maker, is more accurately read as a product of government engineering to transfer earnings from EON to Proton.

What is particularly interesting about this transfer, and the EON reorganization, is that it led to the sidelining from EON of private Malay business groups that were originally included by the state so that they might share in the largesse that was expected to derive from EON activities. Having shared in the profits from distribution thusfar, they were displaced by the government's Ministry of Finance Incorporated (25 percent) and by an MMC subsidiary (30 percent), in the process of an attempt to improve the financial health of Proton (70 percent directly state-owned).[183]

To conclude, at the close of the decade, we find the government's ten-year-old heavy industries initiative a mere shadow of its former self. With the sale and possible dismemberment of HICOM steelmaker Perwaja Trengganu at the hands of the Ministry of Finance, the heavy indebtedness and continued loss-making at Kedah Cement, and the likely sale of SGI, the only shining stars in the heavy industries "galaxy" are the HICOM small engines plants, which are poised to benefit from increased consumer spending on motorcycles.[184]

Although HICOM's results for 1988–1989 include the group's first pretax profit (M$45.9 [US$17] million, on a turnover of M$951 [US$351] million), more than half of this (M$27.35 [US$10] million) came from companies not engaged in industrial production at all, but rather in property development. New initiatives recently undertaken by HICOM include Hicom Engineering, to manufacture compressor parts (for room air-conditioners and other industrial applications) and auto components, beginning in late 1990, and Hicom Diecastings, to produce aluminum die cast parts for motorcycles, autos, and appliances.[185] But these are of very modest scale in comparison with the undertakings that spearheaded the government's heavy-industries initiative in the early 1980s.

Overall, the Mahathir administration appears to have responded to the various HICOM failures, to the 1985–1986 recession, and to subsequent large operating budget deficits—which reached M$3.5 (US$1.4) billion (or 5 percent of GNP) in 1987—with a retreat from activist participation in the economy and urgent calls to non-Malay and foreign managers to rescue the state's industrial holdings from imminent collapse.[186]

Funds earmarked for development spending under the Fifth Malaysia Plan (1986–1990) were reduced by M$10 billion (US$4 billion) or 35 percent in 1987. Although the amount was reinstated in 1988, the spending was redirected away from industrial development towards infrastructure.[187]

And in marked contrast to the abounding faith in state solutions evident in government pronouncements of the early 1980s, Finance Minister Daim signaled in his budget speech of October 1988 that it was now up to the private sector to take the lead as the source of new growth and initiative in the economy in the future.[188]

CONCLUSION

This chapter has been principally concerned with the political determinants of Malaysia's heavy-industries policy (1980 onward), the latest stage in the evolution of that country's post-independence industrial development. This evolution can be represented along a continuum reflecting different degrees of state and private-sector involvement in the process of industrial development. At one end may be placed the market-led strategy pursued during the first decade or so of Malaysia's independence (1957–1969); in the middle stands the mixed market-led/state-regulatory approach adopted during the 1970s, embodying increased levels of state involvement under the NEP; and at the far end is the state-led strategy initiated by Prime Minister Mahathir in the early 1980s, involving the use of state-run heavy industries to spearhead industrial change.

The argument that has been made here is that among the *political* determinants of industrial strategy—specifically strategy concerning the relative weights to be accorded state and private sector initiatives in the achievement of industrial development—relations between communal groups have played a central role. In particular, the nature of the communal settlement and the extent to which it has been considered constraining on state action in the industrial realm have significantly influenced the direction and extent of industrial strategy change from one decade to the next.

At the beginning of the period considered in this chapter, there were two things going on which help explain the timing and character of Mahathir's state-led push into heavy industrialization. On the economic side, government leaders believed that first-stage import-substituting industrialization had run its course and that it was now the responsibility of the state to take the lead in developing new industry, following the nearby NIC model.

This perception by itself is insufficient, however, to explain the strategy's adoption (similar perceptions manifest in earlier eras had prompted only incremental change). Such an explanation requires that attention be paid to the political dimension as well. I have argued here that the perceived intransigence of the (non-Malay) business community, in not providing the opportunities for Malay economic participation mandated under the NEP, encouraged the Malay leadership controlling the state apparatus to embrace a new industrial strategy that was essentially statist in character. The state was prepared to ignore Malaysia's existing industrial capacities and expertise—even at the risk of "reinventing the wheel" in some areas—because of their associations with non-Malay (especially Chinese) interests, and to develop state-led industries which were consciously Malay-led.

The Malay leadership was encouraged to change its approach to industrial development by a belief that, as a result of the ethnic riots of 1969 and the perceived "obstructionist" stance of non-Malay business in the 1970s, the ethnic settlement that underlay Malaysian politics had been abrogated and therefore was no longer to be considered binding on the Malay state. While the UMNO-led governments of Tunku Abdul Rahman, Tun Abdul Razak and Dato Hussein Onn had honored the terms of the agreement that brought leaders of the three major ethnic communities together to form a governing coalition at independence (in particular they foreswore using the state as a weapon against private non-Malay business interests which dominated the economy), Dr. Mahathir not longer felt so bound. The settlement remained, after a fashion, as the basis for the National Front governing coalition, but its central features were perceived by both Malays and non-Malays alike to have been largely eroded away. Chinese business leaders appeared no longer to support the government (they had, after all, been among the most vocal elements in opposing the government's most cherished program—the NEP), so the government felt little hesitation in abandoning its former "kid gloves" approach in dealings with business.

These political motivations, when combined with the economic considerations mentioned above, led to the adoption of an aggressive state strategy of giving state-owned or -run enterprises, in alliance with foreign capital, the leading role in developing industry, thereby marginalizing (in a relative sense) non-Malay commerce and industry. Thus we see in the heavy industries policy the culmination of more than a decade of change towards state intervention in the industrial realm and the usurping of Chinese and Indian domination of the economy by the politically powerful Malay community.

The outcomes of the policy after ten years have fallen well short of expectations. Recent paper profits reported by the state's auto-maker, Proton, and modest sales abroad, have done little to alter the overall impression of heavy indebtedness and poor performance that has accompanied the operation of state-run heavy industries.

Some heavy industries operations have been dismembered or sold and others are being offered for sale. Management of the remaining state-run industries has been passed to the private (foreign and non-Malay) sector in the hope that private managers will be able to save them from sale or liquidation.

With respect to industrial development policy as a whole, the impression one gets from the closing years of the decade (1988–1989) is of a policy interregnum of sorts—the heavy industries initiative remains officially in place, but the government appears resigned to its financial failure and seems to have responded to economic events by effecting a staged withdrawal from direct involvement in industrial development.

The huge budget deficits that followed the severe recession of 1985–1986, and the accumulated indebtedness and losses since recorded by HICOM, suggest that the government has been forced by economic necessity to abandon, perhaps only temporarily, its commitment to state-led industrialization on behalf of Malays. The burgeoning growth of foreign investment in the electronics industry in this sense represents a windfall—industrial development is proceeding apace, little thanks to the government, as Japanese, Taiwanese, Korean, and Hong Kong firms, reacting to exchange rate changes, relative labor costs, and the attraction of back door access to major markets, have flooded MIDA with applications to invest. The fact that growth is occurring in a narrow range of products, that indigenous participation is conspicuously absent, and that Malays are benefiting only at the shop-floor level, through direct employment, has not apparently prompted too much visible hand-wringing among government leaders.

This is especially so since the Malay leaders of UMNO have been embroiled in a furious and all-consuming intra-UMNO leadership struggle since 1987 that has pitted Prime Minister Mahathir against former Finance Minister Tunku Razaleigh and, at one time, former Deputy Prime Minister Musa Hitam, and has led to an unprecedented split in the party (now named New UMNO). While this continuing struggle, in which the Prime Minister has the upper hand, revolves around Mahathir's leadership, and has little direct bearing on industrial policy, it has left government leaders preoccupied and has consumed energy and attention that might otherwise have been devoted to mapping the country's economic future.

As a result, with the beginning of a new decade, Malaysian industrial development policy appears in a state of flux, consisting, for the time being, of little more than a "wait-and-see" attitude. Decision-makers are evidently more than happy to see foreign investors providing the principal source of dynamism in the Malaysian economy because this obviates the necessity for difficult industrial choices, over how to encourage Malay industrial entrepreneurship in the wake of the failure of the state's own heavy industries, which they would prefer to avoid.

6

CONCLUSION: STATE, SOCIETY, AND INDUSTRIAL STRATEGY

This study has been concerned with the general question of why countries choose the industrial development strategies they do, when they do. It was undertaken in response to cross-national studies involving the advanced industrialized countries (AICs) of Western Europe, the United States, and Japan, and implicitly challenges the relevance of the conclusions reached therein to the experience of industrial decision-making in the Third World. The results of this analysis of a middle-income developing country characterized by natural resource dependence and communal differences suggest that most of the variables considered important to explaining choice of industrial development path in AICs are in this Third World context either not relevant or, where they are applicable, do not exhibit sufficient variance to be plausible causes of the variation in strategy observed over time.

Political culture is an example of the former—it is suggested that, for example, the French and the British respond differently to similar crises because of longstanding and deep-seated differences in their cultural orientations. Such an argument can plausibly be made to explain different policy responses between nations; it does not apply, however, when the differences to be explained, are between different, relatively discrete, time periods occurring in the same country.

Structural factors are examples of the latter—change in official industrial strategy cannot be explained in terms of institutional disjucture when (as in the Malaysian case) significant policy realignment has been accompanied by very little institutional change to speak of. Malaysia has in fact experienced a remarkable degree of continuity in institutions, and in those occupying positions within them, with the

Alliance (later National Front) coalition in power for the entire post-colonial period.

In considering existing approaches I have shown, however, that one approach (namely, that focusing on evolving societal group coalitions—Gourevitch's policy coalitions) turns out to be as useful in explaining outcomes in the Third World as it is in the First. Political analysis of Malaysian industrial development strategy suggests that the type of coalition most important in that context is one comprising neither economic actors (workers, capitalists, farmers) nor intermediate associations (political parties, unions), but communal groups. Malay, Chinese, and Indian communities are linked at the top in Malaysia in a coalition that embodies a political settlement of differences—a quid pro quo acknowledging spheres of political and economic influence—that has guided intergroup relations for over thirty years. Changes in the scope of this settlement in successive decades have changed the extent to which the (Malay-dominated) state has felt constrained from using its political power to advance the economic interests of the Malay community. The result has been change in state industrial strategy, from a market-led approach with very limited state involvement during the country's first decade, to a mixed market-led/state-regulatory strategy during the 1970s, and finally to a state-led strategy beginning in 1980.

The most important factor that has varied from one such era to the next has been the extent of state involvement. Lindblom's dictum, that the crucial question we must ask in ascertaining the character of economic policy is "How much state?" (or "How much market?"), is well taken.[1] The Malaysian state's choice of strategy (its answer to Lindblom's question) has taken three different forms in three successive decades and the principal plausible political explanation for this lies in the changing nature of the communal settlement by which Malays, Chinese, and Indians have agreed to live peaceably together.

In this concluding chapter I would like to consider the broader significance of these conclusions for our understanding of how industrial strategy is made in Third World countries. The implications are three-fold.

First, as suggested above, group coalitions play an important political role in shaping strategy choice in the Third World as they do in the First World. But such coalitions in the Third World have quite a different "hue" to those which feature in theories of First World policy choice. Rather than coalitions of economic actors or intermediate associations, they are typically coalitions of communal groups. Moreover, in nonstratified communal societies such as Malaysia, these communal groups (be they ethnically, religiously, or linguistically defined) do not neatly coincide with economic interests—their boundaries instead cut across a range of economic strata. That is to say, these groups are not simply masks for economic interests (in which case the coalitions considered here would simply amount to Gourevitch's economic interest coalitions, only in a different guise); the interests they represent are communal.

This study, then, suggests that a "retooling" of the West European "coalitions" approach is in order to accommodate a wider variety of coalition types and thereby to make it applicable to the task of understanding of how industrial strategy is made in Third World developing societies. Scholars of economic development in India or Pakistan, for example, can profitably employ a communal coalitions approach to their analyses of the politics of industrial strategy choice in those countries.

The objection raised to this line of argument, that communal coalitional arrangements of the sort to which I refer indeed exist in Western Europe and have been well described in, for example, Lijphart's work on consociational democracies,[2] is not valid because such democracies are defined by the presence of *continuing, detailed,* and *explicit* negotiation between the elites of major social groups (the Flems and the Walloons in Belgium, for example) over the terms of economic and political change. This is rarely the sort of relationship that typically exists between communal groups in Third World society.

We are much more likely to find, as in the Malaysian case, broad (often implicit) agreements over respective communal spheres of influence (the military, the economy, the government apparatus, etc.) which prevail for long periods and which serve to keep the peace between potentially antagonistic groups. Periodically, flashpoints occur in the relations between communities which motivate their leaders to reevaluate the status of the communal agreement— how binding it continues to be, and in which spheres it constrains group action—which in turn lead to changes in government policy (in the case of this study, to changes in industrial strategy).

In contrast to consociational arrangements, then, the coalitional communal settlements we witness in the Third World are not subject to *continuing* negotiation (they often stand for years); are rarely *detailed* (usually having more to do with general principles of group interaction than with month-to-month disagreements over policy); and are often not *explicit* (not ratified by formal agreement).

The second respect in which this study is significant is that it reemphasizes the importance of ethnic identity as a factor relevant to the politics of economic decision-making in many Third World societies. In the past, the tendency of some authors to conjure up ethnicity (or culture) as a *deus ex machina* to explain economic "miracles" (the use of Chinese Confucianism to explain the success of Hong Kong, Taiwan, and Singapore is a case in point) has led many analyses of economic development to dismiss the potential relevance of these variables a priori. Consequently, prescriptions for Third World development often overlook a characteristic that may be pivotal. In the Malaysian context, the examples of dramatic strategy change in 1970 and 1980, in response to changing political and economic relations between the major ethnic communities, suggest that we might do well to refocus our attention on ethnicity as a causal variable with potentially powerful influence over choice of development path.

This point is well-illustrated with reference to the controversial topic of World Bank and IMF structural adjustment "conditionality." The Bank has been joined in the 1980s by major donors and lenders in mandating that developing countries embrace free-market (or market-led) economic policies, and a much-reduced role for state enterprises, as a condition for receiving assistance to return their economies to a sounder footing after the oil-related upheavals of the 1970s. Countries like Nigeria have been forced to comply—by adopting structural reforms which have included deep cuts in government spending (especially in social programs), liberalized trade measures, greater incentives and higher prices for farmers for their goods, and major devaluations of their currencies—or face economic collapse.[3]

The Bank, which insists that the reforms are essential to revitalizing dying economies, especially in Africa, and making them more self-reliant, has reported that structural adjustment policies appear to be working in many of the forty-five countries of sub-Saharan Africa. A 1989 Bank study concluded that countries that had adopted adjustment policies were performing slightly better economically than those that had not.[4]

Structural adjustment conditionality, however, is problematic in that even if (and this is debatable) it yields some improvement in economic conditions overall, it appears to have undesirable distributional consequences, at least in the short run. The massive inflation, high unemployment and cuts in government programs, especially in health and education, that almost inevitably attend the imposition of reforms, have placed the burden of "adjustment" more heavily on certain segments of society than on others. Critics[5] have focused in particular on the impact on the poor. But the conclusions of this study point to broader distributional concerns associated with structual adjustment conditionality, the impacts of which have yet to be widely discussed.

While the World Bank claims scrupulous adherence to a neutral policy of nonintervention in the internal affairs of debtor states, it is clear from this study that the free-market policies that the Bank currently prescribes—indeed requires—have direct bearing on the relative balance of economic and political power among groups within recipient societies. Thus, in any society characterized (as are many in Asia and Africa) by major communal divisions, the decision to embrace the Bank's free-market path to economic prosperity (in Lindblom's parlance, to choose "more market" and "less state") carries with it a variety of communal implications. Just as Malaysian Prime Minister Tunku Abdul Rahman's adherence to a market-led industrial development strategy during the 1950s and 1960s had the effect of strengthening the dominant economic position of the ethnic Chinese in commerce and industry, and eventually precipitated what was perceived as a challenge to the political hegemony of the Malay ruling elite, so free-market strategies pursued elsewhere will bolster the positions of those groups already dominant in the commercial sphere and simultaneously undermine the positions of ethnic communities that have wielded political power over the government apparatus (or segments thereof) as an instrument for ensuring the economic security of their members.

The economic technicians that for the most part staff the World Bank appear almost entirely innocent of the intercommunal implications that flow directly from their policy recommendations. Even in the case of a November 1989 Bank report, "Sub-Saharan Africa: From Crisis to Sustainable Growth," which a senior Bank offical claimed, at its release, consciously "goes beyond narrow economic confines" and "attempt(s) to raise some of the major social, cultural and political issues that need to be taken into consideration," these concerns of relative political and economic power between communities are not addressed.[6] The report takes the position that African countries should continue to comply with structural adjustment and had best deal with the social and political ramifications of reform simply by doubling human resource development funding. In addition, harking back to the institutionalist prescriptions of the "modernization" school of economic development in its heyday of the 1950s and 1960s, World Bank President Barber Conable suggested at the announcement of the above-mentioned report that problems of maldistribution of economic reform benefits among different segments of Third World society were really problems of bad government: "Good governance—an efficient and honest public administration—must be provided to complement policies that promote market mechanisms and entrepreneurship."[7] Conable implies that the differential political and economic impact of free-market structural adjustment on communities is not a problem *inherent* to the reforms, but a mere reflection of poor government implementation, which can be reversed with institutional "development."

This study suggests otherwise—that structural adjustment, as a prescription, indeed has inherent, if unintended, side-effects that have far-reaching implications for relations between societal groups. It is this fact that enables us to understand why some countries will and have foresaken badly-needed foreign donor assistance because of the feared repercussions of adopting the Bank's blanket free-market dogma. In this regard, Malaysia provides an example from an earlier era. Attempts by the Bank in the late 1960s to persuade the Malaysian government to "marketize" rural credit met with contemptuous rejection from the government of the time, because of the obvious pro-Chinese and anti-Malay message adoption of such a policy would have sent to largely Malay rural-dwellers.

This study, then, can be seen as a corrective. It suggests that issues relating to ethnicity and communalism have immediate and current import for analyses of Third World economic development strategy choice.

The third implication that may be drawn from this study concerns the viability of East Asian "models" of economic development as alternatives for Third World industrialization. It indeed matters that most Third World societies are structured very differently from those of the NICs and of Japan: specifically, that they are not homogeneous, but instead usually exhibit a myriad of ethnic, religious, caste, and linguistic groups.

Where society is communal and where there are disparities in economic and political power between communities, it is likely that the nature of politics will be very different from that found in Japan or South Korea, for example. Most importantly, settlements between communal groups, acknowledging respective spheres of influence, are likely to constrain the state's ability to pursue industrial strategies of the kind employed by the capitalist developmental states of East Asia.

At crucial junctures in the economic development of the NICs, the state has been able to effect fundamental economic restructuring without constraint from domestic social forces. The point made here is that such opportunities rarely present themselves in the case of a communal Third World industrializing countries, because the ever-present risk of open communal violence, of the kind observed in Lebanon or Sri Lanka, acts as a continuing constraint on state action. Thus an interesting future avenue in the NIC literature might entail exploration of the facilitating role that the relative homogeneity of NIC society has had in their economic success.

These observations ought not be taken to imply, however, that the existence of communal constraint on developmental initiatives of the kinds undertaken in the NICs necessarily precludes national economic successes. In fact, the case considered here must be judged overall as a success story for Third World development.

In the thirty years since Malaysia's independence, the economy has produced relatively high levels of material and social welfare that continue to rise. By comparison with its immediate neighbors, Malaysia's per capita GNP in 1988 (US$2,079) was nearly twice that of Thailand, about three times that of the Philippines, and about six times that of Indonesia.[8] With a real GDP growth rate of 8.7 percent in 1988 (compared with an estimated rate of 5 percent for all low- and middle-income countries),[9] and with more than 25 percent of GDP (and almost 50 percent of exports) accounted for by manufactures,[10] Malaysia's economy may be categorized as rapidly growing, industrializing, and export-oriented. In terms of social indicators, Malaysians have a (1987) life expectancy at birth of 70 years (compared with 51 years for sub-Saharan Africans, 68 years for East Asians and 62 years for the combined populations of all low- and middle-income countries),[11] own (on average) 73 televisions, 934 radio receivers, and 66 telephones per thousand persons, and operate a little under one car per ten persons (there are 1.5 million cars for 17 million people).[12] So, despite following development strategies that have differed in many respects from those of the rapidly industrializing countries of East Asia, Malaysia's communal society has done comparatively well economically.

In contrast, there are many Third World countries which, while communal, are in no position to contemplate pursuit of a NIC-like model. In Africa, countries like Burundi or Zaire, for example, are unlikely to be able to benefit for the foreseeable future from the NIC experience. They lack not only the state institutional capacity to formulate and implement a developmental state strategy, but also the basic infrastructure, trained personnel, and nascent entrepreneurial class ready to respond to state incentives (to name but a few).

There is, however, a stratum of developing nations, among which we might include India, Pakistan, Malaysia, Syria, Kenya, Zimbabwe, and Nigeria, that are both communally divided and have the economic potential to develop considerable industrial strength over the next twenty to thirty years. This study suggests that future analyses of economic strategy choice in these countries could be well-informed by attending to the political implications of different societal structures (communal or noncommunal) and to the nature of group coalitions from which alternative strategies derive.

NOTES

1. Choosing a Development Strategy

1. According to this approach, society may be divided into the three primary categories of economic actor: business, agriculture, and labor (1960s treatments, such as Theodore Lowi's *The End of Liberalism* and Grant McConnell's *Private Power*, share this approach with classic contributions, such as those of Marx and Bentley). Gourevitch argues, however, that we must also consider the actor- or product-*family* (in the case of business and agriculture) or the *type* of employment (in the case of labor) involved, if we are to capture the complexity of preferences in society. Since each category or sub-category of actor has a distinct role in the international or domestic economy, each may be expected to have distinct attitudes and policy preferences. (See Gourevitch, *Politics*, pp. 55–56.)

2. Public choice theorists suggest ways that we can model this behavior using an idealized, game-like contest. Politics is seen as "a competition among individuals [in this case economic actors] whose goals are access to power and scarce resources and whose means are rationally calculated to achieve these ends most efficiently" (Gourevitch, *Politics*, p. 10). Among contributions that have embraced this approach we find Schumpeter's *Capitalism, Socialism and Democracy*, Buchanan and Tullock's *The Calculus of Consent*, and Breton's *The Economic Theory of Representative Government*.

3. Gourevitch, *Politics*, p. 59.

4. Ibid., p. 60.

5. The classic contribution here is that of de Tocqueville (*Democracy in America* and *The Old Regime*). More recently, Katzenstein has used the term "policy networks" to encompass groups of intermediate associations and state institutions. For a critique of this approach, see ibid.

6. Ibid., p. 61. Another family of explanations, group-based models, explains policy as the product of conflict between social groups or classes (on groups, see Truman, *The Governmental Process*; on classes, see Wolfe, *The Limits of Legitimacy*). This approach, while related to economic actor and intermediate association explanations, does not distinguish between economic actors and the organizations that represent them. It argues

that pluralist organizations of economic actors such as farmers or auto manufacturers (i.e., intermediate associations) or social classes and class fractions (i.e., economic actors) form alliances that give rise to policy. From changes in these alliances, we get changes in policy: "A critical factor in the making of a country's political economy is how social classes form alliances in the making of state policy" (Hall, *Governing*, p. 14). Thus alliances between the petty bourgeoisie and either capital or labor have been associated with distinct patterns of policy in Western Europe since World War II.

7. See Krasner, *Defending the National Interest*. Theda Skocpol and John Zysman are two others whose work emphasizes state structure. Skocpol explains differences in welfare systems between countries in terms of state structural variables (see Weir and Skocpol, "State Stuctures"). Zysman (*Governments, Markets*) argues that different formal financial system structures have led different countries to adopt different industrial adjustment policies.

8. Hall, *Governing*, p. 19. Hall's structural analysis is not limited to the organization of the state, but extends to the influence of the organization of capital and labor and of the country's position in the international economy (p. 259). His approach therefore encompasses aspects of the economic actor, intermediate association, and state systems models which are treated separately here.

9. Gourevitch, *Politics*, p. 61; Hall, *Governing*, p. 18. Related to structural theories are those emphasizing the autonomous interests and policy preferences of persons occupying structural positions. State-centric theories, for example, argue that state policy-makers themselves have preferences and often possess the capacity to impose them on others. Their autonomy from societal pressures is greater than either pluralist or Marxist models will admit. See Katzenstein (*Power and Plenty*) and Krasner (*National Interest*). In contrast, Poulantzas (*Political Power*) and Miliband (*Marxism and Politics*), each from very different perspectives, argue that policy-maker preferences are heavily influenced by the organization of the polity and economy, and are therefore not strictly autonomous.

10. Easton, "An Approach," p. 383, quoted in Hall, *Governing*, p. 5.

11. Conservative analysts focus on the needs of the political system (see Parsons, *The Social System*) whereas Marxists emphasize the functional needs of the economic system (see Gough, *Welfare State*, and Holloway and Picciotto, *State and Capital*).

12. As Hall observes, "It might be possible to identify the functions of a given structure, but it is virtually impossible to derive structure from function in a systematic and non-arbitrary way" (Hall, *Governing*, pp. 6–7).

13. Verba defines political culture as "the system of empirical beliefs, expressive symbols and values which defines the situation in which political action takes place. It provides the subjective orientation to politics." See Verba, "Comparative Political Culture," p. 513; Hall, *Governing*, p. 8.

14. Hayward, p. 341, cited in Hall, *Governing*, p. 8. See also Kindleberger, "The Rise of Free Trade," pp. 20–55.

15. Gourevitch alludes to the central weakness of the cultural argument as follows: "Rapid changes within countries . . . , such as the United States of Coolidge contrasted to the United States of FDR, undermine arguments that . . . stress constants over time" (Gourevitch, *Politics*, p. 63).

16. Gerschenkron's contribution, with its emphasis on different types of state role in early and late developing countries, is perhaps the most well-known of the works in this school. Others include works by Cardoso and Faletto (*Dependency and Development*) and Wallerstein (*The Modern World System*).

17. According to this second approach, war, security issues, and military procurement needs arising from a country's strategic position in the international system play a primary role in shaping economic policy choices. Countries drawn into rivalries develop military machines that alter their political systems. See Hintze, "Military Organization"; McNeill, *Pursuit of Power*; Gourevitch, *Politics*, pp. 63–64.

18. Koomsup, *ASEAN Energy Issues*, pp. 68, 89–90.

19. In much of the Third World, important societal actors and the associations that represent them identify their interests in communal rather than economic terms. Labor unions and organizations representing business or agricultural owners exist, but their ability (particularly in the case of labor) to participate in national policy coalitions is in general severely proscribed.

20. Within the context of an overall market-led strategy, for example, there may be segments of the economy subject, for a variety of reasons (national security, historical precedent), to heavy doses of state intervention and direction. Martin Landau has written persuasively on the limitations of analyzing particular policies if one seeks to generate political "knowledge" rather than just to accumulate "information." See Landau, *Political Theory and Political Science*.

21. Zysman characterizes these as model or ideal-typical solutions to the technical-political challenges facing developed societies. His central thesis is that different solutions can be tied to a different types of financial system arrangement. Zysman, *Governments, Markets*.

22. Ibid., p. 309. A similar continuum is suggested by Charles Lindblom's observation that "the greatest distinction between one government and another is in the degree to which market replaces government or government replaces market" (Lindblom, *Politics and Markets*, p. ix). Lindblom's analysis of possible politico-economic alternatives for arranging society posits three main choices: a system based on exchange (i.e., a market system), a system based on persuasion (i.e., a bargained or negotiated system), or a system based on authority (i.e., a bureaucratic or governmental system) [pp. 11–13]. Societies may be arrayed along a continuum depending upon how much they rely on exchange versus persuasion versus authority to order social relations. The different categories of

economic development strategy that are the focus of the present study clearly owe their origins to Lindblom's more elemental description of choices of social organization arranged by degree of market or degree of government.

Following Lindblom, Peter Katzenstein suggests that the three dominant political forms of developed capitalism give rise to a threefold schema of types of national economic strategies (Katzenstein, *Small States,* pp. 23–27). Liberal societies (the United States, for example) tend to rely on macroeconomic policies and market solutions to economic challenges, although on occasions resorting to limited and ad hoc protectionist measures to pass the costs of industrial change to other countries. Corporatist countries (such as Austria and Switzerland) accept industrial change as inevitable, but compensate for it by employing a variety of economic and social policies so as to prevent the costs from leading to political instability. Statist countries (e.g., Japan) confront change by using state institutions preemptorally to transform industrial structures and systematically protect firms as they exploit long-term market trends.

23. "Consensus" or "approval" are terms carrying a positive valence; they imply that actors go along because they are convinced that it is in their *ideal* interests to do so.

24. The definition of power used here is drawn from Talcott Parsons (*The Social System,* p. 121), and is the same as that employed by Etzioni (*Comparative Analysis,* p. 4). The organizational literature on power is vast. The contributions most pertinent to the issue of coercive power, however, are those of Amitai Etzioni, who develops an exhaustive categorization of types of power which includes coercive, utilitarian, and normative power.

25. Etzioni, *Modern Organizations,* pp. 59–60; *The Active Society,* pp. 357, 360.

26. The case of utilitarian compliance can also include situations where ethnic groups calculate that the material costs of noncompliance exceed those of compliance (i.e., where there is no positive payoff, only the possibility of minimizing costs).

27. Some readers might see parallels here with Arend Lijphart's work on consociational democracy in segmented societies of Western Europe. There, Lijphart sees leaders of institutions from each segment of society (in the Netherlands and Austria, for example) forming an elite cartel that makes political decisions satisfactory to members of all segments, so that political stability is ensured through accommodation. He suggests that such consociational arrangements are appropriate instruments for government in other ethnically divided societies, like Malaysia. (See Kasfir, "Explaining," pp. 385–88 for a critique of this conclusion.)

However, the Malaysian situation is crucially different from that analysed by Lijphart because the settlements to which I refer here are overarching settlements, formed and adhered to over long periods, and dealing with overall distributions of types of influence. There is by no means a grand coalition, whose leaders are authorized by, and have the overwhelming support of, their respective communities to make day-to-day policy decisions on all issues that might arise. As Horowitz points out, the Malaysian settlement is made at a very general level. On particular issues community leaders can by no means be assured of their community's support, nor does overall settlement imply agreement between community leaders on specific issues. See Horowitz, *Ethnic Groups,* pp. 569–73.

28. My approach to the definition of ethnicity follows Horowitz (*Ethnic Groups,* pp. 55–57).

29. I here adopt a definition drawn from Schildkrout, "The Ideology of Regionalism," p. 184 n.4, after Horowitz, *Ethnic Groups,* p. 53. This approach draws upon the "primordialist" view of ethnicity but is not inherently in conflict with the alternative "instrumentalist" or rational actor perspective. It shares with the works of primordialists, such as Walker Connor, Clifford Geertz, Pierre van den Berghe, Anthony Smith, and Max Weber, the idea that ethnic groups are distinguishable from other social groups (collectivities of individuals sharing a common identity) by their attachment to "charter myths" of common origin. It also embraces the primordialist position that the culture of an ethnic group (the system of ideas and signs and associations and ways of behaving and communicating shared by members of the group) may be seen as an emblem for the putative common heritage or descent of its members.

But this definition also responds to the instrumentalist view of Dov Ronen, Nelson Kasfir, Paul Brass, Fredrik Bath, and Ernest Gellner, inter alia, that the social definition of identity is more fluid than a rigid primordialist position would suggest, and specifically that ethnic identity is neither necessarily nor fundamentally rooted in heritage or descent— it is as often "chosen" as "given," and is amenable to strategic manipulation by self-interested individuals, groups, and states. Individuals, acting like rational investors seeking to maximize return, may readjust their identities over time (somewhat less frequently, one would imagine, than changing their preferences for brands of beer) in response to the different sets of rewards and costs faced by different ethnic groups (Laitin, "Hegemony and Religious Conflict," pp. 286, 299–301). Similarly, political entrepreneurs may see in ethnic culture and identity a convenient and relatively cheap vehicle for constructing a political power base, bolstering in the process groups with previously tenuous existences (Kasfir, "Explaining," pp. 369, 376). Also, states and colonial powers have proved themselves adept at wielding ethnic identity as an instrument of social control, a means by which to achieve a desired social order.

These variants on the instrumentalist position are primarily concerned with where groups come from. Their perspectives, however, on how an ethnic group may be identified and what makes it cohere once created, are quite compatible with the definition of ethnicity proposed here.

30. Parkin, *Marxism and Class Theory*, p. 31.
31. Nairn, *Breakup*, p. 351.
32. Kasfir, "Explaining," pp. 368–69; Parkin, *Marxism and Class Theory*, p. 4.
33. Gellner, *Nations and Nationalism*, p. 93; Parkin, *Marxism and Class Theory*, p. 36.
34. Parkin, *Marxism and Class Theory*, p. 36.
35. Kasfir, "Explaining," p. 369.
36. For example, Nagata ("The Status of Ethnicity," p. 243) argues that

> while . . . ethnicity and social class are independent in origin and analyt-
> ically distinct in character, they are by no means independent in opera-
> tion. . . . they exist in a dynamic interrelationship, although at any one
> time or on any particular occasion, one principle or idiom (ethnic or
> class) may prevail over the other, and individuals or groups may be
> predisposed to select one identity over the other, depending upon the
> nature of the social situation.

37. Kasfir, "Explaining," p. 378.
38. Nagata, "The Status of Ethnicity," p. 257.
39. Lipset and Rokkan, *Party Systems*, p. 6. Also quoted in Laitin, "Hege-
    mony and Religious Conflict," p. 285.
40. Parkin, *Marxism and Class Theory*, pp. 3, 9. Parkin later (p. 114) general-
    izes his critique:

> There is no general theory that could explain why some societies and
> not others experienced the migratory and demographic movements that
> finally resulted in communal divisions. These have to be treated as 'just
> so' historical facts, not as events to be incorporated into some jumbo
> social theory.

41. Barth, *Ethnic Groups*, p. 27.
42. Ernest Gellner argues that, even given such an arrangement, vertical
    conflict between stratified ethnic groups does not spring, as Marxists
    allege, from differential control (or ownership) of capital, per se. Great
    differences in the extent of ownership may exist, but this is often of little
    social consequence until ethnic divisions, accompanied by obvious cul-
    tural or diacritical marks, accentuate differences in access to education
    and political power and, above all, inhibit the flow of personnel from
    one stratum to the next. Conflict between polarized strata, then, is
    predicated upon the existence of ethnic differences. Such differences are
    not simply an outward manifestation of the conflict itself. Gellner, *Na-
    tions and Nationalism*, p. 96.
43. Smith, *Ethnic Origins*, p. 77.
44. Common language is usually the factor unifying each group. Horowitz,
    Ethnic Groups, p. 23.
45. Parkin, *Marxism and Class Theory*, p. 4.
46. Horowitz, *Ethnic Groups*, p. 25.
47. Parkin, *Marxism and Class Theory*, pp. 4–5.

48. Horowitz, *Ethnic Groups*, p. 7.
49. Ibid., p. 12.
50. The best study so far is that of John Funston on UMNO and PAS. See Funston, *Malay Politics in Malaysia*.
51. For the present purposes, we may define the state as those individuals occupying roles in a set of administrative, policing and military organizations, coordinated by an executive, who are in possession of decision-making authority for the entire society and who monopolize legitimate violence (Haggard, "Pathways From the Periphery," pp. 80–81). The alternative term, government, suffers from multiple referents (parliamentary majority, cabinet, civil service departments).
52. See Dahl and Lindblom, *Politics, Economics and Welfare*.
53. Goran Hyden makes a related point about the state in Tanzania. See *Beyond Ujamaa*.
54. The effects of a narrowing intercommunal consensus are by no means limited to a changing level of constraint on state action in the economic realm. Among the broader political ramifications of such narrowing, witnessed in the Malaysian case over the past decade, have been a decline in democratic institutions, reduced official regard for civil liberties, and direct use of state power to coerce opponents. In short, the changing industrial choices which this study seeks to explain are part of broad political changes whose scope is beyond the purview of the present study.
55. See Harris, *End of the Third World*.
56. In wielding a broad brush and seeking to uncover factors influencing the longer-term evolution of Malaysian industrial strategy, I risk skipping too lightly here over details considered important by country or industry specialists. I believe the payoff, in terms of contributing to the broader debate on the sources of economic strategy choice warrant this effort to generalize from the specifics of the Malaysian experience.
57. Milne, "New Economic Policy," p. 235.
58. Malaya (Federation), *Population Census, 1957*, cited in Lim Mah Hui, "Contradictions," p. 39 n.5.
59. Gale, *Politics and Public Enterprise*, pp. 17–18.
60. Lim Mah Hui, "Contradictions," p. 40; Gale, *Politics and Public Enterprise*, p. 18.
61. Gale, *Politics and Public Enterprise*, p. 17; and Drabble, "Some Thoughts," p. 207, cited in Spinanger, *Industrialization Policies*, p. 8 n.15. This policy was commonplace elsewhere in the British Empire, apparently motivated by a desire to maximize exploitation of raw material wealth and to minimize social friction by enforcing a (sometimes artificial) division of labor, as well as by a paternal concern to protect indigenous cultures from being overwhelmed by more aggressive immigrant communities.
62. Independence was considerably delayed by the demands of a prolonged communist insurgency (the Malayan Emergency, 1948–1960) which had its roots in the Chinese community.

63. Attempts at forming truly multiethnic parties in the 1950s and 1960s all failed.

2. Colonial and Precolonial Malaya

1. In 1874 the population of the Malay Peninsula was estimated at only 300,000, with the largest concentrations in the river valleys of Perak and Negri Sembilan. See Gullick and Gale, *Malaysia*, pp. 2, 35; Khor, *The Malaysian Economy*, p. 34.
2. There was no principle of absolute private ownership of land in traditional Malay society. As one British colonial official noted in 1884: "Land is so abundant in proportion to the population that they scarcely consider it as a subject of right any more than elements of air and water." W.E. Maxwell, "Laws and Customs of the Malays With Reference to the Tenure of Land," *Journal of the Straits Branch of the Royal Asiatic Society* (1884) 13, cited in Hing, "Capitalist Development," p. 298.
3. Goran Hyden makes the same point about possibilities for exit in the case of Tanzania. See Hyden, *Beyond Ujamaa*.
4. Gullick and Gale, *Malaysia*, pp. 34–35. Confiscation was an ever-present threat, as a Malay historian has observed:

    If a man does acquire property or a fine house or a plantation or estate of any size, a Raja is sure to find some way or other to get hold of it, or he may demand a loan or a gift. And if the man refuses, the Raja confiscates his property; if he resists, he and his whole family are killed;

    (Abdullah Allah bin Abdul al-Kadir Munshi, *The Voyage of Abdullah*, translated by A.E. Coope [Oxford: Oxford University Press], quoted in Hing, "Capitalist Development," p. 298.)
5. Gullick and Gale, *Malaysia*, p. 34; Lim Mah Hui, "Contradictions," p. 39.
6. Gullick and Gale, *Malaysia*, pp. 3, 14.
7. Khor, *The Malaysian Economy*, p. 38.
8. Ibid., p. 34.
9. Gullick and Gale, *Malaysia*, p. 15; Gale, *Politics and Public Enterprise*, p. 19.
10. Gullick and Gale, *Malaysia*, pp. 19–20.
11. Ibid., p. 20.
12. Khor, *The Malaysian Economy*, p. 34. In 1830, Singapore became the capital of the newly formed Straits Settlements, a dependency ruled by the British colonial administration of India.
13. Formally independent of British control, these territories were occasionally subject to some measure of British influence. Beyond them, four northern Malay states were tributaries of Siam, although they were allowed considerable freedom by the King of Siam to trade with the Straits Settlements (Gullick and Gale, *Malaysia*, p. 22).
14. Osborn, "Economic Growth," p. 154; Gullick and Gale, *Malaysia*, p. 22.

15. Gullick and Gale, *Malaysia*, p. 34.
16. Hing, "Capitalist Development," p. 299; Gullick and Gale, *Malaysia*, p. 4.
17. Gullick and Gale, *Malaysia*, pp. 23, 34.
18. Ibid., p. 34.
19. Ibid., p. 24.
20. Khor, *The Malaysian Economy*, p. 25; Hing, "Capitalist Development," p. 299. See also Wong, *The Malayan Tin Industry*.
21. Gullick and Gale, *Malaysia*, p. 24.
22. The following discussion of British "intervention" draws on Gullick and Gale, *Malaysia*, pp. 24–26.
23. Ibid., p. 25.
24. Khor, *The Malaysian Economy*, p. 35; Gullick and Gale, *Malaysia*, p. 4.
25. Hing, "Capitalist Development," p. 299.
26. Khor, *The Malaysian Economy*, p. 36.
27. Ibid., pp. 35–36.
28. Official directives were issued in the name of a "Council of Sultans," but their authority was largely derived from that of the British resident general. See Gale, *Politics and Public Enterprise*, pp. 18–19; Gullick and Gale, *Malaysia*, p. 26.
29. Gullick and Gale, *Malaysia*, p. 27.
30. Spinanger, *Industrialization Policies*, p. 8; Gullick and Gale, *Malaysia*, p. 37.
31. Edwards, "Review," p. 156.
32. Khor, *The Malaysian Economy*, p. 36. After twenty years of rapid growth, however, investment faltered during the rubber slump of 1920–1922. The situation in Malaya then came to reflect changes occurring at the global level, specifically changes in the direction of investment flows under the influence of sporadic recession, a continuous drop in prices, and commodity restriction schemes. Investments in commodity production declined worldwide and were increasingly directed to geographic areas closer to the western hemisphere, such as Latin America and Africa, in order to avert the interruptions in supply that were experienced during the first war. Expansion of British investment in rubber continued at a slower rate through the 1920s but leveled off after the world commodity slump of 1932. See Hing, "Capitalist Development," pp. 303–04.
33. Khor, *The Malaysian Economy*, p. 38.
34. Hing, "Capitalist Development," p. 300; Gullick and Gale, *Malaysia*, p. 27.
35. Hing, "Capitalist Development," p. 301.
36. Gullick and Gale, *Malaysia*, p. 37.
37. Meanwhile, heavily capitalized European companies seeking land to establish plantations were able to use loopholes in the act and to benefit from "sympathetic" consideration from the authorities to take over large areas of reserve land. See Hing, "Capitalist Development," p. 301.

38. Lim Mah Hui, "Contradictions," p. 40; Gale, *Politics and Public Enterprise,* pp. 17–18; Spinanger, *Industrialization Policies,* p. 8.
39. Milne, "New Economic Policy," p. 236.
40. Gale, *Politics and Public Enterprise,* p. 20; Gullick and Gale, *Malaysia,* p. 8.
41. Despatch No. 397 from Straits Settlements to Secretary of State, September 24, 1887, cited in Hing, "Capitalist Development," p. 301 n.15.
42. By 1940, almost all foreign-owned tin output was produced by dredges and this output accounted for seventy-two percent of all tin produced in Malaya. See Khor, *The Malaysian Economy,* pp. 36, 38, 55.
43. Mackie, "Changing Patterns," pp. 7–8. Before World War II, the founders of many of today's leading Chinese families and companies in Malaysia were engaged in tin mining, rubber planting (on a very small scale), trade, manufacturing, banking, and shipping. Some of their operations later developed into large Chinese trading groups. See Gale, *Politics and Public Enterprise,* p. 19; Mackie, "Changing Patterns," p. 14.
44. The British accounted for seventy percent of the US$455 million of private western capital sunk in Malaya by 1937. See Khor, *The Malaysian Economy,* p. 38 n.1; Allen and Donnithorne, *Western Enterprise,* p. 290, appendix III.
45. Khor, *The Malaysian Economy,* p. 39.
46. Khor, *The Malaysian Economy,* p. 51; Lee Sheng Yi, *Monetary and Banking Development,* ch. 6.
47. Mackie, "Changing Patterns," p. 10.
48. Khor, *The Malaysian Economy,* p. 52.
49. Allen and Donnithorne, *Western Enterprise,* pp. 210–24; Khor, *The Malaysian Economy,* p. 44.
50. Allen and Donnithorne, *Western Enterprise,* p. 246; Khor, *The Malaysian Economy,* p. 44.
51. Khor, *The Malaysian Economy,* p. 38; Mackie, "Changing Patterns," p. 13.
52. The following section on the impact of British administration on traditional authority structures draws upon Gullick and Gale, *Malaysia,* pp. 26–37.
53. Ibid., p. 30.
54. Gale, *Politics and Public Enterprise,* p. 17.
55. Gullick and Gale, *Malaysia,* p. 29.
56. In the late 1880s, for example, Malay chiefs were sometimes appointed "Malay magistrates" in the districts which they had once governed, so that they might offer advice to the British district officers, who had replaced them. However, lack of a western education, traditional obligations of kinship, and their attachment to the customary perquisites of authority made it difficult for these "magistrates" to fit into the new system of colonial rule.
57. In fact, the role of the councils was simply to rubber-stamp decisions of the adviser and, over time, even this became redundant as policies affecting individual states became increasingly the prerogative of the federal bureaucracy in Kuala Lumpur.

58. Hing, "Capitalist Development," p. 299.
59. Gullick and Gale, *Malaysia*, pp. 28–29.
60. Ormsby Gore, *Report*, p. 21.
61. The following discussion of the CBS and colonial taxation policy draws on Khor, *The Malaysian Economy*, pp. 40–63.
62. From 1906, this rate stood at one straits dollar for two shillings and fourpence sterling.
63. At times during the interwar period, however, the straits dollar was actually backed by almost 200 per cent.
64. Most of Malaya's trade was denominated in sterling.
65. This system was found in various guises in most British dependencies.
66. Khor, *The Malaysian Economy*, p. 48.
67. Ida Cecil Greaves, *Colonial Monetary Conditions* (London: Her Majesty's Stationery Office, 1953), p. 12, cited in Drake, *Financial Development*, p. 32, and reported in Khor, *The Malaysian Economy*, p. 45.
68. Lee Sheng Yi, *Monetary and Banking Development*, p. 32, cited in Khor, *The Malaysian Economy*, pp. 45–48.
69. The exact figures were M$33.17 in Malaya, compared with M$8.99 in Kenya and M$4.30 in India (including Burma). Li, *British Malaya*, p. 25; Khor, *The Malaysian Economy*, p. 49.
70. In Malaya there was neither a company profit tax nor personal income taxes.
71. Revenues not repatriated to Britain were spent on transportation and communications networks and, in particular, on the building of a sophisticated road and rail system on the West Coast of the Malay Peninsula where the tin mines and rubber plantations were to be found. In contrast, expenditures on social services such as education and health-care were tiny. In 1932, they amounted to M$3.2 million and M$4.4 million respectively, whereas by 1934 a cumulative total of over M$235 million had been spent on the railroad alone. In addition a significant proportion of public revenue was drawn off in the form of transfer payments which included contributions to the Imperial War Chest, debt charges, pensions, retirement allowances, and personal emoluments. See Emerson, *Malaysia*, pp. 187, 191; Khor, *The Malaysian Economy*, p. 63.
72. Emerson, *Malaysia*, p. 186; Khor, *The Malaysian Economy*, p. 40.
73. Khor, *The Malaysian Economy*, p. 40.
74. Ibid., p. 41.
75. Lim Chong Yah, *Economic Development*, p. 325, appendix 4.1.
76. Khor, *The Malaysian Economy*, p. 41.
77. Ibid., p. 44.
78. Emerson, *Malaysia*, p. 186; Khor, *The Malaysian Economy*, p. 41.
79. Khor, *The Malaysian Economy*, p. 37.
80. This section on early Malay nationalism draws on Gullick and Gale, *Malaysia*, pp. 42–45.
81. Gullick and Gale, *Malaysia*, p. 43.
82. Ibid., pp. 44–45.

83. Stockwell, *British Policy*, pp. 9–10.
84. Milne and Mauzy, *Politics and Government*, p. 22.
85. Major Fujiwara had formed Fujiwara Kikan, an agency designed to win the local communities of Malaya—in particular, Indians and Malays— to the Japanese cause. See Stockwell, *British Policy*, p. 2.
86. Milne and Mauzy, *Politics and Government*, p. 22.
87. Cheah Boon Kheng, *Red Star*, pp. 19–20.
88. Stockwell, *British Policy*, pp. 4–5.
89. This contrasted with Japanese eagerness to exploit the grievances of opportunists and to fan the aspirations of idealists before and during the Malayan campaign. See Stockwell, *British Policy*, p. 5.
90. Stockwell, *British Policy*, p. 5.
91. Ibid., p. 12.
92. Ibid., p. 6.
93. The philosophy on which it was based, pan-Malayanism, was however to reappear later in the Malay Nationalist Party (see Gullick and Gale, *Malaysia*, p. 80). Some former KMM leaders have claimed that, behind a facade of collaboration with the Japanese, they had formed a clandestine group to secure power as soon was the Japanese grip was relaxed. According to this version of events, Ibrahim Yaacob planned to use for this purpose a Japanese organization of Malay youths propagandized to think in militarist and nationalist terms. PETA (defenders of the fatherland) was controlled by former KMM leaders and only the collapse of the Japanese regime prevented Yaacob from establishing a strong nationalist force. There is no independent corroboration of these claims. See Stockwell, *British Policy*, pp. 12–14.
94. Clutterbuck, *Conflict and Violence*, p. 38.
95. It has been estimated that nearly five thousand Malayan Chinese were executed by the Japanese in February 1942, most of them picked out by hooded informers. See Clutterbuck, *Conflict and Violence*, p. 38; Pye, *Guerrilla Communism*, p. 65.
96. Pye, *Guerrilla Communism*, pp. 64–65.
97. A British liaison officer fighting with the guerrillas reported seeing only one Indian in a regiment of 216, and no Malays. See Clutterbuck, *Conflict and Violence*, p. 38.
98. The graduating classes of 101 Special Training School, which totaled 165 individuals (all Chinese), slipped out of Singapore before the British surrender and formed the nuclei for MPAJA "regiments" in the jungle. See Hanrahan, *Communist Struggle*, p. 32; Clutterbuck, *Conflict and Violence*, p. 37; Pye, *Guerrilla Communism*, p. 65.
99. Pye, *Guerrilla Communism*, p. 67.
100. Clutterbuck, *Conflict and Violence*, p. 38.
101. While fostering the image that it was the new protector of the Chinese community, the MCP, however, had little interest in exposing its followers unnecessarily to the rigors of warfare.
102. Pye, *Guerrilla Communism*, p. 68.

103. Ibid., pp. 68–69.
104. According to its official history, it made some 340 individual raids, of which only 200 were considered major, whereas during a similar period during the Emergency (June 1949 to December 1951), according to British reports, there were some 13,585 actions, of which 4,155 were considered major. See Hanrahan, *Communist Struggle*, p. 44.
105. Hanrahan, *Communist Struggle*, p. 44; Pye, *Guerrilla Communism*, p. 69.
106. Clutterbuck, *Conflict and Violence*, p. 39.
107. Pye, *Guerrilla Communism*, p. 70.
108. Ibid., p. 71.
109. Osborn, "Economic Growth," p. 155.
110. The following discussion of Malayan Union draws on Means, *Malaysian Politics*, pp. 52–59.
111. These English-educated Malays were encouraged in their resistance to Malayan Union by a powerful group of retired British civil servants who exerted pressure on Whitehall and Parliament in London. See Puthucheary, *The Politics of Administration*, p. 31, cited in Gale, *Politics and Public Enterprise*, p. 23.
112. Great Britain, Colonial Office, *Malayan Union*, p. 2; Means, *Malaysian Politics*, p. 52.
113. The rulers, for example, prepared a petition to be sent directly to the King protesting the "annexation of Malaya." See Means, *Malaysian Politics*, p. 54.
114. Puthucheary, *The Politics of Administration*, p. 31, cited in Gale, *Politics and Public Enterprise*, p. 23.
115. Gale, *Politics and Public Enterprise*, pp. 23–24.
116. Ibid., pp. 20, 24.
117. Osborn, "Economic Growth," p. 154; Hing, "Capitalist Development," p. 302.
118. Short, *The Communist Insurrection*, pp. 93–94; Hing, "Capitalist Development," p. 302. Many of these draconian laws outlived the Emergency and remain in force to this day as a potent weapon against unwanted dissent.
119. Thoburn, *Primary Commodity Exports*, p. 60; Spinanger, *Industrialization Policies*, p. 8 n.18. This new roadbuilding had implications for later, post-independent development plans in such areas since the basic infrastructure was already in place.
120. Spinanger, *Industrialization Politics*, p. 6 n.14. These new villages were the prototypes for the fortified hamlets used by U.S. strategists in South Vietnam to isolate the Viet Cong from village support.
121. Lim Mah Hui, "Contradictions," p. 40; Hing, "Capitalist Development," p. 303.
122. Khor, *The Malaysian Economy*, p. 37.
123. Gale, *Politics and Public Enterprise*, p. 24.
124. The MCA was the product of a suggestion by the high commissioner, Sir Henry Gurney, to Tan Cheng Lock that the Chinese form a party

similar to UMNO representing Chinese interests. See Lim Mah Hui, "Contradictions," p. 40 n.8.

125. In the case of the MCA, the British were trying to wean Chinese support from the MCP.
126. Lim Mah Hui, "Contradictions," p. 40.
127. Ibid.
128. Gale, *Politics and Public Enterprise*, p. 24.
129. These religious reformers sought to remove the control over religious matters that had been usurped by traditional rulers during the colonial period.
130. Hing, "Capitalist Development," p. 303.
131. Puthucheary, *The Politics of Administration*, p. 33, cited in Gale, *Politics and Public Enterprise*, p. 25.
132. Allen, *The Malayan Union*, p. 42, quoted in Gale, *Politics and Public Enterprise*, p. 25.
133. Gale, *Politics and Public Enterprise*, p. 25.
134. Milne, "New Economic Policy," p. 236.
135. Gullick and Gale, *Malaysia*, p. 33.
136. This measure was widely misinterpreted as mandating a ratio of Malays to non-Malays in the civil service as a whole of at least 4:1. See Milne, "New Economic Policy," p. 236.
137. Milne, "New Economic Policy," p. 236.
138. Ibid., pp. 236–37; Gale, *Politics and Public Enterprise*, p. 21.
139. Lim Hah Hui, "Contradictions," p. 40; Milne, "New Economic Policy," p. 236; Hing, "Capitalist Development," p. 302.
140. See Osborn, "Economic Growth," pp. 155–56.

3. Ethnic Bargaining and Market-Led Development

1. Bhanoji Rao, *Malaysia: Development Pattern*, p. 83.
2. Hing, "Capitalist Development," p. 304. Calculated from U.N. Monthly Bulletin of Statistics, various issues.
3. Puthucheary, *Ownership and Control*, pp. 26–27.
4. Mackie, "Changing Patterns," p. 8; Lim Mah Hui, "Contradictions," p. 39 n.5.
5. Watson and Caine, *Report*, p. 4.
6. Malaya (Federation), *Draft Development Plan*, pp. 153–54.
7. Malaya (Federation), *Census of Manufacturing*; Southeast Asia Chronicle (special issue), April 1980.
8. Spinanger, *Industrialization Policies*, pp. 5–6, 8.
9. Mackie, "Changing Patterns," pp. 8–14; Lim Mah Hui, "Contradictions," p. 39 n.5.
10. Malaya (Federation), *Census Report 1957*; *Malay Mail*, February 3, 1980, cited in Lim Mah Hui, "Contradictions," p. 39 n.5; Milne, "New Economic Policy," p. 235. Funston, while accepting the likelihood that Malay participation in the urban industrial sector was probably small, ques-

tions the validity of the 1.5 percent figure, for Malay holdings in limited companies, as an indicator of the relative Malay share of wealth in the country:

> In the Malayan context, equity in limited companies cannot . . . be assumed to accurately reflect wealth in the industrial commercial sector; it certainly does not . . . reflect wealth in the community at large. . . . even the racial distribution of share ownership is not at all clear from the figures given [by the government]. (Funston, *Malay Politics*, p. 260).

11. IBRD, *Economic Development of Malaya*, p. 13.
12. Spinanger, *Regional Industrialization*, pp. 22–23; Sundrum, "Manpower and Educational Development," p. 82.
13. Zakaria, "Evolutionary Change," p. 6; Spinanger, *Regional Industrialization*, pp. 22–23.
14. Milne, "New Economic Policy," p. 237; Puthucheary, *The Politics of Administration*, p. 107; Spinanger, *Regional Industrialization*, pp. 23, 28; Spinanger, *Industrialization Policies*, p. 42.
15. Public development expenditure differs from public investment, in that it excludes expenditure on defense, purchases of land, loans and grants to the private sector, and expenditure on the creation of physical assets owned by the private sector. See Malaysia, *Second Malaysia Plan (SMP)*, p. 27.
16. Lim and Canak, "Political Economy," pp. 214–15. Funston points out that most of this 1.3 percent did not involve direct government investment in industrial undertakings but was devoted instead to providing infrastructure and financial institutions in support of private sector development. See Funston, *Malay Politics*, p. 152.
17. Malaysia, *SMP*, p. 28, table 2–4; Lim and Canak, "Political Economy," pp. 214–15.
18. Sundrum, "Manpower and Educational Development," p. 82ff.
19. Spending in these three areas alone accounted for more than three-quarters of public development expenditure on agriculture during the 1960s. But land development, under the auspices of the Federal Land Development Authority (FELDA), was given pride of place; at government expense, new areas were opened up for settlement, each settler receiving ten acres of land (eight for rubber and two for mixed farming). In addition to clearing the land, the government also planted rubber trees and built homes for the settlers, and provided them with a monthly subsidy until the rubber was ready for tapping (at which time they were required to begin repayment of the subsidy, according to an established scale). See Malaysia, *SMP*, p. 11; Spinanger, *Industrialization Policies*, pp. 42, 48.
20. Milne, "New Economic Policy," p. 237; Lim Mah Hui, "Contradictions," pp. 41–42. For example, transport licences for buses, trucks, and taxis were required by the 1958 Road Traffic Ordinance to be issued in proportion to the ethnic composition of the population in each state; in many

states, a Malay contractor could receive a government contract if the tendered price did not exceed that of the most competitive non-Malay tender by more than ten percent; and at least half of all timber concessions were granted to Malays.

21. Malaysia, *SMP*, p. 13.
22. Sundrum, "Manpower and Educational Development," p. 82. The need to expand Malaya's industrial capacity in order to reduce dependence on tin and rubber production was recognized as early as 1950 in the first draft of the colony's first development plan. See Malaya (Federation), *Industrial Development Working Party*, pp. 123–69; Spinanger, *Industrialization Policies*, p. 39.
23. Malaysia, *SMP*, p. 82.
24. Speech by Khir Johari, 1962 (mimeo), n.p., pp. 1, 3; Spinanger, *Regional Industrialization*, pp. 27–28. See also Wheelwright, "Reflections," pp. 66, 69.
25. *Utusan Melayu*, February 2, 1959, .cited in Funston, *Malay Politics*, p. 152.
26. Lim Mah Hui, "Contradictions," p. 42; Spinanger, *Industrialization Policies*, p. 12.
27. Beaglehole, "Malay Participation," p. 218.
28. Funston, *Malay Politics*, pp. 13, 152.
29. This ordinance was recommended by the 1955 World Bank mission (IBRD, *Economic Development of Malaya*) which had urged that the open, free-enterprise nature of the economy be protected, but that diversification of production be promoted by depreciation allowances and a limited amount of tariff protection (the mission discouraged the adoption of tax holidays for pioneer industries as being undesirably "discriminatory"). A subsequent, government-appointed Industrial Development Working Party, in its report of 1957, reiterated most of the Bank report's recommendations but added tax relief for pioneer industries as a way of attracting foreign investors to establish import-substituting industries. This measure thus became part of the new ordinance. See Jomo, *A Question of Class*, pp. 220–21.
30. The period of relief granted under the ordinance was tied to the size of the fixed capital investment, and approval was conditional on a company's ability to provide employment, benefit to the Malayan consumer (a good competitive product) and downstream spinoffs. The ordinance was superseded in 1968 by the Investment Incentives Act. Hing, "Capitalist Development," p. 304; Spinanger, *Industrialization Policies*, pp. 43–44; Spinanger, *Regional Industrialization*, p. 27; diplomatic source dated August 7, 1961.
31. In practice, restrictive conditions for loan eligibility ensured that the main recipients of MIDF loan funds were large, highly capitalized (often foreign) companies—few local enterprises were large or sophisticated enough to qualify. As Drake observed:

To make a [MIDF] application is itself a difficult task and would undoubtedly tax the abilities of all but the best managed local enterprises.
It does not seem rash to suggest that the [MIDF]'s rather sophisticated
application procedure frightens away many smaller firms. (Drake, *Financial Development*, p. 164.)

Thus, up to 1967, MIDF made 145 loans amounting to M$60 million,
but the 64 loans of less than $50,000 totalled less than $2 million. Rather
than help finance smaller local industrial enterprises, as it was ostensibly
intended to, MIDF was in effect subsidizing large foreign-owned companies. See Jomo, *A Question of Class*, pp. 223–24; Spinanger, *Industrialization Policies*, pp. 45–46; diplomatic source dated August 7, 1961.

32. Spinanger, *Industrialization Policies*, pp. 44, 47.
33. The average effective rate of protection for the enumerated manufacturing sector stood at 15 percent in 1962, but subsequently rose to 45
percent in 1966 and 55 percent in 1972. David Lim has argued that this
was still quite low in comparison with other similar economies. See
David Lim, *Economic Growth*, pp. 261–65, and Jomo, *A Question of Class*,
p. 222.
34. A primary government concern at the time was to avoid creation of a
high-priced economy: "High-priced goods are anathema in the Federation [of Malaya]." Diplomatic source dated August 7, 1961. See also
Jomo, *A Question of Class*, p. 221.
35. Spinanger, *Industrialization Policies*, pp. 26–27; Hing, "Capitalist Development," p. 304.
36. Funston, *Malay Politics*, pp. 152, 154.
37. MARA was established in 1966 to supersede the Rural Industrial Development Authority (RIDA—established 1953). Its responsibilities included the provision of technical and financial assistance to Malays in
new and existing businesses and the establishment of new industrial and
commercial projects for later transfer into private Malay hands. Among
concerns set up during MARA's first five years were those involving the
production of batek cloth and clothing, leather goods, handicrafts, sawn
timber and timber products, tapioca starch and pellets, and processed
rubber. In addition, MARA built stores for Malay businesses, ran wholesale supply operations, contracted for the supply of construction materials and operated rural bus services. (Malaysia, *SMP*, p. 15.)
38. Bank Bumiputra was established by the government in 1965 to provide
credit and banking facilities as well as technical and advisory services for
Malays in commerce and industry. By 1970, Bank Bumiputra had assisted with housing development, construction, oil-palm cultivation, logging and saw-milling, import and export businesses, manufacturing, and
small-scale commercial and industrial enterprises. (Malaysia, *SMP*, pp.
15–16.)
39. FAMA was created in 1965 to improve the marketing system for crops

and to ensure that farmers obtained fair prices for their products. At the end of the decade, FAMA was supplemented by another rural institution, Bank Pertanian (the Agricultural Bank), which was established to extend and coordinate credit facilities to farmers on reasonable terms. (Malaysia, *SMP*, p. 12.)

40. Funston, *Malay Politics*, pp. 152, 154.
41. Mackie, "Changing Patterns," p. 7; Hing, "Capitalist Development," p. 304. For this reason the government guaranteed the security of foreign capital by undertaking to pay fair compensation in the event of nationalization. Diplomatic source dated August 7, 1961.
42. Some 57 percent of new enterprises established with the benefit of incentives under the Pioneer Industries scheme were foreign-owned. Among Malayan residents, Malays in particular were hardly in a position to benefit from the scheme because they lacked both financial resources and technical expertise. See Funston, *Malay Politics*, p. 8; Lim Mah Hui, "Contradictions," p. 42; Edwards, "Review," p. 150.
43. Emerson's foreword to King, *The New Malayan Nation*, p. v.
44. Milne and Mauzy, *Politics and Government*, p. 33.
45. Ibid., pp. 36, 129.
46. They agreed, for example, to support Malay as the national language (other languages were, however, not to be suppressed, and English was to continue as an official language until 1967). See Means, *Malaysian Politics* (2nd ed.), p. 198.
47. Morrison, *Japan, U.S.*, p. 7. Means suggests that Malay special rights might have been perceived as only temporary by some non-Malays:

One occasionally would hear rumors to the effect that the Alliance had agreed in principle that Malay "special rights" are inherently unjust, but were temporarily necessary to raise the economic and educational position of the Malays. Officials sometimes hinted that the Malay "special rights" would be reviewed as the economic position of the Malays improved. 1970 and 1972 were both mentioned as tentative dates for the termination of some Malay "special rights." However it seems doubtful that the three Alliance partners ever came to any firm agreement on this issue. (Means, *Malaysian Politics* [2nd ed.], pp. 219–20.)

48. Non-Malays also dominated all categories of professional and skilled labor.
49. Means, *Malaysian Politics* [2nd ed.], p. 198.
50. Milne and Mauzy, *Politics and Government*, pp. 38–39.
51. This allocation of senior positions was designed to compensate for the relatively limited representation accorded the MIC and MCA in the cabinet. See Ratnam and Milne, *The Malayan Parliamentary Election*, p. 196.
52. The component parties brought different strengths to the coalition; while UMNO was expected to provide the bulk of the electoral votes, the MCA

was expected to supply more than its share of financial resources. See Ratnam and Milne, *The Malayan Parliamentary Election*, p. 196.

53. He had threatened to reveal the questionable practices of a senior Chinese civil servant in his Ministry, and thus to undermine the stature of MCA leaders who were closely connected to the individual involved. See Funston, *Malay Politics*, p. 13.

54. Gale, *Politics and Public Enterprise*, p. 22.

55. Milne and Mauzy, *Politics and Government*, p. 323.

56. Milne and Mauzy, *Politics and Government*, p. 131. One firsthand observer has described the Alliance style as "a mutual deterrence model of conflict management." See Esman, *Administration and Development*, p. 258.

57. Funston, *Malay Politics*, p. 13; Beaglehole, "Malay Participation," p. 218; Lim Mah Hui, "Contradictions," p. 42; Means, *Malaysian Politics* (2nd ed.), pp. 195–96.

58. Beaglehole, "Malay Participation," p. 218.

59. Funston, *Malay Politics*, p. 13.

60. Lim Mah Hui, "Contradictions," p. 41; Milne, "New Economic Policy," p. 237.

61. Spinanger, *Industrialization Policies*, p. 42.

62. "Malasia: What Price," *Southeast Asia Chronicle*, p. 21.

63. Spinanger, *Regional Industrialization*, p. 22.

64. There was a small amount of local capital involved in what were generally considered "European" enterprises and a few Malayan Chinese directors of "European" firms, but the process had not advanced very far. Partnerships between local and foreign capital were generally restricted to local companies and there had been little penetration of the former into the metropol ownership structures of the latter. See Mackie, "Changing Patterns," pp. 14–15; Spinanger, *Regional Industrialization*, p. 23.

65. IBRD, *Economic Development of Malaya*; Malaya, *Industrial Development Working Party*, par. 96–147; Spinanger, *Industrialization Policies*, p. 42.

66. Interview, Kuala Lumpur, July 1986.

67. Zakaria, "Evolutionary Change," p. 6.

68. Robinson, *National Control*, p. 30.

69. Zakaria, "Evolutionary Change," p. 11; Gale, *Politics and Public Enterprise*, pp. 21–22, 25–26.

70. As one observer noted of the cultural norms applying in colonial Malaya:

Ordinary Malays mustn't meddle in politics, because politics of the state and its people are in the hands of the Sultan and the traditional elite, who must be given complete loyalty . . . . The term politics was understood to mean 'treason.' It was in the nature of our people to be wholly loyal and submissive to the government, to the authorities, to the rulers; (Roff, *Origins*, p. 218.)

See also Gale, *Politics and Public Enterprise*, p. 21.

71. The Federation of Malaya had became the Federation of Malaysia, en-

compassing Peninsular Malaya, Singapore, Sarawak, and North Borneo (now Sabah) in September 1963. The withdrawal of Singapore two years later was prompted by the advocacy by the Singaporean Chinese leader, Lee Kuan Yew, of a "Malaysian Malaysia" in which all communities would be treated equally and the special preferences and rights accorded Malays removed from the constitution. See Gullick and Gale, *Malaysia*, p. 34; Milne and Mauzy, *Politics and Government*, pp. 67–68.

72. Spinanger, *Industrialization Policies*, p. 47 n.19.

73. IBRD, *Report on the Economic Aspects*, pp. 14, 34–37; Jomo, *A Question of Class*, pp. 221–22.

74. Spinanger, *Regional Industrialization*, p. 45; Spinanger, *Industrialization Policies*, p. 47.

75. Spinanger, *Industrialization Policies*, p. 47; Jomo, *A Question of Class*, p. 225.

76. The act, described by the minister of commerce and industry at its introduction in Parliament as providing "a variety of incentives to induce a greater and more rapid flow of investments" (Lo Sum Yee, *Development Performance*, p. 89), granted companies exemptions from company tax, relief from payroll tax, investment tax credits, accelerated depreciation allowances, and export incentives. In addition, tariff protection and exemption from import duty and surtaxes were granted to facilitate the establishment of new industries. See Malaysia, *SMP*, p. 149; and *Far Eastern Economic Review* (*FEER*), June 16, 1983, p. 102.

77. David Lim, "East Malaysia," p. 158; Ariffin, "Women Workers," p. 49.

78. The figure was even higher (9.6 percent) for the second half of the decade, exceeding the projections in the First Malaysia Plan by over a third. (Malaysia, *SMP*, pp. 10, 21.)

79. Malaysia, *SMP*, p. 15.

80. Malaysia, *SMP*, p. 147.

81. Hoffmann and Tan, *Industrial Growth*, p. 11; Soehoed, "Economic Dimensions," p. 57.

82. Among other goods produced by Malayan industry were prepared foodstuffs, beverages, tobacco products, petroleum products, cement, and rubber and plastic goods. See Malaysia, *SMP*, pp. 15, 149.

83. Malaysia, *SMP*, p. 18. Official statistics on income distribution have, however, been challenged as misleading and inaccurate. See, for example, David Lim, "East Malaysia," p. 158.

84. Milne and Mauzy, *Politics and Government*, pp. 323–24. This use of the term Ali-Baba has no connection, as far as this author is aware, with the parable of the Arabian Nights.

85. Malaysia, *SMP*, pp. 40, 151. The remainder was owned by federal and state governments, nominee companies (in which the composition of ownership is indeterminate), and other individuals. These figures actually understate the relative size of Chinese capital accumulation in comparison to that of Malays since many Chinese small-savers did not consider shares as a safe or attractive way to invest and preferred instead

to put their money into investment circles or to invest in family business activities. Only those with substantial funds tended to invest in public companies. See Mackie, "Changing Patterns," p. 16.

86. Malaysia, *SMP*, p. 151.
87. Gale, *Politics and Public Enterprise*, p. 15; Milne, "New Economic Policy," p. 237.
88. Mahathir, *Malay Dilemma*, p. 42.
89. "Malaysia: What Price," *Southeast Asia Chronicle*, p. 4.
90. Robinson, *National Control*, p. 32. The figure for Indian households was 50 percent.
91. Milton Esman, on the basis of his observations at the time, has illuminated for the writer the full extent of Chinese domination and the nature of the perceived threat this posed to the Malay community.

4. The Settlement Challenged and State Intervention

1. For the Alliance, the victory was a hollow one, as the coalition failed to retain the two-thirds majority (that necessary for passage of constitutional amendments) for which its leaders had campaigned vigorously. Furthermore, in two of the nine states, the government faced the possibility that, for the first time, a state government might be dominated by non-Alliance parties. See Milne and Mauzy, *Politics and Government*, pp. 80–81.
2. Milne and Mauzy, *Politics and Government*, pp. 79–80, 84.
3. Deputy Prime Minister Tun Razak, *Straits Times* (*ST*), May 12, 1969, cited in Milne and Mauzy, *Politics and Government*, p. 164. The following description of the riots and their aftermath draws on author interviews with eyewitnesses and on Milne and Mauzy, *Politics and Government*, pp. 78–83.
4. *The Rocket* (1970) 5, no. 1, cited in Milne and Mauzy, *Politics and Government*, p. 78.
5. Milne and Mauzy, *Politics and Government*, pp. 78–79.
6. Ibid., p. 79. Reports of unrest only a few days after May 14 referred to only scattered incidents (although a brief outbreak of fierce fighting did occur some weeks later, on June 28).
7. Milne and Mauzy, *Politics and Government*, p. 79.
8. In the event, the Sandhurst spirit of senior military officers led them to give primacy to civilian rule. Nevertheless, among members of the National Operations Council which governed the country for almost two years, the military was very well represented.
9. Milne and Mauzy, *Politics and Government*, p. 80. Former prime minister Tunku Abdul Rahman, has emphasized the role of the Malayan Communist Party in his analysis of events. See Abdul Rahman, *May 13*, p. ix.
10. Malaysia, *Parliamentary Debates 1972*, p. 84 (Goh Hock Guan). This statement, though made after the period of immediate crisis, reflects the

nature of the challenge to Malay special rights mounted by the opposition non-Malay parties.

11. *ST,* August 1, 1969, cited in Milne and Mauzy, *Politics and Government,* p. 82.
12. Malaysia, *SMP,* p. 40.
13. David Lim, "East Malaysia," p. 157; "Malaysia: What Price," *Southeast Asia Chronicle,* pp. 21–22; Milne and Mauzy, *Politics and Government,* pp. 82–83.
14. *FEER,* July 10, 1969, p. 119.
15. Morrison, *Japan, U.S.,* p. 7; Milne and Mauzy, *Politics and Government,* pp. 82–84.
16. Milne and Mauzy, *Politics and Government,* p. 100.
17. Ibid., p. 83.
18. Interview, Kuala Lumpur, July 1986.
19. The NEP was first unveiled as the centerpiece of the SMP. However, it was not fully elaborated (nor were supporting statistics provided) until 1973, in the *Mid-Term Review of the Second Malaysia Plan, 1971–1975.* Milne and Mauzy, *Politics and Government,* p. 326.
20. Puthucheary, *The Politics of Administration,* p. 1.
21. Malaysia, *SMP,* p. 3
22. Musa, "Keynote Address," p. 6.
23. Mahathir, "Speech," p. 9.
24. Malaysia, *SMP,* p. 1.
25. There were poor in all communities (for example Indian rubber tappers and Chinese laborers in the tin mines). The Malays were simply the most numerous.
26. Malaysia, *SMP,* p. 1.
27. Milne and Mauzy, *Politics and Government,* p. 325.
28. Malaysia, *SMP,* p. 158.
29. Spinanger, *Regional Industrialization,* p. 66; Malaysia, *SMP,* p. 159.
30. Milne and Mauzy, *Politics and Government,* p. 321.
31. David Lim, "East Malaysia," p. 157; Malaysia, *SMP,* pp. 158–59.
32. Malaysia, *SMP,* p. 158.
33. David Lim, "East Malaysia," p. 157.
34. Malaysia, *SMP,* p. 1.
35. Milne and Mauzy, *Politics and Government,* p. 325.
36. Ibid., pp. 327–28.
37. Ibid., p. 328.
38. The *sense* of constraint is what is important here. In practical terms, the Malays since 1957 had controlled the reins of political power and therefore could have done whatever they liked to impose their wishes on the non-Malays. The price for doing so (the possibility of the disintegration of Malaysian society) was likely to be very high, however, and it is with the *consequences* of such action that Malay leaders were most concerned. After 1969, *not* using the state to assert Malay interests seemed to carry with it costs that were equally as high.
39. Milne and Mauzy, *Politics and Government,* p. 325.

40. Malaysia, *Mid-Term Review SMP*, p. 97; "Malaysia: What Price" *Southeast Asia Chronicle*, p. 22. Interview, Washington, D.C., September 1985.

41. Puthucheary, *The Politics of Administration*, p. 107; Milne and Mauzy, *Politics and Government*, p. 338.

42. Compliance was monitored by the Ministry of Trade and Industry and the Malaysian Industrial Development Authority. Milne and Mauzy, *Politics and Government*, p. 331.

43. Milne and Mauzy, *Politics and Government*, p. 334.

44. Malaysia, *SMP*, p. 7.

45. Milne and Mauzy, *Politics and Government*, p. 336.

46. "Malaysia: What Price" *Southeast Asia Chronicle*, p. 22.

47. Malaysia, *SMP*, p. 7.

48. Puthucheary, *The Politics of Administration*, p. 107.

49. Milne and Mauzy, *Politics and Government*, pp. 336–37.

50. Tham, *Social Science Research*, p. 121; Milne and Mauzy, *Politics and Government*, p. 336.

51. Milne and Mauzy, *Politics and Government*, pp. 335–36.

52. Malaysia, *Mid-Term Review SMP*, pp. 33–35, 197–99. ITM and MARA's vocational institutes were supplemented by those of, inter alia, the National Productivity Centre.

53. Milne and Mauzy, *Politics and Government*, p. 334.

54. Ibid., p. 338.

55. According to a leading Malay politician, in 1975 one offering of shares worth M$18 million by three banks elicited responses from only three Malays who, collectively, could muster just M$150,000. Milne and Mauzy, *Politics and Government*, p. 339.

56. *ST*, January 11, 1972, cited in Milne and Mauzy, *Politics and Government*, pp. 332–33.

57. Senu, *Revolusi Mental*, pp. 87–123.

58. Malaysia, *TMP*, p. 31; "Malaysia: What Price" *Southeast Asia Chronicle*, p. 22; Milne and Mauzy, *Politics and Government*, p. 406.

59. Milne and Mauzy, *Politics and Government*, p. 335. The practice was most prevalent in timber, saw-milling and mining—in 1978, the new Kelantan Chief Minister said that almost 99 percent of the logging companies in that state were run on an Ali-Baba basis.

60. *New Straits Times* (*NST*), August 29, 1975, cited in Milne and Mauzy, *Politics and Government*, p. 337.

61. Milne and Mauzy, *Politics and Government*, p. 337.

62. Ibid., p. 336.

63. Malaysia, *TMP*, p. 190.

64. Ibid.

65. Interview, Kuala Lumpur, June 1986.

66. Lim Yoon Lin, "The New Mood," p. 211.

67. Milne, "New Economic Policy," pp. 255–56. The other successful candidates besides Razaleigh were Mahathir Mohamad and Ghafar Baba, who are today prime minister and deputy prime minister, respectively. Raza-

leigh, Mahathir, and Baba all had the strong backing of the prime minister, Tun Razak.

68. Milne, "New Economic Policy," p. 245.
69. Lim and Canak, "The Political Economy of State Policies," p. 213; Milne, "New Economic Policy," p. 244. What these stalwarts had in common was that they had all been eased out of high government and party posts in the wake of the 1969 riots. See Lim Yoon Lin, "A Troubled Legacy," pp. 146–47.
70. Milne, "New Economic Policy," p. 256.
71. Both Mahathir and Musa had been expelled from the party in 1969 for their strong views favoring Malay progress.
72. Interviews, Kuala Lumpur, June and July 1986.
73. Interview, Kuala Lumpur, July 1986.
74. Diplomatic source dated June 6, 1975.
75. *Malaysian Business* (*MB*), June 1977, p. 10; Milne and Mauzy, *Politics and Government*, p. 331.
76. Associated Chinese Chambers, "Memorandum," p. 1.
77. Diplomatic source dated June 6, 1975.
78. Associated Chinese Chambers, "Memorandum," p. 1; Interview, Kuala Lumpur, July 1986.
79. Associated Chinese Chambers, "Memorandum."
80. According to the act, the minister, in deciding whether or not to grant a license, was to consider if its issuance was "expedient in the national interest" and if it would "promote the orderly development of manufacturing activities." Moreover, the minister had the right to impose such conditions "as he might think fit" on any license. Associated Chinese Chambers, "Memorandum," p. 3.
81. Interview, Kuala Lumpur, July 1986.
82. Malaysia, *SMP*, p. 7.
83. Hussein Alatas, "A Critique," p. 8; Thillainathan, "Distributional Issues," pp. 4, 10, and *NST*, January 30, 1976, cited in Milne and Mauzy, *Politics and Government*, p. 343.
84. Mahathir, "Speech," p. 5. The committee was paralleled by a Consultative Committee on Industrial Coordination comprising officials from the Ministry of Trade and Industry and FIDA, on the one hand, and representatives of business groups such as the ACCCIM, on the other. Diplomatic source dated April 21, 1977.
85. Speech of Prime Minister Onn to the Dewan Rakyat (House of Representatives) launching the TMP, cited in Mahathir, "Speech," p. 9.
86. *NST*, July 20, 1976, and *FEER*, June 10, 1977, pp. 29–30, cited in Milne and Mauzy, *Politics and Government*, p. 342.
87. Interviews, Kuala Lumpur, June and July 1986.
88. Diplomatic source dated April 21, 1977. This announcement was the first indication that Razaleigh's statist views might be falling from favor among other UMNO leaders.
89. Establishments with fixed assets worth less than M$500,000 (represent-

ing about 20 percent of all firms) did not have to satisfy NEP equity requirements to obtain licenses, while those worth less than M$250,000 or having less than twenty-five employees were exempt from the licensing requirement altogether. *MB*, June 1977, p. 11; diplomatic source dated April 21, 1977.

90. *MB*, June 1977, p. 10.
91. Ibid., p. 11.
92. "Malaysia: What Price"v *Southeast Asia Chronicle*, pp. 22–23.
93. Diplomatic source dated September 28, 1977.
94. Malaysia, *TMP*, p. 273.
95. The conference was part of the Chinese response to a series of Bumiputra Economic Congresses held in the 1960s and 1970s that had brought pressure to bear on the government to do more for Malay business.
96. Milne and Mauzy, *Politics and Government*, p. 408. The ICA was amended for a second time in 1979. *FEER*, August 3, 1979, pp. 36–38.
97. Mahathir, "Speech," p. 5.
98. The attraction stemmed from its supply of raw materials and cheap labor, its relatively high standards of honesty and efficiency in public administration and from a generally welcoming official attitude to foreign investment. Milne and Mauzy, *Politics and Government*, p. 348.
99. Milne and Mauzy, *Politics and Government*, p. 348.
100. Malaysia, Ministry of Finance, *Economic Report, 1977–1978*, p. 114; *FEER*, May 16, 1975, pp. 63–66, cited in Milne and Mauzy, *Politics and Government*, p. 349.
101. "Malaysia: What Price" *Southeast Asia Chronicle* (special issue), p. 23; *FEER*, December 10, 1976, pp. 44–45, and December 31, 1976, pp. 37–38, cited in Milne and Mauzy, *Politics and Government*, p. 349.
102. *Wall Street Journal (WSJ)*, September 22, 1975, p. 24; "Malaysia: What Price" *Southeast Asia Chronicle*, p. 23.
103. *NST*, February 3, 1977, cited in Milne and Mauzy, *Politics and Government*, p. 350.
104. *NST*, May 11, 1978, cited in Milne and Mauzy, *Politics and Government*, p. 409.
105. Razaleigh Hamzah, Address, August 26, 1977, cited in diplomatic source dated September 28, 1977.
106. Tan Pek Leng, "Women Factory Workers," pp. 68, 73.
107. Ibid., pp. 65–66.
108. David Lim, "East Malaysia," p. 160.
109. Beaglehole, "Malay Participation," p. 245 n.89.
110. David Lim, "East Malaysia," p. 160; *NST*, March 20, 1978 and April 1, 1978, cited in Milne and Mauzy, *Politics and Government*, p. 408.
111. Milne and Mauzy, *Politics and Government*, p. 408.
112. Puthucheary, *The Politics of Administration*, p. 107.
113. Interview, Kuala Lumpur, July 1986.
114. Puthucheary, *The Politics of Administration*, p. 115.

5. Industrial Aspirations for a Divided Society

1. The basic institutions and policies associated with this heavy industries strategy were the products of Mahathir's initiative. They were put in place in 1980 as a result of his efforts when, as minister of trade and industry and deputy prime minister (he held these positions concurrently during the period 1977–1981), he was given relatively free rein in the industrial sphere. But only when Mahathir succeeded Dato Hussein Onn as prime minister, in 1981, did the new policy, and the campaigns associated with it, become the centerpiece of government economic policy. See Linda Lim, "Charting a Course," p. 5; Bautista, "Recent Shifts," p. 19; Stern, "Growth and Structural Change," p. 30; Kanapathy, "Why Malaysia Needs," pp. 10, 12.

2. Pura, "Doubts," p. 380. As formally stated in the *Mid-Term Review of the Fourth Malaysia Plan, 1981–1985* (p. 250), their primary objectives were

   to reduc[e] the [country's] dependence on foreign countries for the supply of machinery and intermediate inputs, exploit[] forward and backward linkages in industrial development, creat[e] spin-off effects for the growth of small and medium-scale industries, and develop[] the technological capability of the manufacturing sector.

3. The EPU in the Prime Minister's Department was made the principal planning and guiding agency for this new push into state-owned heavy industries. The EPU's role in relation to the heavy industries policy was similar to that of the Ministry of Economic Affairs in Taiwan and the Economic Planning Board in South Korea during implementation of the industrial deepening plans of each country in the 1960s and 1970s.

4. Malaysia, Heavy Industries Corporation of Malaysia (HICOM), *Annual Report 1984*, p. 10.

5. It is worth noting that a number of the industries chosen were also among those chosen by Korean planners when the Heavy and Chemical Industry Plan was formulated a decade before in that country.

6. Planned development allocations for social programs totaled M$6.4 billion for the Fourth Malaysia Plan period, 1981–1985. Malaysia, *Fourth Malaysia Plan*, p. 242. See also Bautista, "Recent Shifts," p. 2; Mukerjee, *Lessons*, p. 82; diplomatic source dated July 6, 1983; Malaysia, Heavy Industries Corporation of Malaysia (HICOM), *Annual Report 1984*, pp. 10, 14, 24; Dhanji, *Structural Change*, p. 39.

7. The initial capital, M$180 million, came from Mitsubishi Corporation (15 percent), MMC (15 percent), and HICOM (70 percent).

8. Malaysia, Heavy Industries Corporation of Malaysia (HICOM), *Annual Report 1984*, p. 18; Tan Bok Huat, "The Malaysian Car Project," p. 5; Ghazali Shafie, remarks made at the Conference on Malaysia, Tufts University, Medford, Mass., November 18–20, 1984.

9. Milne, "New Economic Policy," p. 1377.

10. *Asia Yearbook (AY)*, 1988, p. 182; Malaysia, Heavy Industries Corporation

of Malaysia (HICOM), *Annual Report 1984*, p. 16; Mukerjee, *Lessons*, p. 82.

11. Mukerjee, *Lessons*, p. 82. HICOM's share of the equity in Petro-Pipe Industries, which began production in 1984, was 51 percent. Malaysia, Heavy Industries Corporation of Malaysia (HICOM), *Annual Report 1984*, p. 22.

12. *AY*, 1988, p. 182; Mukerjee, *Lessons*, pp. 81–82.

13. HICOM held 35 percent of the equity involved in Kedah Cement. Malaysia, Heavy Industries Corporation of Malaysia (HICOM), *Annual Report 1984*, pp. 14–16; Mukerjee, *Lessons*, p. 83; *FEER*, June 22, 1989, p. 52.

14. Malaysia, Heavy Industries Corporation of Malaysia (HICOM), *Annual Report 1984*, p. 18.

15. *FEER*, October 26, 1989, pp. 116–18, and February 9, 1989, p. 53.

16. Diplomatic source dated July 6, 1983. After he became Prime Minister in 1981, Mahathir took much more direct control over economic policy-making than any of his predecessors. He made decisions, for example, on those areas in which new initiatives were required and on the broad form that these initiatives would take, and rarely consulted at length with cabinet or party officials on policy matters. *FEER*, April 11, 1985, p. 73.

17. Milne, "New Economic Policy," p. 1379.

18. Diplomatic source dated July 6, 1983.

19. *FEER*, June 11, 1982, p. 38.

20. Diplomatic source dated July 6, 1983.

21. *FEER*, June 14, 1984, p. 113; Bass, "Malaysia in 1983," p. 197; Milne, "New Economic Policy," p. 1373.

22. Pathmanathan, "Malaysia in 1984," p. 226; von der Mehden, "A Political Survey," p. 25; Kanapathy, "Why Malaysia Needs," p. 12.

23. Presumably Musa was referring to the "cold north wind" of depressed commodity prices and sales that swept the South when the developed world reduced its demand for commodities. Diplomatic source dated July 6, 1983.

24. Soesastro, "Japan 'Teacher'," p. 18. See also Mahathir, *Malay Dilemma*.

25. *FEER*, June 14, 1984, p. 113.

26. Diplomatic source dated July 6, 1983.

27. *Asian Wall Street Journal (AWSJ)*, July 13, 1982, cited in Soesastro, "Japan 'Teacher'," p. 17. "Look East" also had concrete manifestations; 582 students and trainees were sent in 1983 to be educated in universities and to receive job-related technical training in large Japanese and Korean corporations, under a program formalized in January of that year. These exchanges were, however, limited in scale in comparison to the numbers of Malaysian students being educated at the time in Western countries (49,000 in 1982). See Mauzy and Milne, "The Mahathir Administration," p. 629, and *FEER*, February 5, 1982, pp. 95–96. High-level exchanges were also expanded (including the visit to Malaysia of Japanese Prime Minister Nakasone). See *FEER*, June 14, 1984, p. 113; Soesastro, "Japan

'Teacher'," p. 22; von der Mehden, "A Political Survey," p. 25; Milne, "New Economic Policy," p. 1373.

28. Milne, "New Economic Policy," pp. 1373, 1380.
29. Soesastro, "Japan 'Teacher'," p. 21.
30. Guthries Corp. was taken over in a "dawn raid" without the knowledge of a majority of shareholders. Subsequently, in a move seen by the Malaysian government as "changing the rules in mid-stream," the Exchange required that shareholders be notified before such a sale could go through. See *FEER*, February 12, 1985, pp. 15–16; von der Mehden, "A Political Survey," pp. 25–26; Milne, "New Economic Policy," pp. 1373–74.
31. Soesastro, "Japan 'Teacher'," p. 10.
32. *Sogoshosha* are corporations created by groups of trading firms to realize economies of scale in export orders and to purchase imports in bulk, thereby reducing unit costs.
33. Malaysia was not alone in adopting the *sogoshosha* format: Korea, Taiwan, and Thailand had also by this time set up their own versions of Japanese *sogoshosha*. Soesastro, "Japan 'Teacher'," pp. 7–8; *FEER*, June 14, 1984, pp. 113–14.
34. "Japan Inc." was coined in the industrialized West, rather than in Japan itself, to characterize the "conspiratorial" alliance of state and private business interests employed by Japan to "breach the barricades" of foreign markets. The use of protection, the non-competitive allocation of markets, and the state-initiated consolidation of firms were some of the examples cited as evidence of a conspiracy. Jomo, "Malaysia in Crisis," pp. 5–6; Pathmanathan, "Malaysia in 1984," p. 227; Bass, "Malaysia in 1983," p. 170; Milne, "New Economic Policy," p. 1374.
35. Privatization, which was becoming increasingly popular elsewhere at the time, notably in Britain under Margaret Thatcher, promised to ease the financial burden that had accompanied the burgeoning size and scope of government in Malaysia. The percentage of the workforce employed in public service was about 45 per cent—much higher than in Thailand or South Korea, for example. It is worth noting that the emergence of this drive to "privatize" was intimately related to progress made towards NEP employment goals. By the early 1980s, the government felt that Malays had shown themselves capable of acting both as managers and as "entrepreneurs" in large state enterprises and that there were sufficient trained Malay businessmen to allow privatization (into Malay hands) to proceed. Milne, "New Economic Policy," p. 1375; Milne, "Ethnic Aspects," p. 119; Jomo, "Malaysia in Crisis," p. 6.
36. Mukerjee, *Lessons*, p. 83. A further Mahathir initiative related to "Look East," which was never really pursued, was a population policy aimed at increasing the number of Malaysians from fifteen to seventy million by the year 2100 in order to create a mass domestic market large enough for Malaysia's enhanced industrial capacity, especially in heavy indus-

tries. See Jomo, "Malaysia in Crisis," p. 4; *Malaysian Digest*, April 30, 1984, p. 1; Milne, "New Economic Policy," p. 1377.

37. *FEER*, March 31, 1983, p. 70; *Asiaweek*, July 8, 1983, p. 54; von der Mehden, "A Political Survey," p. 25; Milne, "New Economic Policy," p. 1374.

38. Even without "Look East," Malaysia, like all of its ASEAN neighbors, had a dependent relationship with Japan—the Japanese were Malaysia's biggest trading partner by far, with both exports to and imports from Japan in 1980 running about 50 percent higher than those with the United States, the next largest partner. *FEER*, September 8, 1983, p. 46.

39. *FEER*, September 8, 1983, p. 46.

40. *FEER*, June 14, 1984, p. 113.

41. Diplomatic source dated July 6, 1983.

42. Jomo, "Malaysia in Crisis," p. 4; diplomatic source dated July 6, 1983; Milne, "New Economic Policy," p. 1376.

43. *FEER*, June 14, 1984, p. 114.

44. Jomo, "Malaysia in Crisis," p. 6.

45. Zakaria, "Evolutionary Change," p. 35; diplomatic source dated July 6, 1983.

46. Industrial growth rates exceeding 10 percent were recorded in the late 1970s. The Fourth Malaysia Plan estimated that manufacturing sector growth in the decade 1981–1990 would average 11 percent per annum. In addition, manufacturing was expected to generate 30 percent of new employment opportunities in the economy (compared with 24 percent for the decade 1971–1980). Malaysia, *Fourth Malaysia Plan*, pp. 161, 169.

47. Mahathir, "The Dilemma," p. 54; Malaysia, Heavy Industries Corporation of Malaysia (HICOM), *Annual Report 1984*, p. 10; diplomatic source dated July 6, 1983.

48. Kanapathy, "Why Malaysia Needs," p. 10.

49. *FEER*, April 21, 1983, p. 55; diplomatic source dated July 6, 1983.

50. *Asian Finance*, October 15, 1981, p. 81.

51. Jomo, "Malaysia in Crisis," p. 1; Interview, Kuala Lumpur, November 1985.

52. Other factors favoring the choice of Korea included the specialized nature of the Hong Kong and Singaporean economies (as entrepôt ports, they had limited value as candidates for emulation) and the fact that, for largely ethnic reasons, Malaysia had no diplomatic relations with Taiwan. Jomo, "Malaysia in Crisis," p. 2.

53. Malaysia, Heavy Industries Corporation of Malaysia (HICOM), *Annual Report 1984*, p. 12.

54. Ibid. One example often given of the inadequacies of commercial calculations of this sort is their failure to include the benefit accruing to the country as a whole from savings in scarce foreign exchange from a plant producing import-substitutes for the domestic market.

55. In point of fact, no official cost-benefit calculation was ever performed

for *any* of the heavy industrial projects. The state's evaluation of their net social worth was essentially qualitative, not quantitative.

56. It made more sense, the argument went, for the country to concentrate its resources on just a few truly world-scale industrial plants and to draw on the best available talent to run them, rather than to allow the existing pool of capital (both human and financial) to be dissipated over a large number of small, inefficient private industries. The best managers, for example, ought to be put to work running just a small number of (state) enterprises. In practice, however, many of these managers were deliberately excluded from positions in the heavy industry projects because they were ethnic Chinese and seen as a threat to Malay control of the state's industrial efforts. *FEER,* June 16, 1983, pp. 103, 106; Kanapathy, "Why Malaysia Needs," p. 10.

57. *FEER,* September 8, 1983, p. 46. The magazine *Malaysian Business* observed that "never before has an intended project been so lambasted and roundly criticized." *MB* went on to report the words of one economist: "I have yet to talk to a single economist who thinks that the project is viable." Cited in *FEER,* February 14, 1985, p. 82.

58. Pura, "Doubts," p. 379.

59. *FEER,* August 3, 1989, p. 40.

60. A suggested alternative was economic diversification, involving state promotion of labor-intensive and agricultural resource-based industries, as well as support for expansion of local small industries. *Asian Wall Street Journal Weekly (AWSJW),* February 1, 1988, p. 14.

61. Jomo, "Malaysia in Crisis," p. 3; Stern, "Growth and Structural Change," pp. 30–31; diplomatic source dated July 6, 1983; Dhanji, *Structural Change,* p. 39.

62. Bautista, "Recent Shifts," p. 21; Stern, "Growth and Structural Change," p. 30; Dhanji, *Structural Change,* p. 39.

63. Bautista, "Recent Shifts," p. 21.

64. Mauzy and Milne, "The Mahathir Administration," p. 629.

65. An example is the price of cement which, at around M$180 (U.S. $66.35) per metric ton, reflects a tariff amounting to 50 percent or M$80 per metric ton, whichever is higher, on imported cement (the world price is M$102). *FEER,* June 22, 1989, p. 52; Jomo, "Malaysia in Crisis," p. 3; Bautista, "Recent Shifts," p. 22; Dhanji, *Structural Change,* p. 39; *FEER,* June 16, 1983, p. 102; Kanapathy, "Why Malaysia Needs," p. 10.

66. Bautista, "Recent Shifts," p. 22.

67. Kanapathy, "Why Malaysia Needs," pp. 9–10.

68. Kanapathy, "Why Malaysia Needs," pp. 11–12; Dhanji, *Structural Change,* p. 39; Jomo, "Malaysia in Crisis," p. 3.

69. *FEER,* June 16, 1983, pp. 102–03.

70. Hall, *Governing the Economy,* pp. 280–81.

71. Pura, "Doubts," p. 380.

72. Chinese support largely took the form of voting for ethnic Chinese candidates belonging to the main Chinese party in the National Front,

the MCA. These votes were aggregated as votes for the governing coalition rather than as votes for the constituent party to which the candidates belonged.

73. Pura, "Doubts," p. 380.
74. von der Mehden, "Malaysia in 1981," p. 215; Mauzy and Milne, "The Mahathir Administration," p. 625.
75. Tunku Abdul Rahman is the son of a sultan, Tun Abdul Razak was one of the four hereditary major chiefs of the state of Pahang, and Tun Hussein Onn was the son, grandson, and great-grandson of former chief ministers of the state of Johor. Gullick and Gale, *Malaysia*, p. 126.
76. Morais, *Mahathir*, p. 1.
77. Ibid., p. 5.
78. Tunku Abdul Rahman and Tun Abdul Razak were both members of the English bar and Tun Hussein Onn, at first a soldier, later trained to become a lawyer also. Gullick and Gale, *Malaysia*, p. 126.
79. Morais, *Mahathir*, p. 7.
80. Menon, *Profile*, p. 12.
81. Morais, *Mahathir*, p. 19.
82. Chung Kek Yoong, *Mahathir Administration*, p. 7; Gale, *Politics and Public Enterprise*, pp. 31, 35; Jomo, *A Question of Class*, p. 254.
83. Chung Kek Yoong, *Mahathir Administration*, p. 7; Gill, *Malaysia Inc.*, p. 93. The Tunku described the letter at the time as "scurrilous." Das, *The Musa Dilemma*, pp. 12–13.
84. Chung Kek Yoong, *Mahathir Administration*, p. 9.
85. Das, *The Musa Dilemma*, p. 13.
86. Hussein Alatas, "Feudalism," p. 586.
87. Mahathir, *The Malay Dilemma*, p. 3.
88. Ibid., pp. 60–61.
89. Ibid., p. 29.
90. Ibid.
91. Ibid.
92. The book was subsequently published in neighboring Singapore, but the ban in Malaysia remained in place until Mahathir became Prime Minister in 1981. Gullick and Gale, *Malaysia*, p. 138.
93. Gale, *Politics and Public Enterprise*, pp. 31, 35, 54; Das, *The Musa Dilemma*, p. 13.
94. Jomo, *A Question of Class*, p. 277; Menon, *Profile*, p. 27; Morais, *Mahathir*, pp. 28–29.
95. Gullick and Gale, *Malaysia*, p. 255.
96. Gill, *Malaysia Inc.*, pp. 93–94.
97. Ibid., p. 93 (original source not cited).
98. Ibid.; Mauzy and Milne, "The Mahathir Administration," pp. 619–20. Chia was the architect of the transformation of United Motor Works (UMW) from a small automotive parts company into a diversified manufacturing and trading company in the short space of fifteen years. Gill, *Malaysia Inc.*, p. 163.

99. Jomo, "Malaysia in Crisis," p. 1. Mahathir has been challenged by, among others, K. Das, for his blanket rejection of Malay traditions:

> There is in business in Malaysia today a coterie of half-educated politicians . . . . These people . . . tend to proclaim from the rooftops their concern about the disability of their own traditions. They like to scold people for being what they regard as old fashioned. Their notions of modernity are almost totally tied to fantasies about the industrial revolution: mass produce and fast, and never mind the smoke-stacks. (Das, *The Musa Dilemma*, p. 5)

100. *FEER*, April 11, 1985, p. 73; Milne, "New Economic Policy," p. 1379.
101. Ohmae is a Japanese economist and consultant and author of *Triad Power*.
102. Interview, economic adviser, Kuala Lumpur, June 1986.
103. We can see a parallel here between the increasingly assertive state role in industry on behalf of Malays (represented by the heavy industries policy) and a state decision to use its holding of shares, rather than that of Malay individuals, as the principal means of achieving the 30 percent Malay ownership target of the NEP. Zakaria suggests that the latter decision was made in 1980, just at the time that the new industrial strategy was being formulated. Both may be seen as a product of frustration at the slow pace at which individual Malays seem to be acquiring equity during the 1970s. See Zakaria, "Malaysia in 1980," p. 210.
104. *FEER*, June 16, 1983, p. 103; Kanapathy, "Why Malaysia Needs," p. 12.
105. *FEER*, June 14, 1984, p. 116.
106. The following discussion of the case of Proton draws on Doner, "The Dilemmas."
107. Automobile Federation of Malaysia (AFM), "Submission of AFM on the Industrial Master Plan," p. 320, cited in ibid.
108. The exact terms of the agreement have never been made public. Ibid., p. 10.
109. Ibid., p. 11.
110. The extreme secrecy made it difficult for outsiders to evaluate the project: "No one outside a small circle in Malaysia and Japan is equipped with enough knowledge of the 'national car' to make a judgement on its viability." *FEER*, December 24, 1982, p. 31; Doner, "The Dilemmas," p. 10.
111. UNIDO, *Japan and Malaysia's Car: Rising Sun or False Dawn of Economic Cooperation?*, quoted in *FEER*, February 14, 1985, p. 82.
112. Doner, "The Dilemmas," p. 11.
113. Ibid.
114. *FEER*, February 14, 1985, p. 80.
115. Doner, "The Dilemmas," p. 12.
116. On the effects of the 1980–1983 slowdown on the Malaysian economy, see Sithambaram, "Economic Decline," pp. 49–50; *FEER*, February 3,

1983, p. 58, and April 21, 1983, pp. 52–55; Navaratnam, "Malaysia's Economy," p. 7; *FEER*, September 27, 1984, p. 120; Bass, "Malaysia in 1982," p. 193.

117. Net government foreign borrowing increased nine-fold, to M$2.9 billion, between 1980 and 1981. This had the effect of accentuating both budget and balance-of-payments deficits, with debt-service claiming 13 percent of all government revenues in 1981. Sithambaram, "Economic Decline," p. 50; *AY*, 1983, p. 198.

118. *AY*, 1985, p. 195.

119. The first quarter of 1984 saw recovery in the prices of commodity exports (except tin), with palm oil, rubber, and cocoa prices reaching levels on average 30 percent higher than a year earlier (although the first two of these subsequently declined). With expanded oil exports, overall export performance exceeded both pre-1981 levels and government forecasts. *FEER*, April 28, 1983, p. 70; *AY*, 1985, p. 195. The result was Malaysia's highest recorded merchandising account surplus and a current account deficit of 5.8 percent of GNP (down from 14.4 percent in 1982). The economy overall grew at a real rate of 7.3 percent and, with the increased revenues this generated and some reduction in government expenditures (to 54 percent of GNP), the federal deficit declined to 10 percent of GNP and annual net foreign borrowing was reduced by 35 percent. *FEER*, September 27, 1984, p. 121, and April 11, 1985, p. 80; Navaratnam, "Malaysia's Economy," p. 6; *Malaysian Digest*, April 15, 1985, p. 6.

120. This vulnerability was exacerbated by a problem with invisibles which, by 1984, had ballooned to the equivalent of 83.4 percent of exports or 51.7 percent of GNP (debt service alone consumed 11.9 percent of export earnings). Invisibles (interest on foreign debt, dividends, insurance, freight, travel, educational fees, royalties, consultancy fees, etc.) amounted to M$9.8 billion in 1984. See *AY*, 1985, p. 194; *FEER*, April 28, 1983, p. 70; *FEER*, September 27, 1984, p. 120, and April 11, 1985, p. 80.

121. *AWSJW*, February 1, 1988, p. 14; *Asiaweek*, February 22, 1987, p. 52.

122. *AWSJW*, December 28, 1987, p. 14; *FEER*, September 1, 1988, p. 56.

123. *AWSJW*, December 28, 1987, p. 14; *FEER*, September 1, 1988, p. 56; *FEER*, August 3, 1989, p. 40.

124. *AY*, 1988, p. 182.

125. Initial production plans had called for Proton to *increase* plant capacity in 1987 by an additional 50 percent, to 120,000 vehicles a year. *FEER*, August 3, 1989, p. 40; *AY*, 1988, p. 182.

126. HICOM owned 51 percent of Perwaja Trengganu.

127. Perwaja Trengganu reported losses of M$118 (US$44) million in the 1987–1988 fiscal year.

128. *AY*, 1988, p. 182; *AWSJW*, December 28, 1987, p. 14; *Business Times* (*BT*), June 4, 1986, p. 1; *FEER*, September 1, 1988, p. 56.

129. Kedah Cement is 35 percent owned by HICOM, 25 percent by the

Kedah State Economic Development Corporation, 10 percent by the Singaporean government's Temasek Holdings, and the remaining ownership shares are split between Nichirin Holdings (Japan), Malaysian Kuwaiti Investment, Lee Rubber Group, and Oriental Holdings. *FEER*, June 22, 1989, p. 53.

130. *AY*, 1988, p. 181; *AWSJW*, December 28, 1987, p. 14.
131. *FEER*, June 22, 1989, p. 52. State efforts to bolster the sagging fortunes of cement producers in general and Kedah Cement in particular by suggesting that new road construction might henceforth be of concrete, rather than the traditional bitumen, sparked some controversy in 1986. *The Star* (*TS*), May 25, 1986, p. 10.
132. *AY*, 1988, p. 182.
133. *FEER*, July 7, 1988, p. 97.
134. *FEER*, September 1, 1988, p. 56.
135. Ibid.
136. Ibid.
137. *FEER*, June 22, 1989, p. 53.
138. APMC wants the government to assume M$590.5 (US$218) million of the two companies' loans, to be repaid over a fifteen-year period. Kedah Cement alone has more than M$650 (US$239.6) million in debts and some M$300 (US$111) million in accumulated losses. *FEER*, June 22, 1989, pp. 53–54.
139. *AY*, 1988, p. 182.
140. *FEER*, March 23, 1989, p. 77.
141. Ibid.
142. Examples of such ties include taxation and visa agreements, official loans, increased trade and investment, annual cultural grants, student exchanges, and visits by Japanese tourists and technical advisers. See Milne, "New Economic Policy," pp. 1373–74; *FEER*, June 14, 1984, pp. 113–14.
143. Milne, "New Economic Policy," p. 1374.
144. *FEER*, June 14, 1984, pp. 113–15.
145. The vehemence of Mahathir's criticism was an unwelcome surprise to Japanese officials. Interview, Ministry of International Trade and Industry, Tokyo, September 1985.
146. *FEER*, October 19, 1989, p. 64. In the Dayabumi case, Petronas was used in 1989 to rescue the owners of the loss-making complex, the Urban Development Administration, by paying almost twice the market value for the building. *FEER*, October 26, 1989, p. 117.
147. *FEER*, May 2, 1985, p. 48; *FEER*, September 27, 1984, p. 121.
148. The offering attracted M$716.7 million worth of applications (i.e., it was oversubscribed by fourteen times). See *AY*, 1986, p. 191.
149. *FEER*, September 1, 1988, p. 53; *AY*, 1988, p. 183; *Asiaweek*, November 9, 1986, p. 71.
150. *TS*, March 18, 1986, p. 8.
151. *AY*, 1988, p. 183; *FEER*, September 1, 1988, p. 53.

152. The Telekoms sale encountered strong opposition from civil-service unions concerned over pension plans, bonuses, compensation for forfeiture of civil service job security, and the resolution of long-standing disputes between Telekoms and its employees. *FEER,* July 20, 1989, p. 66; *BT,* May 30, 1986, p. 1.
153. *FEER,* July 20, 1989, p. 66.
154. *AWSJW,* August 14, 1989, p. 4.
155. *FEER,* September 1, 1988, pp. 52–53.
156. The Economic Planning Unit of the Prime Minister's Department is apparently working on a blueprint for future privatizations. Although this plan has yet to surface, it reputedly recommends the sale, over a decade or more, of some 246 concerns, including electricity and postal services, that are owned and either directly or indirectly managed by federal, state, or local authorities. Motivated in part by a desire to respond to the above-mentioned criticisms of existing privatizations, the planners at EPU are apparently also considering creation of a Federal Regulatory Commission to oversee the targeted enterprises. *AWSJW,* August 14, 1989, p. 4.
157. *AY,* 1985, p. 194; *FEER,* September 4, 1986, pp. 47–48; *Asiaweek,* December 14, 1986, p. 63.
158. On the 1987–1988 recovery, see *AY,* 1989, pp. 171–72; *FEER,* September 7, 1989, p. 96; *FEER,* September 1, 1988, p. 54, also May 4, 1989, p. 81, and July 6, 1989, p. 63.
159. By the end of 1988, industry accounted for 24.2 percent of GDP and it probably exceeded 25 percent in 1989. *AY,* 1989, p. 171.
160. *AWSJW,* November 6, 1989, p. 20, October 2, 1989, p. 30, August 28, 1989, p. 22; *FEER,* November 9, 1989, p. 82.
161. *FEER,* May 4, 1989, p. 81; *AWSJW,* November 6, 1989, p. 20.
162. Nathan, "Malaysia in 1988," pp. 136–37; *FEER,* May 4, 1989, p. 81; *AWSJW,* July 3, 1989, p. 21.
163. *FEER,* September 7, 1989, p. 96.
164. *FEER,* May 4, 1989, p. 81.
165. Ibid.; *FEER,* September 7, 1989, p. 99.
166. *FEER,* September 7, 1989, p. 98.
167. Ibid.
168. *AWSJW,* September 4, 1989, p. 18.
169. *FEER,* September 7, 1989, p. 99.
170. Ibid., pp. 98–99.
171. Ibid.
172. Ibid., p. 99.
173. Ibid.
174. *FEER,* August 25, 1988, p. 72.
175. *FEER,* September 7, 1989, p. 99.
176. The following discussion of Saga exports is drawn from *FEER,* August 3, 1989, pp. 40–41.
177. Ten vehicles were given to China on the occasion of Prime Minister

Mahathir's visit in 1985 (without winterization, however, they performed poorly in the chilly Chinese capital). *AWSJ*, December 19, 1985, p. 1.

178. Even so, it is the second most expensive of the top ten economy cars rated by the London *Sunday Times*. *FEER*, August 3, 1989, p. 40.

179. *FEER*, July 7, 1988, p. 97.

180. Deletion allowances represent the reduction in price that the supplier offers for auto "packs" from which certain components have been omitted. Doner, "Bargaining"; *AWSJ*, December 19, 1985, p. 1; *BT*, May 31, 1986, p. 1; *TS*, January 23, 1986, p. 22.

181. *FEER*, August 3, 1989, pp. 40–41; *AWSJ*, December 19, 1985, p. 1.

182. Proton lost M$58.5 (US$22) million in the 1987–1988 fiscal year. *FEER*, August 3, 1989, p. 40.

183. *FEER*, August 3, 1989, p. 40.

184. *NST*, October 31, 1989, p. 12.

185. Ibid.

186. The total public sector deficit for 1987 (which includes both operating and development expenditures) reached M$12.4 (US$5) billion, or 17.7 percent of GNP, not far short of the 20 percent that is often used as a rule of thumb to identify developing economies experiencing difficulties.

187. *AWSJW*, July 3, 1989, p. 21.

188. Ibid.

6. Conclusion

1. Lindblom, 1977.

2. See, for example, Lijphart, "Consociational Democracy."

3. In the case of Nigeria these reforms, collectively known as the SAP (Structural Adjustment Program), have been made the cornerstone of rule under the four-year government of General Ibrahim Babangida. Donors, including the World Bank, the United States, Japan, and the EEC countries, have responded enthusiastically—at a November 1989 meeting in Paris they agreed to donate over one billion dollars to help fund Nigerian adjustment during 1990. *Washington Post*, December 9, 1989, p. A14.

4. *Washington Post*, November 22, 1989, p. A17.

5. Among those most vociferous in opposing structural adjustment conditionality have been officials at the UN Economic Commission for Africa.

6. *Washington Post*, November 22, 1989, p. A17.

7. Ibid.

8. *FEER*, September 7, 1989, p. 97.

9. *World Development Report*, 1989, p. 147.

10. Ibid., p. 169.

11. Ibid., p. 165.

12. *AY*, 1989, pp. 6–7.

BIBLIOGRAPHY

Abdul Rahman, Tunku. *May 13; Before and After*. Kuala Lumpur: Utusan Melayu Press, 1969.

Allen, G.C., and Audrey G. Donnithorne. *Western Enterprise in Indonesia and Malaya: A Study in Economic Development*. London: Allen & Unwin, 1957.

Allen, J. *The Malayan Union*. New Haven: Yale University Southeast Asia Studies, 1967.

Ariff, Mohamed. "Malaysia in a Recessionary Setting: An Overview." *Southeast Asian Affairs* (1987), pp. 197–216.

Ariff, Mohamed, and Hal Hill. "ASEAN Manufactured Exports: Performance and Revealed Comparative Advantage." *ASEAN Economic Review* (July 1985), vol. 2, pp. 33–55.

Ariffin, Jamilah. "Women Workers in the Manufacturing Industries." In Evelyn Hong, ed., *Malaysian Women: Problems and Issues*, pp. 49–63. Penang: Consumers Association of Penang, 1983.

Asia Yearbook (Hong Kong). Various issues, 1980–1989.

Asian Finance (Hong Kong). Various issues, 1980–1989.

Asian Wall Street Journal (Hong Kong). Various issues, 1980–1989.

Asian Wall Street Journal Weekly (Hong Kong). Various issues, 1980–1989.

Associated Chinese Chambers of Commerce and Industry of Malaysia. "Memorandum to Y.A.B. Dr. Mahathir Mohamad, Chairman of the Cabinet Committee in Investment on the Subject of the Industrial Coordination Act, 1975." (October 4, 1975.)

Aziz, Zeti Akhtar. "Financial Institutions and Markets in Malaysia." In Michael T. Skully, ed., *Financial Institutions and Markets in Southeast Asia: A Study of Brunei, Indonesia, Malaysia, Philippines, Singapore and Thailand*, pp. 110–66. New York: St. Martins, 1984.

Barth, Fredrik, ed. *Ethnic Groups and Boundaries: The Social Organization of Culture Difference*. London: Allen and Unwin, 1969.

Bass, Jerry. "Malaysia in 1982: A New Frontier?" *Asian Survey* (February 1983), vol. 23, pp. 191–200.

Bass, Jerry. "Malaysia in 1983: A Time of Troubles." *Asian Survey* (February 1984), vol. 24, pp. 167–77.

Bautista, Romeo M. "Recent Shifts in Industrialization Strategies and Trade

Patterns of ASEAN Countries." *ASEAN Economic Bulletin* (July 1984), vol. 1, pp. 7–25.

Beaglehole, J.H. "Malay Participation in Commerce and Industry: The Role of RIDA and MARA." *Journal of Commonwealth Political Studies* (November 1969), vol. 7, pp. 216–45.

Berghe, Pierre van den. *The Ethnic Phenomenon.* New York: Elsevier, 1979.

Bhanoji Rao, V. V. *Malaysia: Development Pattern and Policy, 1947–1971.* Singapore: Singapore University Press, 1980.

Bhanoji Rao, V. V. *National Accounts of West Malaysia 1947–1971.* Singapore: Heinemann, 1976.

Bowie, Alasdair. "Redistribution With Growth? The Dilemmas of State-Sponsored Economic Development in Malaysia." *Journal of Developing Societies* (Spring 1988), vol. 4, pp. 52–66.

Bradford, Colin I., Jr. "Trade and Structural Change: NICs and Next Tier NICs as Transitional Economies." *World Development* (March 1987), vol. 15, pp. 299–316.

Brass, Paul R., ed. *Ethnic Groups and the State.* London; Sydney: Croon Helm, 1985.

Breton, A. *The Economic Theory of Representative Government.* London: Macmillan, 1974.

Buchanan, J., and G. Tullock. *The Calculus of Consent.* Ann Arbor: University of Michigan Press, 1962.

Business Times (Kuala Lumpur). Various issues, 1980–1986.

Cardoso, Fernando H., and Enzo Faletto. *Dependency and Development in Latin America.* Berkeley: University of California Press, 1979.

Cheah Boon Kheng. *Red Star Over Malaya: Resilience and Social Conflict During and After the Japanese Occupation, 1941–1946.* Singapore: Singapore University Press, 1983.

Chee Peng Lim. "The Malaysian Car Industry at the Crossroads: Time to Change Gear?" In Lim Lin Lean and Chee Peng Lim, eds., *The Malaysian Economy at the Crossroads: Policy Adjustment or Structural Transformation,* pp. 436–54. Kuala Lumpur: Malaysian Economic Association and Organisational Resources Sdn. Bhd., 1984.

Chee Peng Lim. "Malaysian Sogoshoshas: No Go So Far." In K.S. Jomo, ed., *The Sun Also Sets,* pp. 369–76. Petaling Jaya, Selangor: Institute for Social Analysis (INSAN), 1985.

Chee Peng Lim. "Regulating the Transfer of Technology: An Analysis of Malaysia's Experience." *Contemporary Southeast Asia* (June 1985), vol. 7, pp. 13–33.

Chee Peng Lim. "The Role of Government in Malaysian Industrial Development." *South East Asian Economic Review* (April 1985), vol. 6, pp. 29–38.

Chee Peng Lim. *Small Industry in Malaysia.* Kuala Lumpur: Berita, 1986.

Chia Oai Peng. "The Chinese Chambers of Commerce and the New Economic Policy." Paper presented at the 40th Meeting of the Association for Asian Studies, San Francisco, March 25–27, 1988.

Ching Teik Goh. *The May Thirteenth Incident and Democracy in Malaysia*. Kuala Lumpur: Oxford University Press, 1971.

Chung Kek Yoong. *Mahathir Administration: Leadership and Change in a Multiracial Society*. Petaling Jaya, Selangor: Pelanduk, 1987.

Clutterbuck, Richard. *Conflict and Violence in Singapore and Malaysia, 1945–1983*. Rev. ed. Boulder, Colo.: Westview, 1985.

Connor, Walker. "Nation-Building or Nation-Destroying?" *World Politics* (April 1972), vol. 24, pp. 319–55.

Connor, Walker. "The Politics of Ethnonationalism." *Journal of International Affairs* (1973), vol. 27, pp. 1–21.

Crone, Donald K. "State, Social Elites, and Government Capacity in Southeast Asia." *World Politics* (January 1988), vol. 40, pp. 252–68.

Dahl, Robert, and Charles E. Lindblom. *Politics, Economics and Welfare*. New York: Harper, 1953.

Das, K. *The Musa Dilemma*. Kuala Lumpur: K. Das, 1986.

Development Cooperation (Paris). Various issues, 1980–1989.

Dhanji, F., et al. *Malaysia: Structural Change and Stabilization*. Washington: World Bank, 1983.

Doner, Richard F. "Bargaining In the Malaysia National Car Project: The Dilemma of State Autonomy." Discussion paper. Kuala Lumpur: Institute of Strategic and International Studies (ISIS), 1986.

Doner, Richard F. "The Dilemmas and Limits of State Autonomy in Malaysia: The Case of the National Car Project." Paper presented at the 40th Meeting of the Association for Asian Studies, San Francisco, March 25–27, 1988.

Drabble, J.H. "Some Thoughts on the Economic Development of Malaya Under British Administration." *Journal of Southeast Asian Studies* (1974), vol. 5, pp. 199–208.

Drake, P.J. *Financial Development in Malaya and Singapore*. Canberra: Australian National University Press, 1969.

Easton, David. "An Approach to the Analysis of Political Systems." *World Politics* (April 1957), vol. 9, pp. 383–400.

Edwards, Chris. Review of *The Malaysian Economy - Structures and Dependence*, by Khor Kok Peng. *Kajian Malaysia* (December 1984), vol. 2, pp. 142–59.

Emerson, Rupert. *Malaysia: A Study in Direct and Indirect Rule*. New York: Macmillan, 1937.

Emmerson, Donald K. "Rediscovering the State: Notes Toward the Comparative Study of Political Institutionalization in Southeast Asia." Paper presented at a Conference on Development, Stability, and Security in the Asian-Pacific Region, University of California, Berkeley, March 17–21, 1984.

Enloe, Cynthia. *Ethnic conflict and Political Development*. Boston: Little, Brown, 1973.

Esman, Milton J. *Administration and Development in Malaysia: Institution Building and Reform in a Plural Society*. Ithaca: Cornell University Press, 1972.

Etzioni, Amitai. *The Active Society: A Theory of Societal and Political Processes.* New York: The Free Press, 1968.

Etzioni, Amitai. *A Comparative Analysis of Complex Organizations: on Power, Involvement, and Their Correlates.* Rev. and enl. ed. New York: The Free Press, 1975.

Etzioni, Amitai. *Modern Organizations.* Englewood Cliffs, N.J.: Prentice Hall, 1964.

Evans, Peter. "Class, State and Dependence in East Asia: Lessons for Latin Americanists." In Frederic C. Deyo, ed., *The Political Economy of the New Asian Industrialism,* pp. 203–26. Ithaca: Cornell University Press, 1987.

Evans, Peter. *Dependent Development: The Alliance of Multinational, State and Local Capital in Brazil.* Princeton: Princeton University Press, 1979.

Far Eastern Economic Review (Hong Kong). Various issues, 1980–1989.

Fisk, E.K., and H. Osman-Rani. *The Political Economy of Malaysia.* Kuala Lumpur: Oxford University Press, 1982.

Fong Chan Onn. *Technological Leap: Malaysian Industry in Transition.* Singapore: Oxford University Press, 1986.

Fong Chan Onn and Lim Kok Cheong. "Investment Incentives and Trends of Manufacturing Investments in Malaysia." *The Developing Economies* (December 1984), vol. 22, pp. 396–418.

Fong Chan Onn and Lim Kok Cheong, eds. *Malaysian Industrialization, Problems and Prospects: Towards an Industrialized Nation.* Kuala Lumpur: Kajian Ekonomi Malaysia, 1986.

Freeman, John R., and Ernest J. Wilson. "It Isn't Enough to Bring the State Back In." Paper presented at the 82nd meeting of the American Political Science Association, Washington, D.C., August 27–29, 1986.

Funston, Neil John. *Malay Politics in Malaysia: A Study of UMNO and Party Islam.* Kuala Lumpur: Heinemann Educational Books, 1980.

Gale, Bruce. "PETRONAS: Malaysia's National Oil Corporation." *Asian Survey* (November 1981), vol. 21, pp. 1129–44.

Gale, Bruce. *Politics and Public Enterprise in Malaysia.* Singapore: Eastern Universities Press, 1981.

Garnaut, Ross, ed. *ASEAN in a Changing Pacific and World Economy.* Canberra: Australian National University Press, 1980.

Geertz, Clifford. "The Integrative Revolution: Primordial Sentiments and Civil Politics in the New States." In Clifford Geertz, ed., *Old Societies and New States: The Quest for Modernity in Asian and Africa,* pp. 105–57. New York: The Free Press, 1963.

Gellner, Ernest. *Nations and Nationalism.* London: Basil Blackwell, 1983.

Gerschenkron, Alexander. *Economic Backwardness in Historical Perspective.* Cambridge, Mass.: Harvard University Press, 1962.

Gill, Ranjit. *The Making of Malaysia Inc: A 25 Year Review of the Securities Industry of Malaysia and Singapore.* Petaling Jaya, Selangor: Pelanduk, 1985.

Glassburner, Bruce. "ASEAN's 'Other Four': Economic Policy and Economic Performance Since 1970." Paper presented at a Conference on Development, Stability, and Security in the Pacific-Asian Region, University of California, Berkeley, March 17–21, 1984.

Glassburner, Bruce. "Southeast Asia: Economic Problems and Prospects." In Robert A. Scalapino and Jusuf Wanandi, eds., *Economic, Political and Security Issues in Southeast Asia in the 1980s*, pp. 33–51. Berkeley: Institute for East Asian Studies, University of California, 1982.

Golay, Frank H. "Malaya." In Frank H. Golay, ed., *Underdevelopment and Economic Nationalism in Southeast Asia*, pp. 341–89. Ithaca: Cornell University Press, 1969.

Gough, I. *The Political Economy of the Welfare State*. London: Macmillan, 1978.

Gourevitch, Peter. *Politics in Hard Times: Comparative Responses to International Economic Crises*. Ithaca: Cornell University Press, 1986.

Great Britain. Colonial Office. *Malayan Union and Singapore*. London: His Majesty's Stationery Office, 1946 (command paper 6724).

Gullick, J.M. *Indigenous Political Systems in Western Malaya*. London: University of London, The Athlone Press, 1958.

Gullick, J.M. *Malaysia: Economic Expansion and National Unity*. Boulder, Colo.: Westview, 1981.

Gullick, J.M., and Bruce Gale. *Malaysia: Its Political and Economic Development*. Petaling Jaya, Selangor: Pelanduk, 1986.

Haggard, Stephan Mark. "Pathways From the Periphery: the Newly Industrializing Countries in the International System." Ph.D. dissertation, University of California, Berkeley, 1983.

Hall, D.G.E. *A History of Southeast Asia*. 3rd ed. New York: St. Martins, 1968.

Hall, Peter A. *Governing the Economy: The Politics of State Intervention in Britain and France*. Cambridge: Polity, 1986.

Hanrahan, Gene Z. *The Communist Struggle in Malaya*. New York: Institute of Pacific Relations, 1971.

Harris, Nigel. *The End of the Third World: Newly Industrializing Countries and the Decline of an Ideology*. London: Tauris, 1986.

Hartley, William D. "Malaysia Scares Away Foreign Capital With Rules for Redistributing Wealth." *Wall Street Journal* (Pacific ed.), September 22, 1975, p. 24.

Hauser, Philip M., Daniel B. Suits, and Naohiro Ogawa, eds. *Urbanization and Migration in ASEAN Development*. Tokyo: National Institute for Research Advancement, 1985.

Hayward, Jack. "Institutional Inertia and Political Impetus in France and Britain." *European Journal of Political Research* (December 1976), vol. 4, pp. 341–59.

Heng Pek Koon. "Chinese Business Elites of Malaysia." Paper presented at the Conference on Industrializing Elites in Southest Asia, Sukhothai, Thailand, December 9–12, 1986.

Heussler, R. "Why Study the Colonial Service." *Corona* (May 1961), vol. 8, pp. 165–68.

"Hicom Looking for New Business Ventures." *New Straits Times*, October 31, 1989, p. 12.

Higgott, Richard A., and Richard Robison, eds. *Southeast Asia: Essays in the Political Economy of Structural Change.* London; Boston: Routledge and Kegan Paul, 1985.

Hing Ai Yun. "Capitalist Development, Class and Race." In S. Husin Ali, ed., *Ethnicity, Class and Development in Malaysia*, pp. 296–328. Kuala Lumpur: Persatuan Sains Sosial Malaysia, 1984.

Hintze, Otto. "Military Organization and the Organization of the State." In Felix Gilbert, ed., *The Historical Essays of Otto Hintze*, pp. 178–215. New York: Oxford University Press, 1975.

Hirono, R. *Malaysia Country Study: Study of the Bank's Operational Priorities and Plans for the 1980s.* Washington: Development Planning Office, International Bank for Reconstruction and Development, 1982.

Hirschman, Charles. "The Meaning and Measurement of Ethnicity in Malaysia: An Analysis of Census Classifications." *Journal of Asian Studies* (August 1987), vol. 46, pp. 555–82.

Hoffmann, Lutz, and Tan Siew Ee. *Industrial Growth, Employment and Foreign Investment in Peninsular Malaysia.* Kuala Lumpur: Oxford University Press, for Institut fur Weltwertschaft, Kiel, 1980.

Holloway, J., and S. Picciotta, eds. *State and Capital: A Marxist Debate.* London: Edward Arnold, 1978.

Horowitz, Donald L. *Ethnic Groups in Conflict.* Berkeley: University of California Press, 1985.

Howell, Llewellyn D., et al. "The International Attitudes of Southeast Asians: An Evolutionary Perspective." *Annals* (Southeastern Regional Conference of the Association for Asian Studies) (January 1983), vol. 5, pp. 63–77.

Hua Wu Yin [pseud.]. *Class and Communalism in Malaysia: Politics in a Dependent Capitalist State.* London: Zed Books, 1983.

Husin Ali, S., ed. *Ethnicity and Class in Malaysia.* Kuala Lumpur: Persatuan Sains Sosial Malaysia, 1984.

Hussein Alatas, Syed. "Feudalism in Malaysian Society: A Study in Historical Continuity." *Civilisations* (1968), vol. 18, pp. 579–92.

Hussein Alatas, Syed. *The Second Malaysia Plan 1971–1975: A Critique.* Singapore: Institute of Southeast Asian Studies, 1972.

Hyden, Goran. *Bejond Ujamaa in Tanzania: Underdevelopment and an Uncaptured Peasantry.* Berkeley: University of California Press, 1980.

Information Malaysia (Kuala Lumpur). Various issues, 1980–1989.

International Bank for Reconstruction and Development. *The Economic Development of Malaya.* Baltimore: Johns Hopkins University Press, for IBRD, 1955.

International Bank for Reconstruction and Development. *Report on the Economic Aspects of Malaysia.* Kuala Lumpur: Government Printer, 1963.

James, Kenneth. "The Malaysian Economy: The Shadows of 1990." *Southeast Asian Affairs* (1986), pp. 208–22.

Johnson, Chalmers. *MITI and the Japanese Miracle: The Growth of Industrial Policy 1925–1975.* Stanford: Stanford University Press, 1982.

Jomo, Kwame Sundaram. "Contemporary Ethnic Relations in Malaysia: Implications for National Unity and Security." Paper presented at the First Institute of Strategic and International Studies National Conference on Security entitled "Comprehensive Security: Challenges and Responses." Kuala Lumpur, July 15–17, 1986.

Jomo, Kwame Sundaram. "Malaysia in Crisis." Unpublished manuscript, 1986.

Jomo, Kwame Sundaram. *A Question of Class: Capital, the State and Uneven Development in Malaya.* Singapore: Oxford University Press, 1986.

Jomo, Kwame Sundaram, ed. *Malaysia's New Economic Policies: Evaluation of the Mid-Term Review of the Fourth Malaysia Plan.* Kuala Lumpur: Malaysian Economic Association, 1985.

Jomo, Kwame Sundaram, ed. *The Sun Also Sets: Lessons in 'Looking East.'* 2nd ed. Petaling Jaya, Selangor: INSAN, 1985.

Jomo, Kwame Sundaram, and R.J.G. Wells, eds. *The Fourth Malaysia Plan: Economic Perspectives.* Kuala Lumpur: Malaysian Economic Association, 1983.

Joseph, Richard A. "Class, State and Prebendal Politics in Nigeria." In Nelson Kasfir, ed., *The State and Class in Africa,* pp. 21–38. Totawa, N.J.: Cass, 1984.

Kanapathy, V. "Why Malaysia Needs an Industrial Policy." *UMBC Economic Review* (1981), vol. 17, pp. 5–22.

Kasfir, Nelson. "Explaining Ethnic Political Participation." *World Politics* (April 1979), vol. 31, pp. 365–88.

Katzenstein, Peter J. *Corporatism and Change: Austria, Switzerland and the Politics of Industry.* Ithaca: Cornell University Press, 1985.

Katzenstein, Peter J. *Small States in World Markets: Industrial Policy in Europe.* Ithaca: Cornell University Press, 1985.

Katzenstein, Peter J., ed. *Between Power and Plenty.* Madison: University of Wisconsin Press, 1978.

Khor Kok Peng. *The Malaysian Economy: Structures and Dependence.* Kuala Lumpur: Marican and Sons, for Institut Masyarakat, 1983.

Kindleberger, Charles. "The Rise of Free Trade in Western Europe, 1820–1975." *Journal of Economic History* (1975), vol. 35, pp. 20–55.

King, Frank H.H. *The New Malayan Nation: A Study of Communalism and Nationalism.* New York: Institute of Pacific Relations, 1957.

Konggeres Ekonomi Bumiputra Kedua. *Laporan-Laporan Atas Perlaksanaan Usul-Usul Konggeres Ekonomi Bumiputra Pertama.* Kuala Lumpur: Jabatan Cetak Kerajaan, 1968.

Konggeres Ekonomi Bumiputra Kedua. *Memorandum Dari Persaorangan.* Kuala Lumpur: Jabatan Cetak Kerajaan, 1968.

Konggeres Ekonomi Bumiputra Malaysia. *Kertas-Kertas Kerja.* Kuala Lumpur: Jabatan Cetak Kerajaan, 1965.

Koomsup, Praipol, ed. *ASEAN Energy Issues: Proceedings of the 6th Conference of the Federation of ASEAN Economic Associations, Bangkok, Thailand, Novem-*

ber 12–14, 1981. Bangkok: Thammasat University Press, for the Thai Economic Society, 1984.

Krasner, Stephen D. *Defending the National Interest: Raw Materials Investments and U.S. Foreign Policy*. Princeton: Princeton University Press, 1978.

Laitin, David. "Hegemony and Religious Conflict: British Imperial Control and Political Cleavages in Yorubaland." In Peter Evans, Dietrich Rueschemeyer, and Theda Skocpol, eds., *Bringing the State Back In*, pp. 285–316. Cambridge: Cambridge University Press, 1986.

Landau, Martin. *Political Theory and Political Science: Studies in the Methodology of Political Inquiry*. New York: Macmillan, 1972.

"LDC Capital Flight." *World Financial Markets* (Morgan Guarantee Trust), March 1986, pp. 13–15.

Lee Hock Lock. *Public Policies and Economic Diversification in West Malaysia, 1957–1970*. Kuala Lumpur: University of Malaya Press, 1978.

Lee Poh Ping. "Malaysian Perceptions of Japan Before and During the 'Look East' Period." *Asia Pacific Community* (Summer 1985), vol. 29, pp. 97–108.

Lee Sheng Yi. *The Monetary and Banking Development of Malaysia and Singapore*. Rev. and enl. ed. Singapore: Singapore University Press, 1974.

Lee Soo Ann. *Economic Growth and the Public Sector in Malaysia and Singapore 1948–1960*. Singapore: Oxford University Press, 1974.

Lee, Susan, and Tatiana Pouschine. "The Rising Stars." *Forbes*, May 5, 1986, pp. 106–12.

Li Dun Jen. *British Malaya: An Economic Analysis*. New York: The American Press, 1955.

Lijphart, Arend. "Consociational Democracy." *World Politics* (January 1969), vol. 21, pp. 207–25.

Lijphart, Arend. *The Politics of Accommodation; Pluralism and Democracy in the Netherlands*. Berkeley: University of California Press, 1968.

Lim Chong Yah. *Economic Development of Modern Malaya*. Kuala Lumpur: Oxford University Press, 1967.

Lim, David. "East Malaysia in Malaysian Development Planning." *Journal of Southeast Asian Studies* (March 1986), vol. 17, pp. 156–70.

Lim, David. *Economic Growth and Development in West Malaysia 1947–1970*. Kuala Lumpur: Oxford University Press, 1973.

Lim, David. "Export-Oriented Industrialization: A Case Study of Malaysia." *Kajian Ekonomi Malaysia* (December 1970), vol. 7, pp. 17–25.

Lim, David, ed. *Further Readings on Malaysian Economic Development*. Kuala Lumpur: Oxford University Press, 1983.

Lim, David, ed. *Readings on Malaysian Development*. Kuala Lumpur: Oxford University Press, 1975.

Lim Hua Sing. "Japanese Perspectives on Malaysia's 'Look East' Policy." *Southeast Asian Affairs* (1984), pp. 231–45.

Lim Lin Lean. "The Erosion of the Chinese Economic Position." Paper presented at a Political Seminar organized by the MCA Headquarters, Kuala Lumpur, June 28, 1987.

Lim Lin Lean and Chee Peng Lim, eds. *The Malaysian Economy at the Cross-*

roads: Policy Adjustment or Structural Transformation. Kuala Lumpur: Malaysian Economic Association and Organisational Resources Sdn. Bhd., 1984.

Lim, Linda. "Charting a Course for Industry in the Eighties." *ASEAN Business Quarterly* (1981), pp. 3–6.

Lim, Linda. "The Electronics Industry in Southeast Asia: Confounding the Critics." Paper presented at the 40th Meeting of the Association for Asian Studies, San Francisco, March 25–27, 1988.

Lim, Linda, and L.A. Peter Gosling, eds. *The Chinese in Southeast Asia.* 2 vols. Singapore: Maruzen Asia, 1983.

Lim Mah Hui. "Contradictions in the Development of Malay Capital: State, Accumulation and Legitimation." *Journal of Contemporary Asia* (1985), vol. 15, pp. 37–63.

Lim Mah Hui. *Ownership and Control of the 100 Largest Corporations in Malaysia.* Singapore: Oxford University Press, 1981.

Lim Mah Hui and William Canak. "The Political Economy of State Policies in Malaysia." *Journal of Contemporary Asia* (1981), vol. 11, pp. 208–24.

Lim Yoon Lin. "Malaysia: The New Mood." *Southeast Asian Affairs* (1976), pp. 211–33.

Lim Yoon Lin. "Malaysia: A Troubled Legacy." *Southeast Asian Affairs* (1977), pp. 145–59.

Lindblom, Charles E. *Politics and Markets: The World's Political Economic Systems.* New York: Basic Books, 1977.

Lipset, Seymour M., and Stein Rokkan. *Party Systems and Voter Alignments: Cross-National Perspectives.* New York: The Free Press, 1967.

Lo Sum Yee. *The Development Performance of West Malaysia 1955–1967: With Special Reference to the Industrial Sector.* Kuala Lumpur: Heinemann Educational Books, 1972.

Lowi, Theodore. *The End of Liberalism.* New York: Norton, 1969.

McConnell, Grant. *Private Power and American Democracy.* New York: Knopf, 1966.

McNeill, William H. *The Pursuit of Power: Technology, Armed Force, and Society Since A.D. 1000.* Chicago: University of Chicago Press, 1982.

Machado, Kit G. "Malaysian Cultural Relations With Japan and South Korea in the 1980s: Looking East." *Asian Survey* (June 1987), vol. 27, pp. 638–60.

Mackie, J.A.C. "Changing Patterns of Chinese Big Business in Southeast Asia." Paper presented at the Conference on Industrializing Elites in Southeast Asia, Sukhothai, Thailand, December 9–12, 1986.

Mahathir bin Mohamad. "The Dilemma of Developing Countries Wishing to Industrialize." *Foreign Affairs Malaysia* (March 1984), vol. 17, pp. 50–54.

Mahathir bin Mohamad. *Guide for Small Businessmen.* Petaling Jaya, Selangor: Eastern Universities Press, 1985.

Mahathir bin Mohamad. *The Malay Dilemma.* Singapore: Donald Moore, for Asia Pacific Press, 1970.

Mahathir bin Mohamad. "Memorandum to Heads of Departments from Datuk Mahathir." (June 28, 1983).

Mahathir bin Mohamad. "Speech by Y.A.B. Dr. Mahathir Mohamad, Deputy

Prime Minister/Education Minister, at the Opening of the Federation of Malaysian Manufacturers Seminar on the Third Malaysia Plan." Kuala Lumpur, August 26, 1976.

Malay Mail (Kuala Lumpur). Various issues, 1957–1989.

Malaya (Federation). *Census of Manufacturing Industries in the Federation of Malaya, 1959.* Kuala Lumpur: Government Printer, 1961.

Malaya (Federation). *Draft Development Plan of the Federation of Malaya.* Kuala Lumpur: Government Printer, 1950.

Malaya (Federation). *Pioneer Industries (Relief From Income Tax) Ordinance 1958.* Kuala Lumpur: Government Printer, 1958.

Malaya (Federation). *Population Census, 1957.* Kuala Lumpur: Government Printer, 1958.

Malaya (Federation). *Report by the Federation of Malaya Constitutional Conference held in London in January and February 1956.* London: Her Majesty's Stationery Office, 1956.

Malaya (Federation). *Report of the Industrial Development Working Party.* Kuala Lumpur: Government Printer, 1957.

Malaysia. *First Malaysia Plan, 1966–1977.* Kuala Lumpur: Government Printer, 1965.

Malaysia. *Mid-Term Review of the First Malaysia Plan, 1966–1977.* Kuala Lumpur: Government Printer, 1969.

Malaysia. *Second Malaysia Plan, 1971–1975.* Kuala Lumpur: Government Printer, 1971.

Malaysia. *Mid-Term Review of the Second Malaysia Plan, 1971–1975.* Kuala Lumpur: Government Printer, 1973.

Malaysia. *Third Malaysia Plan, 1976–1980.* Kuala Lumpur: Government Printer, 1976.

Malaysia. *Mid-Term Review of the Third Malaysia Plan, 1976–1980.* Kuala Lumpur: Government Printer, 1979.

Malaysia. *Fourth Malaysia Plan, 1981–1985.* Kuala Lumpur: Government Printer, 1981.

Malaysia. *Mid-Term Review of the Fourth Malaysia Plan, 1981–1985.* Kuala Lumpur: Government Printer, 1984.

Malaysia. *Fifth Malaysia Plan, 1986–1990.* Kuala Lumpur: Government Printer, 1986.

Malaysia. *Industrial Co-ordination Act (Act 177).* Kuala Lumpur: Government Printer, 1985.

Malaysia. *Industrial Co-ordination (Amendment) Act 1977.* Kuala Lumpur: Government Printer, 1977.

Malaysia. *Investment Incentives Act.* Kuala Lumpur: MDC Legal Advisors, 1985.

Malaysia. *Parliamentary Debates 1972.* Kuala Lumpur: Government Printer, 1972.

Malaysia. *Petroleum Development Act.* Kuala Lumpur: Petronas, 1974.

Malaysia. Bank Negara. *Annual Report.* Various issues, 1957–1988. Kuala Lumpur: Government Printer.

Malaysia. Heavy Industries Corporation of Malaysia (HICOM). *Annual Report 1984*. Kuala Lumpur: Government Printer, 1985.

Malaysia. Ministry of Finance. *Economic Report*. Various issues, 1957–1988. Kuala Lumpur: Government Printer.

Malaysia. National Operations Council. *The May 13 Tragedy: A Report by the National Operations Council*. Kuala Lumpur: Government Printer, 1969.

"Malaysia: What Price Success?" *Southeast Asia Chronicle* (April 1980), vol. 72, pp. 1–28.

Malaysian Business (Kuala Lumpur). Various issues, 1980–1989.

Malaysian Digest (Kuala Lumpur). Various issues, 1980–1989.

Mauzy, Diane K., ed. *Politics in the ASEAN States*. Kuala Lumpur: Maricans, 1984.

Mauzy, Diane K., and R.S. Milne. "The Mahathir Administration in Malaysia: Discipline Through Islam." *Pacific Affairs* (Winter 1983), vol. 56, pp. 617–48.

Means, Gordon P. "Ethnic Preference Policies in Malaysia." In Neil Nevitte and Charles H. Kennedy, eds., *Ethnic Preferences and Public Policy in Developing Societies*, pp. 95–118. Boulder, Colo.: Lynne Rienner, 1986.

Means, Gordon P. *Malaysian Politics*. London: Hodder and Stoughton, 1970.

Means, Gordon P. *Malaysian Politics*. 2nd ed. London: Hodder and Stoughton, 1976.

Means, Gordon P. "'Special Rights' as a Strategy For Development: the Case of Malaysia." *Comparative Politics* (1972), vol. 1, pp. 29–61.

Mehmet, Ozay. *Development in Malaysia: Poverty, Wealth and Trusteeship*. London: Croon Helm, 1986.

Menon, T.H., ed. *Profile of Dato' Seri Dr. Mahathir Mohamad*. Kuala Lumpur: Federal Department of Information, Ministry of Information, 1982.

Miliband, R. *Marxism and Politics*. New York: Oxford University Press, 1977.

Miller, Harry. *Jungle War in Malaya: The Campaign Against Communism 1948–60*. London: Barker, 1972.

Milne, R.S. "Corporatism in the ASEAN Countries." *Contemporary Southeast Asia* (September 1983), vol. 5, pp. 172–84.

Milne, R.S. "Ethnic Aspects of Privatization in Malaysia." In Neil Nevitte and Charles H. Kennedy, eds., *Ethnic Preferences and Public Policy in Developing States*, pp. 119–34. Boulder, Colo.: Lynne Rienner, 1986.

Milne, R.S. "Malaysia—Beyond the New Economic Policy." *Asian Survey* (December 1986), vol. 26, pp. 1364–84.

Milne, R.S. *Politics in Ethnically Bipolar States: Guyana, Malaysia, Fiji*. Vancouver: University of British Columbia Press, 1981.

Milne, R.S. "The Politics of Malaysia's New Economic Policy." *Pacific Affairs* (Summer 1976), vol. 49, pp. 235–61.

Milne, R.S. "Technocrats and Politics in the ASEAN Countries." *Pacific Affairs* (Fall 1982), vol. 55, pp. 403–29.

Milne, R.S., and Diane K. Mauzy. *Malaysia: Tradition, Modernity and Islam*. Boulder, Colo.: Westview, 1985.

Milne, R.S., and Diane K. Mauzy. *Politics and Government in Malaysia*. Rev. ed. Vancouver: University of British Columbia Press, 1980.

Mohamad Ariff, K. A., and Hal Hill. *Export-Oriented Industrialisation: The ASEAN Experience*. Sydney: Allen and Unwin, 1985.

Mohamed bin Burhanuddin. "The Manufacturing Sector in the Malaysian Economy." *UMBC Economic Review* (June 1985), vol. 21, pp. 6–11.

Moli Siow. "Problems of Ethnic Cohesion Among the Chinese in Peninsular Malaysia: Intraethnic Divisions and Interethnic Accommodation." In Linda Lim and L. A. Peter Gosling, eds., *The Chinese in Southeast Asia*, vol. 2: *Identity, Culture and Politics*, pp. 170–88. Singapore: Maruzen Asia, 1983.

Montgomery, John D., and Milton J. Esman. *Development Administration in Malaysia: Report to the Government of Malaysia*. Kuala Lumpur: Government Printer, 1966.

Morais, J. Victor. *Mahathir, A Profile in Courage*. Singapore: Eastern Universities Press, 1982.

Morrison, Charles E. *Japan, the United States, and a Changing Southeast Asia*. New York: University Press of America and the Asia Society, 1985.

Mukerjee, Dilip. *Lessons From Korea's Industrial Experience*. Kuala Lumpur: Institute of Strategic and International Studies, 1986.

Munir Majid. "Ethnic Slowdown and Implications for National Security." Paper presented at the First Institute of Strategic and International Studies National Conference on Security entitled "Comprehensive Security: Challenges and Responses." Kuala Lumpur, July 15–17, 1986.

Musa Hitam. "Keynote Address." Speech delivered at the Conference on Malaysia, Tufts University, Medford, Mass., November 18–20, 1984.

Nagata, Judith. *The Reflowering of Malaysian Islam: Modern Religious Radicals and Their Roots*. Vancouver: University of British Columbia, 1984.

Nagata, Judith. "The Status of Ethnicity and the Ethnicity of Status: Ethnic and Class Identity in Malaysia and Latin America." *International Journal of Comparative Sociology* (September-December 1976), vol. 17, pp. 242–60.

Nairn, Tom. *The Break-up of Britain: Crisis and Neo-nationalism*. London: NLB, 1981.

Nathan, K.S. "Malaysia in 1988: The Politics of Survival." *Asian Survey* (February 1989), vol. 29, pp. 129–39.

Navaratnam, Dato' Ramon V. "Malaysia's Economy: Domestic and International Prospects." Paper presented at the Conference on Malaysia, Tufts University, Medford, Mass., November 18–20, 1984.

Nevitte, Neil, and Charles H. Kennedy, eds. *Ethnic Preferences and Public Policy in Developing Societies*. Boulder, Colo.: Lynne Rienner, 1986.

New Straits Times (Kuala Lumpur). Various issues, 1957–1989.

New York Times (New York). Various issues, 1980–1989.

Ohmae, Kenichi. *Triad Power*. New York: The Free Press, 1985.

Ong, Michael. "Malaysia: The Limiting of a Limited Democracy." Paper presented at a workshop on "The Political System and Nation-Building in ASEAN." Singapore, January 23–25, 1986.

Ong, Michael. "Malaysia in 1983: On the Road to Greater Malaysia." *Southeast Asian Affairs* (1984), pp. 197–230.

Ong, Michael, and Lee Kam Hing. "Malaysia." In Myron Weiner and Ergun Ozbudun, eds., *Competitive Elections in Developing Countries*, pp. 112–46. Durham, N.C.: Duke University Press, for the American Enterprise Institute, 1987.

Ongkili, James P. *Nation-Building in Malaysia 1946–1974*. Singapore: Oxford University Press, 1985.

Ormsby Gore, W.G.A. *Report by the Right Honourable W.G.A. Ormsby Gore, M.P. (Parliamentary Under-Secretary of State for the Colonies), on his visit to Malaya, Ceylon and Java During the Year 1928*. London: His Majesty's Stationery Office, 1928 (command paper 3235).

Osborn, James. "Economic Growth With Equity? The Malaysian Experience." *Contemporary Southeast Asia* (September 1982), vol. 4, pp. 153–73.

Osman-Rani, Hassan. "Manufacturing Industries." In Ernest Kevin Fisk and Hassan Osman-Rani, eds., *The Political Economy of Malaysia*, pp. 260–86. Kuala Lumpur: Oxford University Press, 1982.

Osman-Rani, Hassan, Jomo Kwame Sundaram, and Ishak Shari, eds. *Development in the Eighties: With Special Emphasis on Malaysia*. Bangi: Fakulti Ekonomi, Universiti Kebangsaan Malaysia, 1981.

Parkin, Frank. *Marxism and Class Theory: A Bourgeois Critique*. New York: Columbia University Press, 1979.

Parsons, Talcott. *The Social System*. Glencoe, Ill.: The Free Press, 1951.

Pathmanathan, Murugesu. "Malaysia in 1984: A Political and Economic Survey." *Southeast Asian Affairs* (1985), pp. 211–34.

Poulantzas, N. *Political Power and Social Classes*. London: Verso, 1976.

Pura, Raphael. "Doubts Over Heavy Industrialization Strategy." In K.S. Jomo, ed., *The Sun Also Sets*, pp. 377–82. Petaling Jaya, Selangor: INSAN, 1983. Reprinted from *Asian Wall Street Journal*, June 10–11, 1983.

Purcell, Victor. *The Chinese in Southeast Asia*. 2nd ed. London: Oxford University Press, 1965.

Puthucheary, James J. *Ownership and Control in the Malayan Economy*. Singapore: Donald Moore, for Eastern Universities Press, 1960.

Puthucheary, Mavis. *The Politics of Administration: the Malaysian Experience*. Kuala Lumpur; New York: Oxford University Press, 1978.

Pye, Lucian W. *Guerrilla Communism in Malaya: Its Social and Political Meaning*. Westport, Conn.: Greenwood Press, 1956.

Rabushka, Alvin, and Kenneth A. Shepsle. *Politics in Plural Societies: A Theory of Democratic Instability*. Columbus, Ohio: Charles Merrill Publishing, 1972.

Rachagan, S. Sothi. "The 1986 Parliamentary Elections in Peninsular Malaysia." *Southeast Asian Affairs* (1987), pp. 217–35.

Ratnam, K.J., and R.S. Milne. *The Malayan Parliamentary Election of 1964*. Singapore: Oxford University Press, 1967.

Ratnam, K.J., and R.S. Milne. "Politics and Finance in Malaya." *Journal of Commonwealth Political Studies* (1965), vol. 3, pp. 182–98.

Robinson, Richard D. *National Control of Foreign Business Entry: A Survey of Fifteen Countries.* New York: Praeger, 1976.

Roff, Margaret E. *The Politics of Belonging.* Kuala Lumpur: Oxford University Press, 1974.

Roff, William R. *The Origins of Malay Nationalism.* 2nd ed. New Haven: Yale University Press, 1974.

Ronen, Dov. *The Quest for Self-Determination.* New Haven: Yale University Press, 1979.

Rothchild, Donald. "Hegemonial Exchange: An Alternative Model for Managing Conflict in Middle Africa." In Dennis L. Thompson and Dov Ronen, eds., *Ethnicity, Politics and Development*, pp. 65–104. Boulder, Colo.: Lynne Rienner, 1986.

Rothschild, Joseph. *Ethnopolitics.* New York: Columbia University Press, 1981.

Saw Swee Hock and Lee Soo Ann, eds. *Economic Problems and Prospects in ASEAN Countries.* Singapore: Singapore University Press, 1977.

Scalapino, Robert A., Seizaburo Sato, and Jusuf Wanandi, eds. *Asian Political Institutionalization.* Berkeley: Institute for East Asian Studies, University of California, 1986.

Schildkrout, Enid. "The Ideology of Regionalism in Ghana." In William A. Shack and Elliot P. Skinner, eds., *Strangers in African Societies*, pp. 183–207. Berkeley: University of California Press, 1979.

Schumpeter, Joseph. *Capitalism, Socialism and Democracy.* New York: Harper and Row, 1947.

Scott, James C. *Political Ideology in Malaysia: Reality and the Beliefs of an Elite.* New Haven: Yale University Press, 1968.

Selvaratnam, V. "Malaysia in 1981: A Year of Political Transition." *Southeast Asian Affairs* (1982), pp. 245–72.

Senu bin Abdul Rahman et al. *Revolusi Mental.* Kuala Lumpur: Penerbitan Utusan Melayu, 1971.

Short, Anthony. *The Communist Insurrection in Malaya, 1948–60.* London: Muller; New York: Crane, Russak, 1975.

Sieh Lee Mei Ling. "Emerging Corporate Groups in Malaysia: Response to the New Economic Policy." Paper presented at the Conference on Industrializing Elites in Southeast Asia, Sukhothai, Thailand, December 9–12, 1986.

Sieh Lee Mei Ling. "The Scheme for Bumiputra Investment in Malaysia: Some Implications." In K.S. Jomo and R.J.G. Wells, eds., *The Fourth Malaysia Plan: Economic Perspectives*, pp. 92–97. Kuala Lumpur: Malaysian Economic Association, 1983.

Sieh Lee Mei Ling. *Ownership and Control of Malaysian Manufacturing Corporations.* Petaling Jaya: University of Malaya Cooperative Bookstore Publications, 1982.

Sieh Lee Mei Ling and Chew Kwee Lyn. "Redistribution of Malaysia's Corporate Ownership in the New Economic Policy." *Southeast Asian Affairs* (1985), pp. 236–58.

Simandjuntak, B. *Malayan Federalism 1945–1963: A Study of Federal Problems in a Plural Society*. Kuala Lumpur; New York: Oxford University Press, 1969.

Sithambaram, Subramaniam. "Economic Decline: Causes and Consequences." *Aliran Quarterly* (1982), vol. 2, pp. 47–51.

Skully, Michael T. *ASEAN Financial Cooperation: Developments in Banking, Finance and Insurance*. London: Macmillan, 1985.

Skully, Michael T. *Financial Institutions and Markets in Southeast Asia: A Study of Brunei, Indonesia, Malaysia, Philippines, Singapore and Thailand*. London: Macmillan, 1984.

Skully, Michael T. *Merchant Banking in ASEAN: A Regional Examination of its Development*. New York: Oxford University Press, 1983.

Smith, Anthony D. *The Ethnic Origins of Nations*. Oxford; New York: Basil Blackwell, 1986.

Smith, Anthony D. *The Ethnic Renewal*. Cambridge; New York: Cambridge University Press, 1981.

Smith, Wendy. "A Japanese Factory in Malaysia: Ethnicity as a Management Ideology." In K.S. Jomo, ed., *The Sun Also Sets*, pp. 278–304. Petaling Jaya, Selangor: INSAN, 1985.

Snodgrass, Donald R. *Inequality and Economic Development in Malaysia*. Kuala Lumpur: Oxford University Press, 1980.

Snyder, Louis L. "Nationalism and the Flawed Concept of Ethnicity." *Canadian Review of Studies in Nationalism* (Fall 1983), vol. 10, pp. 253–65.

Soehoed, A.R. "Economic Dimensions of Security in the ASEAN Region." In Robert A. Scalapino and Jusuf Wanandi, eds., *Economic, Political and Security Issues in Southeast Asia in the 1980s*, pp. 52–59. Berkeley: Institute for East Asian Studies, University of California, 1982.

Soesastro, Hadi. "Japan 'Teacher'-ASEAN 'Pupils': Can It Work?" Paper presented at the Conference on Development, Stability, and Security in the Pacific-Asian Region, Berkeley, March 17–21, 1984. Published under same title: Robert A. Scalapino, Seizaburo Sato, and Jusuf Wanandi, eds., *Asian Economic Development-Present and Future*, pp. 114–30. Berkeley: Institute for East Asian Studies, University of California, 1985.

Spinanger, Dean. *Industrialization Politics and Regional Economic Development in Malaysia*. Singapore: Oxford University Press, 1986.

Spinanger, Dean. *Regional Industrialization Policies in a Small Developing Country: A Case Study of West Malaysia*. Kiel: Institute for World Economics, 1980.

The Star (Penang). Various issues, 1980–1989.

Stern, Joseph J. "Malaysia: Growth and Structural Change." Paper presented at the Conference on Malaysia, Tufts University, Medford, Mass., November 18–20, 1984.

Stockwell, A.J. *British Policy and Malay Politics During the Malayan Union Experiment, 1942–1948*. Kuala Lumpur: The Malaysian Branch of the Royal Asiatic Society, 1979.

Straits Times (Singapore). Various issues, 1957–1989.

Straits Times Weekly (Singapore). Various issues, 1988.

Sundrum, R.M. "Manpower and Educational Development in East and Southeast Asia: A Summary of Conference Proceedings." *Malaysian Economic Review* (Singapore) (October 1971), vol. 16, pp. 78–90.

Tan Bok Huat. "The Malaysian Car Project: A Financial Economic/Social Cost-Benefit Analysis." Kuala Lumpur: Institute of Strategic and International Studies (working paper), 1985.

Tan Loong Hoe. "The State and Distribution of Wealth Within Malay Society in Peninsular Malaysia." *Southeast Asian Affairs* (1981), pp. 217–34.

Tan Pek Leng. "Women Factory Workers and the Law." In Evelyn Hong, ed., *Malaysian Women: Problems and Issues*, pp. 64–78. Penang: Consumers Association of Penang, 1983.

Tan Tat Wai. *Income Distribution and Determination in West Malaysia.* Kuala Lumpur: Oxford University Press, 1982.

Tham Seong Chee. *Social Science Research in Malaysia.* Singapore: Graham Brash, 1981.

Thillainathan, R. "Distributional Issues and Policies in Malaysia." Paper delivered at the second Malaysian Economic Convention of the Malaysian Economic Association, Kuala Lumpur, March 26–30, 1974.

Thoburn, John T. *Primary Commodity Exports and Economic Development: Theory, Evidence and a Study of Malaysia.* London; New York: Wiley, 1977.

Thompson, Dennis L., and Dov Ronen, eds. *Ethnicity, Politics and Development.* Boulder, Colo.: Lynne Rienner, 1986.

Thompson, Robert J., and Joseph R. Rudolph, Jr. "Ethnic Politics and Public Policy in Western Societies: A Framework for Comparative Analysis." In Dennis L. Thompson and Dov Ronen, eds., *Ethnicity, Politics and Development*, pp. 25–63. Boulder, Colo.: Lynne Rienner, 1986.

Thong Yaw Hong. "Balance of Payments Issues and Implications." *UMBC Economic Review* (1985), vol. 21, pp. 20–25.

Tocqueville, Alexis de. *Democracy in America.* 2 vols. Rev. ed. New York; London: The Colonial Press, 1899.

Tocqueville, Alexis de. *The Old Regime and the French Revolution.* New York: Doubleday, 1955.

Todd, Halinah. "Sales Drive Aims to Boost Malaysia's Car." *Asian Business* (November 1986), vol. 22, pp. 59–60.

Truman, David. *The Governmental Process.* New York: Knopf, 1951.

United Nations Monthly Bulletin of Statistics (New York). Various issues, 1950–1989.

Verba, Sidney. "Comparative Political Culture." In Lucian Pye and Sydney Verba, eds., *Political Culture and Political Development*, pp. 512–60. Princeton: Princeton University Press, 1965.

Von der Mehden, Fred R. "Communalism, Industrial Policy and Income Distribution in Malaysia." *Asian Survey* (March 1975), vol. 15, pp. 247–61.

Von der Mehden, Fred R. *Industrialization in Malaysia: A Penang Micro-Study.* Houston: Rice University Program of Development Studies, 1973.

Von der Mehden, Fred R. "Malaysia: A Political Survey." Paper presented at the Conference on Malaysia, Tufts University, Medford, Mass., November 18–20, 1984.

Von der Mehden, Fred R. "Malaysia in 1981: Continuity and Change." *Asian Survey* (February 1982), vol. 22, pp. 212–18.

Von Vorys, Karl. *Democracy Without Consensus: Communalism and Political Stability in Malaysia*. Princeton: Princeton University Press, 1975.

Wallerstein, Immanuel. *The Modern World System*. New York: Academic, 1974.

Wall Street Journal (New York). Various issues, 1970–1989.

Washington Post (Washington, D.C.). Various issues, 1989.

Watson, G.M., and Sir Sydney Craine. *Report on the Establishment of a Central Bank in Malaya*. Kuala Lumpur: B.T. Fudge, Acting Government Printer, 1956.

Weber, Max. *Economy and Society: An Outline of Interpretive Sociology*. 2 vols. Guenther Roth and Claus Wittich, eds. New York: Bedminster Press, 1968.

Weinstein, Franklin B. "Japan and Southeast Asia." In Robert A. Scalapino and Jusuf Wanandi, eds., *Economic, Political and Security Issues in Southeast Asia in the 1980s*, pp. 184–94. Berkeley: Institute for East Asian Studies, University of California, 1982.

Weir, M., and Theda Skocpol. "State Structures and the Possibilities for 'Keynesian' responses to the Great Depression in Sweden, Britain and the United States." In Peter Evans, Dietrich Rueschemeyer, and Theda Skocpol, eds., *Bringing the State Back In*, pp. 107–63. Cambridge: Cambridge University Press, 1986.

Wheelwright, E.L. *Industrialization in Malaysia*. Melbourne: Melbourne University Press, 1965.

Wheelwright, E.L. "Reflections on Some Problems of Industrial Development in Malaya." *Malayan Economic Review* (April 1963), vol. 8, pp. 66–80.

Wolfe, A. *The Limits of Legitimacy*. New York: The Free Press, 1977.

Wong Lin Ken. *The Malayan Tin Industry to 1914*. Tucson: University of Arizona Press, 1965.

World Development Report. Various issues, 1980–1989.

Yap Koon See, ed. *Who's Who in Malaysian Business and Directory*. Kuala Lumpur: Budayamas, 1985.

Young, Kevin, Willem C.F. Bussink, and Parvez Hasan. *Malaysia: Growth and Equity in a Multiracial Society*. Baltimore: Johns Hopkins University Press, for World Bank, 1980.

Zakaria Haji Ahmad. "Evolutionary Change and Political System Development: The Malaysian Case." Paper presented at the Conference on Development, Stability, and Security in the Pacific-Asian Region, University of California, Berkeley, March 17–21, 1984. Published as "Evolution and Development of the Political System in Malaysia." In Robert A. Scalapino, Seizaburo Sato, and Jusuf Wanandi, eds., *Asian Political Institutionalization*, pp. 221–40. Berkeley: Institute for East Asian Studies, University of California, 1986.

Zakaria Haji Ahmad. "Malaysia in 1980: A Year of Political Consolidation and Economic Developments." *Southeast Asian Affairs* (1981), pp. 201–16.

Zakaria Haji Ahmad. "Malaysia in 1984: No More Free Lunches?" *Asian Survey* (February 1985), vol. 25, pp. 206–13.

Zakaria Haji Ahmad, ed. *Government and Politics of Malaysia.* Singapore: Institute of Southeast Asian Studies, 1987.

Zakaria Haji Ahmad, ed. *Selected Readings in Malaysian Politics and Government.* Kuala Lumpur: Oxford University Press, 1985.

Zysman, John. *Governments, Markets and Growth: Financial Systems and the Politics of Industrial Change.* Ithaca: Cornell University Press, 1983.

INDEX